THIS COULD GET MESSY

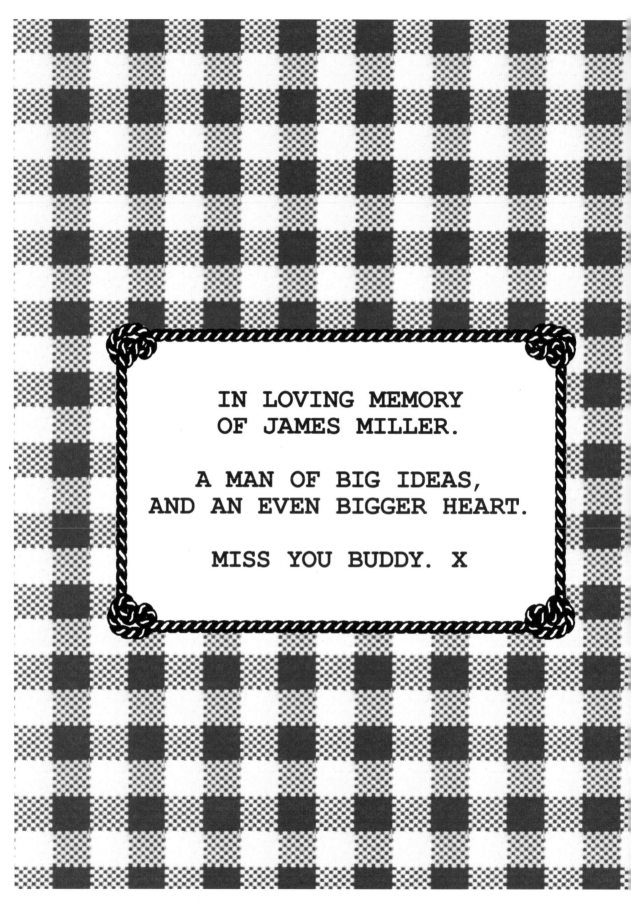

IN LOVING MEMORY
OF JAMES MILLER.

A MAN OF BIG IDEAS,
AND AN EVEN BIGGER HEART.

MISS YOU BUDDY. X

THIS COULD GET MESSY

A GUIDE TO EATING.
TO DRINKING.
TO DOING BOTH AT
THE SAME TIME.

JAMES WIRTH

MURDOCH BOOKS

CONTENTS

WELCOME TO OUR WORLD

This is the loosest, most non-judgy recipe book you'll ever own. So crack open a beer, thumb through this little number, then fire up the deep-fryer — you're going to need it!

Drink'n'Dine wasn't something we planned. It was very much an accident. I mean for starters, when we began, none of the people in our own weird band of non-hostile pub-takeover mercenaries were chefs or veterans of the hospitality industry. Somehow, though, we found ourselves thrown together finding pubs and venues in Sydney that had done their dash in former lives; redesigning and reimagining them into fresh, new and slightly odd things.

In the space of two years, Drink'n'Dine progressed from a few beers and a handshake in a dive bar, to a hospitality management concept currently responsible for six venues and 200 staff. All nine of our venues, alive or dead — The Norfolk, The Carrington, The Abercrombie, The Forresters, Santa Barbara, Queenies, The Oxford Tavern, House of Crabs and Chica Linda — have been the proud results of our accidental endeavours. You could say we've stumbled on a way of doing things that, in its own highly unorthodox fashion, works.

Each of our venues embodies a distinct personality, a strong identity — something we realised through trial and error that we were good at creating, even though we didn't really know much in the beginning about all the other stuff that comes after The Idea.

So I suppose I should explain who 'we' are, and how we came to own and run this rowdy bunch of pubs and venues.

To start with, the Australian electronic music scene is indirectly responsible for this book. I fell into DJing some time around the early 2000s and, with my crew of extremely loose human beings,

the Bang Gang Deejays, we spent a good deal of time travelling around the world, partying and abusing musical genres by throwing them together to form our own style. We played with big acts like Daft Punk, The Prodigy, and even Vanilla Ice (when he attempted his comeback)… In short, we generally had a criminally good time being paid to travel around the world and wreak our own special brand of havoc.

In 2011, I met James Miller, who would become one of my partners in crime. Our mutual friend Greggy (Greg Magree), who introduced us, had 'just bought this pub', The Norfolk, in Sydney's Surry Hills. Greggy and I became friends because he'd come to the clubs I was playing at. He can pull serious shapes on the dance floor and likes a drink or two. In short, my kinda guy. He's also a pretty gifted property developer who can see the potential in a space before anyone else can. Sydney was, at the time, undergoing a slow and sad death when it came to pubs, and naturally he saw the potential in this downturn. Pubs at that time mostly fell into one of three categories:

- working-class pubs that had lost their charm in favour of poker machines, big-beer-company-branded everything, and no soul
- ugly, shiny monstrosities that didn't know if they were a club, a pub or a restaurant
- classic old school — the kind nobody hates and that you shouldn't mess with.

Several pub groups had also gone bust, leaving the door open just a crack for people with a little bit of money and zero sense to get into the game. The Norfolk fell into category number one. It was the quintessential stinky old pub with not much by way of charm or character going for it, and Greggy was looking for tenants to take the place over. At the time, my DJ career was winding down and

I was attempting to go legit by being a partner in another Sydney pub called The Flinders Hotel. James was running yet another pub called Ruby, having just moved on from the surprising success of a salad chain he started, called Sumo Salad. We were both looking for new projects to fill our time and found ourselves set up on a blind date by Greggy. At The Norfolk over a few beers, ideas began to form.

What came out of those few beers was the beginning of a partnership. James would crunch the numbers, and I would work on the conceptual stuff. We enlisted the help of Michael Delany, the magical unicorn responsible for transforming my half-baked ideas into a physical reality. As a designer responsible for some of the most respected clubbing venues in Melbourne in the 2000s (Honky Tonks, 3rd Class, Sorry Grandma), we'd known each other for a debaucherous decade, and I knew he'd be able to understand what I was trying to achieve. Tropical Caribbean meets American dive motel? Got it. Los Angeles Latino ghetto street food? Too easy.

As a team, we figured we had the ingredients to make this thing work. It was simple enough: create the kind of pub *we* wanted to go to. Something that honoured its own pub-ness, with an energetic atmosphere (aka 'The Vibe'), an emphasis on fun, and of course good food and drink. But back to the important bit: The Vibe.

I was in charge of said vibe. Imagine that on a business card: Vibe Master. Okay, maybe not. Coming up with ideas isn't an exact science and some of our best ideas have been the direct result of a bad joke, a late-night drinking session, or a random email rant. However they come, I document them in a Google folder, which is my version of an inspiration board for ideas, then develop them and bounce them off friends for feedback. Sometimes they work, and other times they're met with stone-cold silence, which means back to the drawing board. From bad Colombian wall murals to Instagram photos, I collect anything that captures a feeling or an atmosphere. Particularly if it's a bit crap.

Crap, my friends, is good.

Australians have a good handle on what pub food is about. In most places, it's about steaks, schnitzels, burgers, chips. We wanted to honour that. There's nothing worse than going to a pub and not being able to get a decent burger and fries: why screw with that logic? We decided then and there that any menu we created needed to have those key components that make pub food great; the concept just needed a bit of a shake-up.

In our collective travels, as well as our former (or imagined) lives, we'd each spent a bit of time stateside in the US as well as South America and Europe, and we drew on that collection of real or researched experience to form The Idea. From American diner gems to Spanish tapas and Jamaican barbecue, we'd use something small (but mighty) as the basis from which to flavour the style, atmosphere, food and drink. The major criteria was that it had to be, above all things, fun. To our surprise, one by one, each venue opportunity sprang to life and people came. What's more, they left us with clean plates and smiles on their faces.

So somehow along the way, looking for something to do, we found ourselves in the business of food and drink. And while we like to play around a lot with crazy notions, we take food and drink very seriously. As none of us had a culinary background, we needed someone who could, like Mike Delany, understand our crazy ideas and bring them to life.

Which is how Jamie Thomas came into our lives. A Brit by birth, he's worked at far more legit places, like the iconic St John in London, as well as renowned gastro pub The Anglesea Arms and a host of other high-profile places. Sometimes we do wonder why he chooses to put up with our nonsensical ideas of what food could be, but we love him and we suspect he might love us back.

You could say I'm a backseat chef. Just call me Miss Daisy. I can see in my mind what I want a menu to be, but how to get there is not really my territory. As group head chef, Jamie's role is to translate my half-baked ideas into things people actually want to eat. This is sometimes challenging, given that I don't really speak 'chef'. I know how something should look and taste, but I can't always tell Jamie why, how, or what's missing. Sometimes I'll email him a 'so crazy it could work' idea. Sometimes he'll answer me. Sometimes I get a diplomatic 'Er, oh. Yeah?' — he's nothing if not a stand-up guy and a gentleman.

Our food is an unapologetic mash-up of places, cultures, flavours and ideas. So you could say that what I spent so many years doing with Bang Gang rubbed off in the way Drink'n'Dine blends together anything that feels like a good idea. It seems like a bit of a pot-luck way to go, but as in music, here the same logic seems to have prevailed.

Over time Jamie has become accustomed to me saying, 'It needs… *something*.' When I say this, he usually knows how to bring the 'something' that's missing, which is one of the great things about Jamie: he just gets it. His technical background blends with a flexible attitude towards creating new dishes, so although he occasionally rolls his eyes when we say things like, 'How can we make a Chinese taco?', he'll usually humour us by helping us get to where we want to go… and most of the time, the punters seem to like it.

While each of our venues is distinct, there are a couple of constants we hold on to. Firstly, everything we do is deliberately a bit rough around the edges. At least aesthetically. In the business of pubs, the last thing you want is polished perfection.

You could also say that our style is 'so wrong it's right'. Given this, how do we know when it's 'so wrong it's wrong'?

The answer is simple: if we knew, we wouldn't do it. But it's easy to know when something's not going to work, once it's in motion. You can feel it in the first few days if a concept is being received well, or not. Now, after nine venues, the test we put our ideas through is based on something James Miller once said: 'You gotta be famous for something.' In other words, if a customer can't describe to their friends in one

sentence what your place is about and why you'd go there, then chances are they won't get it (and they won't go).

Santa Barbara (RIP) is a good illustration. One publication described it as 'USA BBQ meets Asian Street Food', with cocktails. And a nightclub. You wouldn't be the first person to find that idea a bit confusing, and within a few short months, we knew it was time to pull the plug. House of Crabs, people get: you go there, you get messy, you wear a bib, eat boiled crabs and have a laugh. Simple.

The other thing we ask ourselves is, 'What do people like to eat in pubs?' It sounds obvious, but you'd be surprised how many publicans think sashimi is a good idea. You know, for the ladies. I'll just put it out there and say that sashimi on a pub menu isn't a great idea. Forget how many people want to be healthy — when they enter a pub, eight out of ten people will want some component of their meal deep-fried, baby.

So, this book is an ode to the places and spaces we've created. It's about food that's fun, that's designed to be shared, and in many cases, designed to be enjoyed with a tropical drink in one hand. It's divided into drinking snacks, shared plates, weekend backyard barbecue wonders, burgers, tacos, 3pm breakfasts, couch comfort food, substantial salads, cocktails and more.

Most of all, it's an ode to fun, because in our minds food and drink is about having a good time with people you like: it shouldn't be hard, but it should be tasty. And if you screw up a recipe, just give it another go. We don't judge.

James Wirth

DRINKING LOVES COMPANY

This chapter is the beginning. The beginning of a big night out, that is. The beginning of a meal. Of good times. It's about mouthwatering snacks: small bites to accompany a few (or more than a few) drinks with mates. All good drinking food requires salt, spice, fat, frying… and only a small amount of effort. Most of these recipes are designed to be made with one hand — so that you can hold a drink in the other while making them. One-handed recipes: the future? Most probably. Welcome.

TOSTONES with HUANCAÍNA SAUCE

PREPARATION: 15 MINUTES // COOKING: 20 MINUTES // SERVES 4–6

Tostones are known throughout the Latin world under different names, but what they all equate to is fried plantain goodness. There's something about the mixture of salty, spice-coated plantains that works so well with the rich, South American cheesy dipping sauce: it's one of our favourite odd couples, hands down.

Depending on where in the world you happen to live, plantains can sometimes be difficult to get hold of. In that case, green unripe bananas work well as a substitute.

vegetable oil, for deep-frying

lime wedges, to serve

TOSTONES

1 teaspoon garam masala

1 teaspoon smoked paprika

1 tablespoon sea salt flakes

1 teaspoon curry powder

4 plantains (see glossary) or
   green bananas, peeled using
   a sharp knife

HUANCAÍNA SAUCE

1 tablespoon vegetable oil

1 garlic clove, chopped

½ small brown onion, diced

2 pickled aji chillies
   (see glossary)

95 g (3¼ oz/⅓ cup) cottage
   cheese

125 ml (4 fl oz/½ cup) evaporated
   milk

juice of 1 lime

10 water cracker biscuits,
   roughly broken

small pinch of ground turmeric

To make the huancaína sauce, heat a small frying pan over medium heat. Add the vegetable oil and sweat off the garlic and onion for 2–3 minutes, or until translucent. Remove from the heat and set aside to cool.

Scrape the cooled onion mixture into a blender. Add the remaining ingredients and blitz until smooth, then season with sea salt to taste. Transfer to an airtight container and refrigerate until required. The sauce will keep for 2–3 days in the fridge; bring to room temperature for serving.

For the tostones, combine the garam masala, paprika, salt and curry powder in a small mixing bowl and set aside. Using a sharp knife, very thinly slice the plantains, about 5 mm (¼ inch) thick.

Fill a deep-fryer or large heavy-based saucepan one-third full of vegetable oil (no higher, or the oil will overflow when the plantain discs are added). Heat over medium heat until it reaches 180°C (350°F) when tested with a cooking thermometer, or until a cube of bread dropped into the oil turns golden brown in 15 seconds.

Working in batches, fry the plantain slices in the hot oil for 2–3 minutes, or until crisp and golden, stirring them around a bit with a metal spatula (not plastic, as it may melt) to stop them sticking together. Remove with the spatula and drain on paper towel.

Serve hot, sprinkled to taste with the spice mixture, with the huancaína sauce and lime wedges on the side.

PRETZELS with JALAPEÑO MUSTARD

PREPARATION: 1 HOUR + 6½–7½ HOURS PROVING // COOKING: 40 MINUTES
MAKES 16 LARGE PRETZELS

Nothing really goes with beer quite like pretzels. And pretzels taste SO MUCH better when you make them yourself. The jalapeño mustard is the missing link: combined with pretzels and beer, it unleashes a force previously unknown to man.

THE PRETZELS
2 teaspoons dried yeast
1 kg (2 lb 4 oz) plain (all-purpose) flour
250 ml (9 fl oz/1 cup) milk
80 g (2¾ oz) unsalted butter
2 tablespoons sea salt or salt flakes
1 tablespoon malt extract

Put the yeast in a large mixing bowl with 100 g (3½ oz/⅔ cup) of the flour and 250 ml (9 fl oz/1 cup) lukewarm water. Mix to combine, then cover with plastic wrap. Leave in a warm place for 5–6 hours to let the yeast do its work.

Gently heat the milk and butter in a small saucepan until lukewarm. Add to the yeast mixture, along with the salt, malt extract and remaining flour. Mix together, then turn out onto a lightly floured surface and knead to form a firm dough; this will generally take about 10 minutes. Place in a clean bowl, cover with plastic wrap and leave for about 1½ hours, or until the dough has doubled in size and feels springy to the touch.

Punch the dough down with your fist to release the air, then turn out onto a bench and knead it back into shape. Divide the dough into 16 even portions, then roll them into batons around 2.5 cm (1 inch) thick and 30 cm (12 inches) long. Ask Uncle YouTube how to throw them into traditional pretzel shapes.

TO FINISH THE PRETZELS
3 tablespoons bicarbonate of soda
   (baking soda)
sea salt flakes, for sprinkling
50 g (1¾ oz) butter, melted

To cook the pretzels, bring 1.5 litres (52 fl oz/6 cups) water to the boil in a large heavy-based saucepan.

Add the bicarbonate of soda. Cooking them one at a time, gently drop in your pretzels and cook for 5–10 seconds, until they rise to the surface. Fish them out with a slotted spoon or sieve and place on trays lined with baking paper, leaving them near a fan or an open window to catch a cool breeze. This will help to create a skin on the pretzels, giving them that distinctive chewy texture.

Leave the pretzels alone for 20 minutes or so. Meanwhile, preheat the oven to 200°C (400°F).

Score the top of the pretzels with a knife and sprinkle some sea salt on them. Transfer to the oven and bake for 15–20 minutes, or until they've turned a deep golden brown.

Remove from the oven and cool on a wire rack. The pretzels can be stored in the fridge overnight if needed.

JALAPEÑO MUSTARD
60 g (2¼ oz/½ cup) pickled jalapeño
   chillies (see glossary), drained
185 g (6½ oz/¾ cup) American mustard

Use a blender to blitz the jalapeños and mustard into a coarse paste — or if you prefer the texture a bit more rustic, you can dice the jalapeños by hand and fold them into the mustard.

TO SERVE
When you're ready to chow down, preheat the oven to 160°C (315°F).

Place the pretzels on a baking tray and warm them in the oven for about 10 minutes. Remove the pretzels from the oven and brush with melted butter.

Grab a six-pack of beer. Sit on the couch. Eat the lot, dipping the pretzels into the jalapeño mustard as you go.

PORK CHIPS with ONION DIP

PREPARATION: 20 MINUTES // COOKING: 1 HOUR 40 MINUTES + 12 HOURS SLOW ROASTING
SERVES 4-6

Deep-fried pork bits: does life get much better? From English pubs to Filipino street stalls, they're a global drinking snack for a reason. Don't take shortcuts with these, or you'll end up with chewy pork bits even your dog won't want to know about. When they're prepared and consumed correctly, you will feel like mowing the lawn, shooting a duck and doing burnouts, all at the same time. The onion dip is our take on the French onion variety popular way back in the 1970s. But better.

PORK CHIPS

1 piece of pork skin, from the top of the loin section, measuring about 50 x 30 cm (20 x 12 inches); if you ask nicely, your butcher may even give it to you for free!

Place the pork skin in a large stockpot and cover with cold water. Bring to the boil, then reduce the heat and simmer for 1 hour. Remove the pork skin from the pot and lay it on a baking tray to cool.

Meanwhile, preheat the oven to 70°C (150°F). Once cool enough to handle, place the pork skin fat side up. Scrape away and discard all the fat, so you are left with just the skin. Place the skin on a wire rack, set over a large baking tray.

Transfer to the oven and bake for a minimum of 12 hours. When done, the skin should resemble hard, shiny plastic. If it still looks or feels soft, leave it in the oven to dehydrate further.

ONION DIP

2 tablespoons olive oil
235 g (8½ oz/1½ cups) thinly sliced brown onion
¾ teaspoon kosher salt, sea salt flakes or pink salt
375 g (13 oz/1½ cups) sour cream
185 g (6½ oz/¾ cup) whole-egg mayonnaise
2 teaspoons garlic powder
½ teaspoon ground white pepper

Heat the olive oil in a frying pan over medium–low heat. Add the onion and ¼ teaspoon of the salt. Gently cook the onion until caramelised — this should take about 20 minutes, and you'll need to stir frequently to stop the onion burning. Remove from the pan and set aside to cool.

In a serving bowl, mix together the remaining ingredients. Give the cooled caramelised onion a quick chop, then stir it through.

Cover and refrigerate for up to 2 hours. Stir again just before serving.

TO FINISH

vegetable oil, for deep-frying
salt flakes, for sprinkling over the chips — or you could try the Curry salt or Paprika salt (see page 145), or shichimi togarashi (see glossary)

When ready to serve, break the dried pork skin into small chips. (On frying, the chips will expand exponentially — they will grow 10 times bigger! — so keep this in mind…)

Fill a deep-fryer or large heavy-based saucepan one-third full of vegetable oil. Heat over medium heat until it reaches 180°C (350°F) when tested with a cooking thermometer, or until a cube of bread dropped into the oil turns golden brown in 15 seconds.

Drop in a piece of pork skin to test if you have your intended chip size right. Once your chips are the right size, fry them in small batches for 4–5 minutes, or until puffed, light and airy. Remove with a slotted spoon and drain on paper towel.

Sprinkle with salt flakes or whatever seasonings you like, and serve with the onion dip. The chips are best served warm, but are also fine the next day if left to cool and stored in an airtight container.

CUCUMBER SNACKS

PREPARATION: 10 MINUTES + 5 MINUTES MARINATING // SERVES 4–6

We like serving up free little bites of this spicy, refreshing cucumber snack, just as people sit down and start looking at the menu. It gets the mouth in the mood for food and freshens the breath.

Shichimi togarashi is a Japanese seven-spiced chilli pepper condiment that you can pick up these days from any good supermarket or Asian grocer. We reckon it ought to be a kitchen pantry staple.

Trim the ends off the cucumbers, then peel if you wish. Cut them into halves or thirds, then into batons. Place in a bowl and sprinkle with the smoked salt. You can leave them in the fridge for 5 minutes to soften a little, if you'd like.

Drain any moisture that has seeped out, then sprinkle with a good shake of shichimi togarashi.

We serve ours in a plastic beer glass, with a little pile of smoked salt on the side for salt fiends to dip into.

3 telegraph (long) cucumbers
1 tablespoon smoked salt (see glossary), plus extra to serve
80 ml (2½ fl oz/⅓ cup) rice vinegar
shichimi togarashi (a Japanese chilli spice mix; see glossary), for sprinkling

CHILLI FRUIT

PREPARATION: 10 MINUTES + 30 MINUTES MARINATING // SERVES 4

All over Los Angeles and Mexico, you'll find street vendors carting around little stalls filled with ice and fruit — usually looking bored, reading a five-year-old magazine. When it's hot and you've been pounding the pavement all day, nothing is more refreshing than a bag of chilli fruit from one of these roadside heroes. It's essentially just chilled, freshly cut tropical fruit, seasoned with chilli and salt — an underrated combination of sweet, salt and spice that whets the appetite and cools you down.

Use any fruit you like, but we find it works best if you keep it tropical.

Peel the pineapple, watermelon, rockmelon and apples. Cut the flesh into bite-sized pieces and place in a large zip-lock bag.

Pour in the salt and chilli flakes, then seal the bag. Shake so that the fruit is evenly coated. Taste and adjust the seasoning to your preference.

Allow the fruit to steep in the fridge for 30 minutes before serving it up.

10 cm (4 inch) chunk of pineapple
10 cm (4 inch) chunk of watermelon
10 cm (4 inch) chunk of rockmelon
2 crisp apples
1 teaspoon salt flakes
1 teaspoon mild chilli flakes

MAHOLO POPCORN

PREPARATION: 10 MINUTES // COOKING: 15 MINUTES // SERVES 4-6

'Hello popcorn'? Yes, we realise this is probably the worst name for a recipe or dish ever. What's worse, when we put it on one of our menus, we didn't even spell it right. Genius.

What we did get right, though, is how this popcorn tastes, and how well it goes with booze (obviously). It's popcorn, Hawaiian–Japanese style: bacon and pineapple for a luau factor, Japanese seasonings and a whole lotta butter. It's a bit of a train wreck to look at, but when it's destined to be hoovered, who really cares.

1 tablespoon black sesame seeds

1 tablespoon white sesame seeds

220 g (7¾ oz/1 cup) popping corn

4 bacon rashers, rind removed, finely diced

50–100 g (1¾–3½ oz) melted butter (depending on how much you like butter)

4 tablespoons finely diced dried pineapple

50 g (1¾ oz/½ cup) powdered parmesan cheese

1 teaspoon gochugaru (Korean red chilli flakes; see glossary)

a few shakes of furikake (Japanese seasoning mix; see glossary)

Add all the sesame seeds to a small dry frying pan. Toast over medium heat for about 3 minutes, or until they darken and become fragrant, shaking the pan frequently and keeping an eye on them so they don't burn. Tip them into a bowl and set aside.

Follow the instructions on the popcorn packet and pop that corn!

Meanwhile, heat a frying pan over medium–high heat. Fry the bacon for 4 minutes, or until super crispy. Remove with a slotted spoon, drain on paper towel and set aside.

Pour the hot popcorn into a large bowl. Mix together with the bacon, melted butter, pineapple, parmesan and the rest of the seasonings, in any combination that suits you. Serve hot.

BUFFALO CELERY

PREPARATION: 15 MINUTES // COOKING: 1 HOUR // SERVES 4-6

The great American classic, buffalo chicken, got that way because of the celery and blue cheese, just sayin'. For this bar snack, we decided to ditch the chicken and get straight to the point: celery, buffalo sauce, blue cheese — no messing about...

The vinaigrette makes a little bit more than you'll need, so bottle the rest and keep it in the fridge. It's great as a dipping sauce, marinade or dressing and will become your new favourite go-to sauce.

Preheat the oven to 180°C (350°F).

To make the hot sauce vinaigrette, slice the tops off each garlic bulb, then place each bulb on a piece of foil. Drizzle generously with olive oil and a good sprinkling of sea salt flakes, then wrap the foil up and place on a baking tray. Roast for between 45 minutes and 1 hour, or until the garlic is soft. Remove from the oven and leave to cool.

Squeeze the garlic cloves from their skins, into a blender. Blitz to a soft purée. Scrape the garlic purée into a small bowl and whisk in the 2 tablespoons olive oil, along with the spring onion and hot sauce. Cover and refrigerate until required. The vinaigrette can be made a day ahead; bring to room temperature for serving.

When ready to serve, toss the celery sticks in a bowl with about 250 ml (9 fl oz/1 cup) of the hot sauce vinaigrette. Add half the peanuts and all the cheese and lightly mix together, until the celery is coated.

Pile the mixture into small serving dishes and scatter with the remaining peanuts. Garnish with some celery leaves and serve.

HOT SAUCE VINAIGRETTE

3 garlic bulbs

2 tablespoons olive oil, plus extra for drizzling

sea salt flakes, for sprinkling

6-8 spring onions (scallions), thinly sliced

250 ml (9 fl oz/1 cup) spicy cayenne pepper sauce, such as Frank's RedHot sauce or Tabasco sauce

THE REST

8-10 celery stalks, peeled and sliced on the diagonal into 1 cm (½ inch) chunks, plus a small handful of celery leaves, to garnish

115 g (4 oz/¾ cup) salted peanuts, roughly chopped

50 g (1¾ oz) mild blue cheese (we use Gorgonzola 'dolce'), broken into small chunks

PICK IT UP

AND EAT IT

Snacks. Canapés. Bites. Starters. Shares. Smalls.

Call them what you want, we love 'em. So naturally, all our menus have a large selection of the tasty little buggers on them. It's where we can get a bit weird, have some fun and jump around between flavours/cuisines/countries. People always seem more open to try new things when the dish comes in a small size, so get amongst it. This is your opportunity to freak people out and get them eating something they wouldn't otherwise try.

We highly encourage mixing, matching and creating your own versions of these. Go on, don't be scared: make a selection for your next house party, a bunch to share for a quick dinner, or a few for a one-man eating bonanza.

This chapter moves from finger food to double-handed wrap-your-laughing-gear-around-it pleasure, so use it to choose your own adventure, depending on how hungry your hordes are.

DEEP-FRIED PICKLES
with RANCH DRESSING

PREPARATION: 20 MINUTES + 10 MINUTES RESTING // COOKING: 20 MINUTES // SERVES 6

When we think of this dish, Barbra Streisand's 'The Way We Were' plays in the back of our minds. This was the first snack on the first menu in our first pub, and it's never come off since.

The combination sounds weird, but trust me, it's one of the best things you will ever put in your mouth. It's also super simple to make and will change the way you or anyone else feels about pickles (unless you are already obsessed). It's kind of like a cheeseburger, without the cheeseburger.

vegetable oil, for deep-frying

375 g (13 oz) dill pickles, drained well, then sliced on the diagonal into bite-sized pieces

50 g (1¾ oz/⅓ cup) plain (all-purpose) flour, for dusting

Quick ranch dressing (see page 274), to serve

BATTER

140 g (5 oz) plain (all-purpose) flour

85 g (3 oz/⅔ cup) cornflour (cornstarch)

2½ teaspoons sea salt

1 teaspoon smoked paprika

¼ teaspoon cayenne pepper

330 ml (11¼ fl oz/1⅓ cups) of your favourite beer

To make the batter, combine the flour, cornflour, salt, paprika and cayenne pepper in a bowl. Make a well in the centre, then whisk in your beer until you have a smooth batter. Let the batter rest for 10 minutes.

Meanwhile, fill a deep-fryer or large heavy-based saucepan one-third full of vegetable oil. Heat over medium heat until it reaches 180°C (350°F) when tested with a cooking thermometer, or until a cube of bread dropped into the oil turns golden brown in 15 seconds.

Make sure your dill pickles are well drained. Working in batches, toss them in the flour, drop them in the batter, then gently add them to the hot oil, being careful not to overcrowd the deep-fryer.

Cook each batch for 3–4 minutes, or until golden brown and crisp, using a slotted spoon to move the pickles around in the oil to stop them sticking together.

Remove the pickles and drain on paper towel. Serve immediately, with the ranch dressing.

BARBECUE JERK CORN and COCONUT

PREPARATION: 15 MINUTES // COOKING: 20 MINUTES // SERVES 4-6

As far as we're concerned, you can never go wrong with coconut. This dish has more coconut than you can throw a coconut at (that's a lot of coconut).

Almost everyone loves this snack, probably because it tastes like a vacation. Or maybe because it looks like a cute poodle? Or a lamington? Who knows. Jamaican jerk seasoning adds to the tropical vibe, and the mayo ties it all together. It's a great dinner party snack because it's quick and simple to make, and is guaranteed to draw nods of approval all round.

Our tip: when you think there's too much coconut, you should probably add more. Yep, just a tiny bit more.

Heat a frying pan over medium heat. Add the coconut and cook for 3–4 minutes, or until golden brown, tossing regularly so it doesn't burn. Tip into a mixing bowl and set aside.

Meanwhile, bring a saucepan of lightly salted water to the boil. Add the corn cobs and cook for 7–8 minutes, or until tender. Drain and leave to cool.

Now use the open flame of a gas hob or barbecue to slightly char the corn on each side for 2 minutes. (Alternatively, you could char them on a stovetop chargrill pan over medium heat.) Set aside until cool enough to handle.

In a mixing bowl, combine the mayonnaise with as much of the jerk paste as you can handle — it will mellow out a little by the time you use it, so be bold!

To serve, you can chop each nicely charred corn cob into a few pieces for daintier handling, or not. Using a pastry brush, smother each piece of corn with the jerk mayonnaise, then toss the corn pieces in the toasted coconut. Serve with lime wedges for squeezing over.

130 g (4½ oz/2 cups) shredded coconut (fresh coconut is best, but dried coconut is also fine)

4 corn cobs, husks and silks removed

250 g (9 oz/1 cup) whole-egg mayonnaise

125–250 g (4½–9 oz/½–1 cup) Jerk paste (see page 273)

2 limes, cut into wedges

BUFFALO CAULIFLOWER

PREPARATION: 20 MINUTES + 30 MINUTES CHILLING // COOKING: 30 MINUTES
SERVES 4-6

Rest assured no buffalo were harmed in the making of this dish.

Originating in Buffalo, New York, these little snacks are actually all about the classic cayenne-spiced vinegary sauce used to coat chicken wings eaten at pubs, clubs and football matches all across the great nation. But the vinegary sauce is not just good for wings. We've tried putting it on everything (bloody marys, steaks, babies), and it's all good.

This is a great vegetarian snack to add to your dinner party repertoire, and we promise any self-respecting American will give it the thumbs-up.

1 cauliflower, cut into bite-sized florets
250 g (9 oz/1⅔ cups) plain (all-purpose) flour
3 free-range eggs, beaten
120 g (4¼ oz/2 cups) panko (Japanese breadcrumbs; see glossary)
375 ml (13 fl oz/1½ cups) spicy cayenne pepper sauce, such as Frank's RedHot sauce or Tabasco sauce
150 g (5½ oz) cold butter, diced
250 g (9 oz/1 cup) sour cream
100 g (3½ oz) Gorgonzola cheese, or other blue cheese
vegetable oil, for deep-frying
3-4 celery stalks, peeled and cut into long batons

In a large saucepan of lightly salted boiling water, cook the cauliflower florets for 5–6 minutes, or until just tender. Drain in a colander, refresh under cold running water, then set aside to cool.

Line up three mixing bowls. Place the flour in the first bowl, the beaten eggs in the second bowl, and the breadcrumbs in the third.

Working in small batches, toss the cauliflower florets in the flour, then the egg, then the crumbs, placing them all on a tray or large plate. When all the florets have been given this treatment, cover with plastic wrap and chill in the fridge for at least 20–30 minutes, to help the crumb coating adhere to the cauliflower.

In a saucepan over medium–low heat, warm the hot sauce. When it is nearly simmering, whisk in the cold cubes of butter until incorporated. Set aside.

In a blender, blitz together the sour cream and blue cheese, then decant into a serving bowl.

When ready to serve, fill a deep-fryer or large heavy-based saucepan one-third full of vegetable oil. Heat over medium heat until it reaches 180°C (350°F) when tested with a cooking thermometer, or until a cube of bread dropped into the oil turns golden brown in 15 seconds.

Fry the crumbed cauliflower florets in small batches for 3–4 minutes each time, or until golden brown and crisp, taking care that they don't clump together. Remove with a slotted spoon and drain on paper towel.

Once all the florets have been deep-fried, toss them in the buttery hot sauce and serve immediately, with the celery sticks and blue cheese sour cream sauce.

PAELLA ONIGIRI

PREPARATION: 45 MINUTES + OVERNIGHT CHILLING // COOKING: ABOUT 45 MINUTES
ON DAY ONE + 45 MINUTES ON DAY TWO // SERVES 4–6

We are not normal people. So we didn't want to have 'just another paella'
on the menu. Paella is so overplayed and often underwhelming that it's hard to
not snore when you see it on a menu. But after eating at a Japanese takeaway
joint, we had the idea of making stuffed rice balls out of paella.

The idea eventually evolved into this: we press the paella into onigiri shapes,
whack some fried squid and saffron mayo on top, and voilà: Spananese!

This recipe can be made two or three days ahead of time, making it
a low-stress entertainer's dream.

THE PAELLA

1.5 litres (52 fl oz/6 cups) vegetable,
chicken or ham stock — whatever you
can get your hands on

1–2 tablespoons olive oil, for
pan-frying

2 small red onions, finely diced

2 garlic cloves, crushed

1 fennel bulb, white part finely diced

1 red capsicum (pepper), finely diced

250 g (9 oz) chorizo sausages,
finely diced

550 g (1 lb 4 oz/2½ cups) paella rice,
washed

2 tablespoons squid ink (see glossary)

1 bunch (80 g/2¾ oz) flat-leaf (Italian)
parsley, leaves picked and finely
chopped

vegetable oil, for pan-frying

THE SQUID

vegetable oil, for deep-frying

60 g (2¼ oz/½ cup) cornflour
(cornstarch)

50 g (1¾ oz/⅓ cup) plain (all-purpose)
flour

1 teaspoon sea salt

4–6 small squid tubes, cleaned and
sliced into rings (if you like,
you can ask your fishmonger to do
all this for you)

SAFFRON MAYONNAISE

a few saffron threads

1 tablespoon hot water

125 g (4½ oz/½ cup) whole-egg mayonnaise

To make the paella, dig out a large heavy-based saucepan with a tight-fitting lid, a 35 x 25 cm (14 x 10 inch) tray that is at least 6 cm (2½ inches) deep (to spread your paella in), and a slightly smaller tray that fits inside your paella tray (this one will sit on top of your paella and compress it).

Pour the stock into another saucepan and leave it to warm up over medium–low heat.

In your paella saucepan, heat a little olive oil over low heat, then slowly cook the onion and garlic for about 10 minutes, or until soft and translucent. Add the fennel and capsicum and continue to cook gently for another 10 minutes, until everything is soft, stirring occasionally.

Throw in the chorizo and turn up the heat a little. Cook the mixture for 5–7 minutes, or until the oil starts to leach out of the sausage. Add the rice and mix thoroughly until the rice is nicely coated. Now add the squid ink and give the big pot one last stir, so that everything goes Rolling Stones ('Paint It Black').

Gradually stir in the warm stock. Turn the heat down low and pop on the lid. Set a timer for 4-minute intervals. Each time the alarm goes off, take off the lid and give the rice a gentle stir — you will need to do this four times (for a total of 16 minutes), or until you're happy the rice is nearly done. (Remember that the rice will be cooked a little more later on, so it doesn't hurt to be slightly undercooked at this point.)

Toss the parsley through. Taste for seasoning and sprinkle in a little sea salt or freshly ground black pepper if necessary.

Get your deep-sided baking tray and line it with plastic wrap. Carefully turn the rice out onto the tray and smooth it out. Cover with another layer of plastic wrap, then sit the smaller tray on top. Place some heavy jars or bottles on top of the smaller tray to weigh it down.

Now refrigerate the paella overnight.

THE NEXT DAY

Preheat the oven to 150°C (300°F).

Remove the compressed paella sheet from the fridge and turn it out onto a chopping board. Cut your 'onigiri' into triangular pieces — small for canapés, or larger if there are fewer people; we cut ours into 7 cm (2¾ inch) squares, then cut the squares on the diagonal to get the triangles.

Heat a little vegetable oil in a frying pan over medium–high heat. Working with 4–5 triangles at a time (you'll have more chance of staying in control if you resist the temptation to crowd the pan!), fry the paella pieces in batches for 4–5 minutes on each side to create a crust — a traditional feature of a classic paella (aka the 'socarrat').

Place the newly crusted paella triangles on a baking tray and warm them in the oven until heated through — 10 minutes should do it.

Meanwhile, cook the squid. Fill a deep-fryer or medium-sized heavy-based saucepan one-third full of vegetable oil. Heat over medium heat until it reaches 180°C (350°F) when tested with a cooking thermometer, or until a cube of bread dropped into the oil turns golden brown in 15 seconds.

Sift the flours and salt together, into a bowl. Working in small batches, dust the squid rings in the flour mixture, then immediately drop them into the hot oil. Cook for 2–3 minutes, or until golden. Remove and drain on paper towel.

To make the saffron mayonnaise, place the saffron threads in a ramekin or small bowl and pour the hot water over. Allow the saffron to infuse for a minute or so, then mix the water and threads into the mayonnaise until combined.

TO SERVE

Remove the paella triangles from the oven. Place a dollop of saffron mayonnaise on each onigiri and top with the squid rings, securing them in place with small bamboo skewers if you like.

Serve immediately.

KOREAN BARBECUED PIZZAS

PREPARATION: 25 MINUTES + 1 HOUR PROVING // COOKING: 10 MINUTES // SERVES 6-8

Barbecued pizza dough: it's a thing. Think of the best wood-fired pizza you've ever had — fire and wheat are best friends forever! Add a few exotic saucy numbers and an angelic halo of haloumi and you have one killer boozing buddy.

PIZZA DOUGH

4 teaspoons dried yeast

1 tablespoon golden caster (superfine) sugar

80 ml (2½ fl oz/⅓ cup) extra virgin olive oil

1 kg (2 lb 4 oz) strong flour (also called bread-making flour)

1 teaspoon fine sea salt

THE REST

olive oil, for brushing

250 ml (9 fl oz/1 cup) Quick ranch dressing (see page 274)

125 ml (4 fl oz/½ cup) Tomatillo salsa verde (see page 277)

125 g (4½ oz/½ cup) gochujang (Korean hot red pepper paste; see glossary)

250 g (9 oz) block of haloumi

1 tablespoon black or white sesame seeds, or a mix of both

To make the pizza dough, put the yeast and sugar in a jug. Pour in the olive oil and 685 ml (23½ fl oz/2¾ cups) lukewarm water and mix to combine. Leave for 10 minutes for the yeast to activate (it will begin to foam).

Sift the flour and salt onto a clean work surface and make a well in the middle. Pour the yeast mixture into the well. Using a fork, gradually bring the flour in from the sides, swirling it into the liquid. Keep mixing, drawing larger amounts of flour in. When it all starts to come together, work in the rest of the flour with clean, flour-dusted hands. Knead for 10 minutes, or until you have a smooth, springy dough.

Place the dough in a large, flour-dusted bowl. Sprinkle a little more flour on top. Cover with a damp cloth and place in a warm spot for 1 hour, or until doubled in size.

Turn the dough out onto a flour-dusted work surface and knead it around a bit to push the air out — this is called knocking back the dough. You can use it immediately, or wrap in plastic wrap and keep in the fridge or freezer until required. We're using it straightaway, so divide the dough into 200 g (7 oz) balls; you should get five balls, each about the size of a baseball. Flatten each ball out, rolling it or just pushing and gently stretching it into any shape you like. It doesn't have to be round; think about the shape of your chargrill pan or barbecue and follow that.

Fire up your chargrill pan — or even better, the grill bars on your barbecue — to medium–high heat.

Working in batches if you need to, lightly oil the pizza dough portions and stick the oiled side on the grill. Leave for a minute or so, until there are nice deep grill marks underneath the bread — you want a little char on the dough, because that gives it the smoky taste we're after. Flip the dough over and grill the other side.

Remove the pizzas from the grill and get creative: alternate drizzling a little of the ranch dressing, salsa verde and gochujang, so that the sauces are layered and each bite gets a little of each. Finely grate the haloumi over the top, coating the pizza in a light dusting of cheesy snow. Garnish with the sesame seeds, cut into slices and serve.

SEAN PAUL CEVICHE

PREPARATION: 30 MINUTES // COOKING: 10 MINUTES // SERVES 6

Either the best or worst name for a dish we've ever come up with. Somebody once told us Sean Paul (of the iconic dancehall hit 'Temperature') is Indian–Jamaican, so when we came up with this Caribbean-style ceviche served on poppadoms, naturally we named it after him. (You'd have done the same, right? RIGHT?) As it turns out, Sean Paul apparently has no Indian heritage, which takes the name of this dish to a whole other level of stupid. Still, this dish is awesome. And Sean Paul is awesome. So there's that.

12 poppadoms, each 13 cm
    (5 inches) across
Curry salt (see page 145),
    for sprinkling
24 super-fresh scallops,
    roe removed
8 limes
sea salt flakes, for sprinkling
extra virgin olive oil,
    for drizzling
3 avocados
125 g (4½ oz) cherry tomatoes
1 small red onion
3 red bird's eye chillies, seeded
    if desired
1 bunch (60 g/2¼ oz) coriander
    (cilantro), leaves picked
    (save the roots and stems
    for the Black bean purée)

BLACK BEAN PURÉE
400 g (14 oz) tin black beans,
    drained and rinsed
juice of 2 limes
1 teaspoon ground cumin
50 ml (1¾ fl oz) olive oil
pinch of sea salt
reserved coriander (cilantro)
    roots and stems, from the bunch
    used above
1 garlic clove, peeled
1 tablespoon squid ink
    (optional; see glossary)

Place all the black bean purée ingredients in a blender and whiz to a smooth, silky purée. Add a little more olive oil if needed, but make sure you balance the oil with a little more lime juice. Cover and refrigerate until required, bringing the purée to room temperature for serving; the purée will keep in the fridge for up to 2 days.

Near serving time, cook the poppadoms according to the packet instructions. Immediately sprinkle with a little curry salt and set aside.

Using a very sharp knife, slice your scallops lengthways, into very thin round discs; depending on their size, you should be getting about 4–6 thin slices off each. Arrange all your lovely white scallop discs on a large plate, making sure they are not overlapping. Cover with plastic wrap and chill until you're ready to serve, but no longer than 2 hours, pulling them out of the fridge 10 minutes before serving.

Squeeze the juice from six of the limes and sprinkle all over the scallop discs, making sure each one is evenly dressed (this is the 'cooking' bit — the acid in the lime juice will 'cure' the scallop flesh). Add a little pinch of salt flakes to each scallop disc and a drop of extra virgin olive oil.

While the scallops are doing their thing — 3–4 minutes is long enough — stone the avocados and cut the flesh into slices. Cut the cherry tomatoes into quarters, and slice the onion and chillies as thinly as possible.

Break each poppadom into two or three pieces and arrange on a serving platter or individual plates.

Now it's just a case of building the ceviche however you like. So, dab a little spoonful of the bean purée here and there, add a slice of avocado here, and some onion slices there, scattering a few bits of tomato around. Place your scallop discs in all the gaps and add some chilli and coriander leaves. Add a final squeeze of juice from the remaining limes, a good sprinkle of curry salt and eat!

VOODOO WINGS

PREPARATION: 20 MINUTES + OVERNIGHT MARINATING // COOKING: 25 MINUTES // SERVES 4

We could talk about the merits of UFC (ultimate fried chicken) all year long. We have about ten varieties on our menus, all with their own charms, personalities and flavour dimensions. This version sits on the mouth-tingling, slightly sweaty, 'I might cry!' spectrum: it packs some serious heat, so be warned. The voodoo sauce is fairly lethal to the senses, so use gloves when making it, avoid splashing it around, and rinse your hands afterwards. It lasts forever, so keep the leftovers in a bottle in the fridge (it's great on scrambled eggs when you're hungover). The coconut cooler is a must, to temper the heat. It's the only known voodoo antidote!

Put the cayenne pepper and paprika in a small sieve and sift into a mixing bowl. Whisk in the buttermilk. Submerge the wings in the mixture, tossing to coat well. Cover with plastic wrap and marinate in the refrigerator overnight.

To prepare the voodoo sauce, first pop on a pair of disposable gloves. Have a clean squeeze bottle at hand, ready to pour the voodoo sauce straight into.

Put the sauce ingredients in a bowl or blender and carefully whisk or blend together. Slowly pour into a clean squeeze bottle, avoiding splashes. Refrigerate until required; the sauce will keep in the fridge indefinitely.

Whisk all the coconut cooler, ingredients together in a mixing bowl. Cover and refrigerate until needed; the mixture will keep in the fridge for up to 3 days.

TO SERVE

Fill a deep-fryer or large heavy-based saucepan one-third full of vegetable oil. Heat over medium heat until it reaches 180°C (350°F) when tested with a cooking thermometer, or until a cube of bread dropped into the oil turns golden brown in 15 seconds.

Combine the flour, oregano, salt and pepper in a mixing bowl. Drain the chicken wings from the buttermilk mixture and dredge them through the seasoned flour mixture.

Working in small batches, cook the floured wings for 5–7 minutes, or until golden and cooked through. Remove and drain on paper towel.

Toss the fried wings with some voodoo sauce, ensuring they are evenly coated. (If you're a bit of a wimp, you can serve the voodoo sauce on the side — but you're not a wimp, are you?)

Serve immediately, with the coconut cooler on the side as a life-saving dipping sauce.

1 heaped teaspoon cayenne pepper
1 heaped teaspoon smoked paprika
250 ml (9 fl oz/1 cup) buttermilk
1 kg (2 lb 4 oz) chicken wings — the largest ones you can find

VOODOO SAUCE
500 ml (17 fl oz/2 cups) spicy cayenne pepper sauce, such as Frank's RedHot sauce or Tabasco sauce
125 ml (4 fl oz/½ cup) Scotch bonnet sauce (see page 275)
3 drops chilli pepper extract (see glossary; we use a hot one, with 2.3 million Scoville units!)

COCONUT COOLER
250 g (9 oz/1 cup) Greek-style yoghurt
60 ml (2 fl oz/¼ cup) coconut milk
2 teaspoons shredded coconut, toasted
1 teaspoon caster (superfine) sugar

THE REST
vegetable oil, for deep-frying
600 g (1 lb 5 oz/4 cups) plain (all-purpose) flour
2 heaped teaspoons dried oregano
1 teaspoon sea salt
1 teaspoon ground white pepper

PRAWN and MANGO ROLLS

PREPARATION: 15 MINUTES // COOKING: 5 MINUTES // SERVES 8–10

If there's one thing that Aussies love, it's prawns. If there are two things that Aussies love, they are prawns and mangoes. Put them together and it's a fair bet that most Aussies will lose their minds. Put those two things together on a small, sweet roll with some mayo, and faces start melting.

For an even more luxurious version, feel free to substitute the prawns with a few chunks of cooked crabmeat.

The buns we're using here are the kind you find at Chinese bakeries — the sort that give you trays and tongs to select your sugar-stuffed cakes and savouries.

1 kg (2 lb 4 oz) cooked prawn (shrimp) meat (no heads or shells) — we use the meat from small 'cocktail' prawns, but if yours are larger, just chop them up a bit

125 g (4½ oz/½ cup) Chipotle mayo (see page 271)

salt flakes, for seasoning

ground white pepper, for seasoning

8–10 small Asian brioche buns, or Soft burger buns (see page 87)

½ iceberg lettuce, finely shredded

celery salt, for sprinkling

Mango salsa (see page 273), to serve

Place the prawn meat in a mixing bowl and toss with enough of the chipotle mayo to coat (reserve some of the mayo for spreading on the buns). Season with a pinch of salt flakes and ground white pepper to taste.

Gently split the buns and toast them — as these brioche-style buns are full of sugar, they burn easily, so be warned.

Spread a thin layer of the remaining chipotle mayo on the cut sides of each bun. On the bottom half lay down some lettuce, then the prawn mix. Sprinkle with a little celery salt, then add a spoonful of the mango salsa.

Place the bun lids on, then quickly put in face!

COCONUT SOFT-SHELL CRAB
with HOTSTEPPER SAUCE

PREPARATION: 20 MINUTES // COOKING: 25 MINUTES // SERVES 6

Somehow we distilled the entire essence of a tropical island holiday into a pile of deep-fried crab. There is nothing about this dish that doesn't scream tanning lotion, sunsets, romance, piña coladas and getting caught in the rain. Don't worry about planning a tropical holiday this year; cook this instead.

The hotstepper sauce is our version of a Thai nahm jim. She's a spicy little number, so watch your back! One other thing: make sure you wring out your crabs properly before you get going or they'll taste like a dark corner of the Mekong River. Which is not a nice thing, just sayin'.

6 frozen soft-shell crabs, thawed
350 g (12 oz/2 cups) rice flour
1 quantity Tempura batter
   (see page 277)
vegetable oil, for deep-frying

HOTSTEPPER SAUCE
125 ml (4 fl oz/½ cup) fish sauce
2 garlic cloves, peeled
juice of 4 limes
170 g (6 oz/¾ cup) caster
   (superfine) sugar
1 bunch (60 g/2¼ oz) coriander
   (cilantro), washed thoroughly,
   roots removed
2 tablespoons shredded coconut
2 tablespoons sambal oelek
   (see glossary)

TO SERVE
Curry salt (see page 145),
   for sprinkling
coriander (cilantro) sprigs,
   to garnish
1 red bird's eye chilli, chopped
   into thin rings
toasted shredded coconut,
   for sprinkling (optional)
2 limes, cut into wedges

To make the hotstepper sauce, put the fish sauce, garlic, lime juice, sugar and coriander in a blender and blitz to a rough paste. Decant into a small bowl and mix in the coconut and sambal oelek. Taste and adjust the seasoning if needed. Set aside while preparing the crab; this sauce is best made close to serving time.

Squeeze the thawed crabs to remove the excess water, then cut each one into quarters. Place the rice flour in a large bowl, and the tempura batter in another large bowl.

Fill a deep-fryer or large heavy-based saucepan one-third full of vegetable oil. Heat over medium heat until it reaches 180°C (350°F) when tested with a cooking thermometer, or until a cube of bread dropped into the oil turns golden brown in 15 seconds.

Working and cooking in batches, gently dredge each crab segment through the rice flour, then dip into the tempura batter, making sure it is completely covered. Let the excess batter drip off before gently lowering the crabs into the hot oil. Give the pieces a little jiggle to discourage them from sticking together, then don't touch them for 2–3 minutes. Give the pieces another jiggle, then cook for a further 2–3 minutes, so they become nice and crisp.

Remove from the hot oil using tongs, drain on paper towel and immediately sprinkle with curry salt. Arrange the crab pieces on a serving plate and garnish generously with coriander sprigs. Sprinkle with the chilli slices, and shredded coconut if desired.

Serve immediately, with the hotstepper sauce on the side for dipping into, and the lime wedges for squeezing over the crab.

KINGFISH PASTRAMI and RYE CRISPS

PREPARATION: 40 MINUTES + 2 DAYS CURING + EXTRA 12 HOURS MARINATING
COOKING: 10 MINUTES // SERVES 4-6

A loose riff on one of our favourite sandwiches, pastrami on rye. The fish is cured with the same ingredients used for pastrami, but we lose the bread for air-thin rye crisps. Combined with kohlrabi slaw and a pickle, it's a winner, folks. We use kingfish as it takes on flavour really well, but you can use salmon if that's your jam.

CURING THE KINGFISH

1 x 500–700 g (1 lb 2 oz–1 lb 9 oz)
  kingfish fillet, skin on
30 ml (1 fl oz) lemon juice
65 g (2¼ oz/½ cup) sea salt flakes
55 g (2 oz/¼ cup) raw or demerara sugar
1½ tablespoons freshly cracked black
  pepper, coarsely ground

Rub the fish all over on both sides with the lemon juice. Place the fish, skin side down, in a glass dish. In a small bowl, combine the salt flakes, sugar and pepper, then rub the mixture all over the top of the fish. Cover the fish loosely with plastic wrap and cure in the fridge for 2 days.

PASTRAMI GLAZE

2 tablespoons molasses
2 bay leaves, roughly torn
¼ teaspoon cayenne pepper
1 teaspoon caraway seeds
1 teaspoon coriander seeds
1 teaspoon sweet paprika
1 teaspoon freshly ground black pepper

After the fish has cured for 2 days, it's time for stage two. In a small saucepan, combine the molasses, bay leaves and cayenne pepper. Bring to a simmer over medium–high heat, then simmer for 1 minute, or until well combined. Remove from the heat and allow to cool to room temperature.

Place a small dry frying pan over medium heat. Lightly toast the caraway and coriander seeds, shaking the pan regularly for about 1 minute, or until the seeds become fragrant. Transfer the seeds to a mortar and let them cool completely, before crushing them as finely as you can. (Alternatively,

you can use a spice grinder.) Stir in the paprika and black pepper.

Remove the fish from the refrigerator and gently scrape off the curing rub. Place the fish on a plate, skin side down, and brush with the molasses mixture, picking out the bay leaves as you go. Sprinkle the ground spices evenly over the fillet. Return the fish to the fridge, uncovered. Leave overnight, or for up to 12 hours.

THE REST

2 kohlrabi
1 tablespoon wholegrain mustard
1 tablespoon dijon mustard
250 g (9 oz/1 cup) whole-egg mayonnaise
juice of 1 lemon
½ loaf of rye bread
a handful of dill pickles or cornichons,
  thinly sliced

Preheat the oven to 150°C (300°F).

Meanwhile, peel the kohlrabi and coarsely grate into a bowl. Add the wholegrain and dijon mustards. Gradually add the mayonnaise, stopping once you're happy you've created a good-looking slaw. Add the lemon juice, then season to taste with sea salt and freshly ground black pepper.

Thinly slice the rye bread and lay the slices on a baking tray. Pop them in the oven and bake for 6–8 minutes, or until crisp. Remove from the oven and leave to cool slightly.

Meanwhile, using a sharp knife, thinly slice your kingfish pastrami.

Arrange the rye crisps on a serving platter. Top with a small pile of the kohlrabi slaw and a few kingfish slices. Garnish with thin dill pickle slices and serve.

GRILLED WATERMELON

PREPARATION: 15 MINUTES // COOKING: 15 MINUTES // SERVES 8

Grilled fruit can be a bit of a divisive topic. Some people LOVE IT and some people really HATE IT. Hot fruit is not to everyone's taste, it would seem.

We are, however, front-row fans of grilled watermelon. This dish is all about grilling the watermelon for the right amount of time. It needs long enough for the sugars to cook, the texture to transform, and to pick up a strong char taste. When cooked correctly, the watermelon takes on a totally unexpected, almost tuna steak–like texture. Well, we think so anyway…

Heat a stovetop chargrill pan or the grill bars of a barbecue to the highest possible heat.

Grill the watermelon slices for 2–3 minutes on each side, until both sides have achieved char marks and the sugars in the watermelon have started to caramelise.

While the watermelon is grilling, make the salad, by combining all the remaining ingredients in a mixing bowl.

Serve the hot watermelon slices straight off the grill, piled high with some of the salad.

8 rectangular watermelon slices, each measuring about 15 x 8 cm (6 x 3¼ inches), and about 3 cm (1¼ inches) thick

½ bunch (30 g/1 oz) coriander (cilantro), leaves picked

½ bunch (40 g/1½ oz) mint, leaves picked

1 long red chilli, cut into thin rings, seeded if desired

1 green mango, or ½ a small green papaya, thinly sliced, then cut into matchsticks

juice of 1 lime

generous pinch of Paprika salt (see page 145)

CHOOK SAN CHOY BAU

PREPARATION: 30 MINUTES + 3 HOURS MARINATING // COOKING: 15 MINUTES // SERVES 6–8

We started doing versions of this much-loved pseudo-Chinese classic when people started telling us our menus were 'all fried food' or had 'nothing healthy on them'. We just put the words 'lettuce cups' on the menu, and overnight the health nuts became our best buddies again.

For the rest of you, this is basically a taco in a salad leaf — a great flavour burst for those scared of carbs and glutens, which to our knowledge don't actually exist. (Just kidding. Okay, carbs and glutens do exist... we just don't think people should freak out about them quite as much as they do.)

1 kg (2 lb 4 oz) boneless chicken thighs

1 quantity Achiote marinade (see Barbecued chicken tacos recipe, page 59)

2 iceberg lettuces

250 g (9 oz/1 cup) Salsa roja (see page 274)

140 g (5 oz/1 cup) crushed toasted peanuts, tossed with a pinch of chilli powder

JICAMA & CUCUMBER SALAD

1 bunch (60 g/2¼ oz) coriander (cilantro), leaves picked

1 jicama (see glossary), peeled and cut into very thin matchsticks; if unavailable, use a green mango or a small green papaya

1 Lebanese (short) cucumber, cut into very thin matchsticks

2 long red chillies, seeded and cut into very thin strips

1 small red onion, thinly sliced

juice of 1 lime

Put the chicken in a large mixing bowl. Add the achiote marinade and massage it into the chicken. Cover and leave to marinate in the refrigerator for 3 hours.

Near serving time, heat a chargrill pan or barbecue to a medium–high heat.

Meanwhile, prepare your lettuce cups by removing the centre core of each lettuce. The best way is to hold the lettuce upright, then bang it violently — just once — on the kitchen bench, and the core should just pop out. Wash the lettuce heads in icy-cold water, then carefully peel the leaves apart. Cut the leaves into cups using scissors. Allow to drain on paper towel.

When the chargrill pan or barbecue is hot, grill the marinated chicken thighs for 6–7 minutes, or until cooked through. Remove from the heat, season with sea salt and set aside until cool enough to handle.

Meanwhile, in a mixing bowl, combine the jicama and cucumber salad ingredients. Season with a little sea salt and toss to combine.

Slice up the grilled chicken pieces. In the bottom of each lettuce cup, put a good dollop of salsa roja, then some grilled chicken, followed by another dollop of salsa roja. Serve immediately, topped with the salad and a sprinkling of the chilli crushed peanuts.

KOREAN SALTEÑAS

PREPARATION: 45 MINUTES + 30 MINUTES MARINATING + 30 MINUTES RESTING

COOKING: 3 HOURS FOR THE RIBS, 25 MINUTES FOR THE SALTEÑAS // SERVES 10–12

'Fusion' is considered a dirty word in modern dining, which is just fine by us. We see no shame in combining the best bits of different cuisines together in the blender of life.

For this dish we take some short ribs that have been slathered in a Korean-style chilli paste, then barbecued, and jam it inside a salteña (a Bolivian fried empanada). We're advocating international relations right here.

KOREAN SHORT RIBS

2 tablespoons garlic powder

2 tablespoons onion powder

1 tablespoon sea salt

2 teaspoons freshly ground black pepper

2 teaspoons chilli powder

1 teaspoon Chinese five spice

500 g (1 lb 2 oz/2 cups) gochujang (Korean hot red pepper paste; see glossary)

100 ml (3½ fl oz) cola

4 kg (9 lb) beef short ribs

a handful of wood chips, suitable for smoking (optional)

Heat a hooded barbecue on low heat — around 130°C (250°F).

While the barbecue is heating up, marinate the ribs. In a mixing bowl, combine the garlic powder, onion powder, salt, pepper, chilli powder and five spice. Add the gochujang and cola and mix to a paste. Wearing gloves, and using a pastry brush, spread a thick, even amount of the spice mixture onto both sides of the ribs and place them on a large tray. Allow to marinate for 30 minutes at room temperature.

If you are using the wood chips to smoke the ribs on the barbecue, soak them in water while the ribs are marinating; check the packet directions for the recommended soaking time.

Place the ribs on the barbecue (along with the wood chips in a smoker box, if using). Close the lid. For the first hour, turn and baste the ribs every 15 minutes.

For the next 2 hours, check, turn and baste the ribs every 30 minutes. The ribs are done when the meat comes away from the bone with a fork, without too much effort.

Remove the ribs from the heat and set aside. Eat a few (because that's the cook's treat) and leave the rest to cool.

Shred the meat from the ribs and set aside. (The meat, by the way, can be barbecued a few days ahead and refrigerated until needed; the salteñas are also a great dish for using up left-over barbecued meat.)

PASTRY

450g (1 lb/3 cups) plain (all-purpose) flour

1 teaspoon baking powder

100 g (3½ oz) cold butter, diced

½ teaspoon sea salt

1 teaspoon ground turmeric

40 ml (1½ fl oz) orange juice

125–170 ml (4–5½ fl oz/½–⅔ cup) chilled sparkling water

The pastry recipe makes more than you need for these salteñas, but the left-over pastry freezes really well.

Sift the flour and baking powder into the bowl of an electric mixer. Add the butter, salt and turmeric and mix to a breadcrumb consistency.

CONTINUED OVER

49

CONTINUED FROM PREVIOUS PAGE

Add the orange juice, and enough of the chilled water to form a dough.

As soon as the mixture has come together, remove the dough to a clean, floured surface and knead for 2 minutes. Cover with plastic wrap and chill in the fridge for 30 minutes to allow the dough to rest.

Then, roll the chilled dough out as thinly as you can — around 1.5 mm (1⁄16 inch) is ideal. Using a 9 cm (3½ inch) round pastry cutter, cut out as many discs as possible.

Start with one pastry disc and do a trial run. Put a heaped teaspoon of the shredded rib meat in the middle of the pastry. Wet the edge along one half of the disc and fold the pastry over. You should be able to comfortably seal the disc into a semicircle — if not, remove a little stuffing and try again. Use a fork to 'crimp' the edges shut. Repeat with the remaining pastry rounds and filling.

The salteñas can be shaped 3–4 hours ahead and kept in the fridge until required; remove them from the fridge 30 minutes before cooking them.

TO SERVE

vegetable oil, for deep-frying

sliced spring onions (scallions),
  to garnish

Quick ranch dressing (see page 274)
  or Korean red pepper dressing
  (see page 273), to serve

When you're ready to serve, fill a deep-fryer or large heavy-based saucepan one-third full of vegetable oil. Heat over medium heat until it reaches 180°C (350°F) when tested with a cooking thermometer, or until a cube of bread dropped into the oil turns golden brown in 15 seconds.

Fry the salteñas in small batches for about 4–5 minutes, or until crisp and golden. Remove and drain on paper towel.

Serve hot, sprinkled with spring onion slices, and with little bowls of your choice of dressing on the side for dipping into.

TUNA POKE with CASSAVA CRACKERS

PREPARATION: 30 MINUTES // COOKING: 10–15 MINUTES // SERVES 6

Sure, we like to deep-fry things… who doesn't? We run pubs, and no matter what people say about diet regimes, when they've 'had a few' everyone loves deep-fried food. But — and it's a big but — in a concerted effort to maintain balance, we also like to make food for the ladies/people who don't like deep-fried food/people who like it 'fresh'.

Poke (pronounced 'pock-kay'), is a Japanese–Hawaiian dish that generally consists of sashimi-grade seafood, diced and tossed with a soy-based dressing, raw onion and other seasonings. Which is exactly what this is.

Ours is tangy, packed with spice, and the cassava crackers give it nice crunch. Which really puts the 'lad' in 'ladies'. Or, to keep it really fresh, you can serve the poke in lettuce cups instead of the crackers.

Cook the cassava crackers in the vegetable oil following the packet instructions, keeping them as flat as possible. Drain on paper towel and set aside.

Take your piece of tuna and pat it firmly with paper towel to make sure it's nice and dry. Using a very sharp knife, cut the tuna into 1 cm (½ inch) cubes. Cover with plastic wrap and set aside in the refrigerator until needed, but no longer than 3–4 hours.

In a mixing bowl, combine the spring onion, shallot and ginger. Add the sesame seeds, soy sauce, sesame oil and sriracha and mix together well. Now add the tuna and give everything a good mix to ensure the tuna is nicely coated.

Top each cassava cracker with a spoonful of the tuna mixture, and a small teaspoonful of mango salsa if desired. Serve immediately.

12 cassava crackers (see glossary)

vegetable oil, for frying the cassava crackers

300 g (10½ oz) piece of sashimi-grade tuna

3 spring onions (scallions), green part only, thinly sliced

1 French shallot, thinly sliced

1 thumb-sized knob of fresh ginger, thinly sliced into matchsticks

1 tablespoon sesame seeds, lightly toasted

80 ml (2½ fl oz/⅓ cup) Japanese soy sauce

1 teaspoon sesame oil

1 tablespoon sriracha hot chilli sauce (see glossary)

½ quantity of Mango salsa (optional; see page 273)

TALKING TACO

We are such fans of tacos that we have a version of them on every one of our menus. There is just something about eating everything on your plate — including the plate — that people can't seem to ever get enough of, so why fight it? The good news is that it doesn't always take two to taco. And if you don't know how to taco, look no further. This chapter will teach you how to make your own real-deal corn tortillas, and enough about meats, salsas and hot sauces to cover all bases.

There's a bit of a knack to eating a taco properly. It's not rocket science, but lots of people mess it up. All you do is grab a napkin; no knife or fork. Bring sides of taco together, then raise taco to mouth. Insert end of taco in mouth, then bite/chew/swallow (you choose). Repeat until no taco is left… then clean yo-self!

What we've learnt about tacos is not authentic. It does, however, come from a lot of time spent hungry, drunk and/or hungover in Los Angeles, Mexico and New York. So it's basically the traveller's guide to tacos — or rather, what we remembered when we got back.

When we talk tacos, we're not just on about corn tortilla numbers, but also bammies, bings, arepas and things in between — tacos and their cousins, basically. Mix and match as much as you like. Swap a bing meat for a bammy salsa, a taco seasoning for an arepa hot sauce, as you see fit. Get mingling, while we make you fluent in taco.

BUILDING FROM THE BASE UP

TORTILLAS

Unless you are Mexican and/or obsessed with the food from that amazing place in the world, you will probably need to go shopping to get yourself a few special implements and ingredients to make your own tortillas at home.

Thanks to the magic of the interwebs, you can usually find these things online; otherwise, if you're lucky enough to live within striking distance of a gourmet specialty store or spice grocer that features Latin ingredients, you should be able to find them without too much trouble. We promise it'll be worth it.

TACO FLOUR: Stock up on a flour known as masa harina, a maize-based flour that is used in an innumerable array of Latin dishes, from making tortillas to tamales. ('Masa' basically means 'dough' in Spanish.) Masa harina undergoes a lime-slaking treatment process that makes it specifically geared for these uses, so using other flours just won't do.

TORTILLA PRESS: Chances are you'll find one of these to suit your budget, ranging from cheap (just a few bucks) to a quality cast-iron press. If you can afford it, a cast-iron press will last longer and do the job better.

TORTILLA WARMER: This last one is just for kicks. Great to have, but if you haven't, we find a Chinese bamboo steamer set over a saucepan of simmering water will keep your tortillas soft and warm while waiting to be used.

BAMMIES

A bammy, for the uninitiated, is a type of Jamaican flatbread that is made from cassava — a yam-like root that is grated, pressed and then baked.

We took that idea and perverted it slightly, soaking the cassava in coconut milk and then giving it a quick deep-fry. The result is a thinner, crisper and sweeter version of the original, which we like to use as a Jamaicanised taco substitute. So, it's not really an authentic bammy… but we can't say we're sorry about it.

You can buy fresh cassava from most good markets and grocers, but it is also readily available frozen. If you can find the grated stuff frozen, use that — it will take most of the work out of this recipe, which we're always a fan of.

Just a heads-up here: you'll need a 15 cm (6 inch) round pastry mould to help shape your bammies; you'll also need to cut out 16 rounds of baking paper, to fit snugly inside the pastry mould.

BINGS

A 'bing' is otherwise known as a Peking/Beijing pancake. In our eyes, that means it can be used/abused in the same way you would a tortilla, arepa or bammy. What's great about them, though, is that they're thinner and lighter than a tortilla, and a little more subtle in flavour, which means you can make it all about the filling.

The store-bought ready-made pancakes, which you can find at any Asian grocer and some good supermarkets, are excellent: they come frozen and can be steamed or flash barbecued to bring them alive. They're a good thing to have on hand at all times, so you're always ready for an after-party/midnight feast any day of the week.

AREPAS

Think of these little dudes as tortilla's South American cousins.

Arepas are essentially a cake or patty made out of cornmeal, so they have a similar flavour and texture to fresh tortillas, pupusas and tamales. They're quick and simple to make and can be served just topped with butter, or split partway like a pide and stuffed (which is what we like to do).

REAL-DEAL CORN TORTILLAS

PREPARATION: 40 MINUTES // COOKING: 20 MINUTES // MAKES 16

360 g (12¾ oz/2 cups) masa harina
(see glossary)

500 ml (17 fl oz/2 cups) warm
water, approximately

Place the masa harina in a large mixing bowl. Gradually add about 375 ml (13 fl oz/1½ cups) of the warm water and start mixing (flours vary, so check the packet instructions for more specific directions on how much water you'll need). Once combined, let the dough rest for about 5 minutes.

Begin to knead the dough in the bowl, working it with your fingers and palms as if you are kneading bread dough. If the dough seems a bit dry, add a little more warm water to moisten the mixture. Once kneaded thoroughly, break the dough into 55 g (2 oz) balls, the size of golf balls. Set aside under a clean damp tea towel (dish towel) until ready to use; they can be kept under a damp cloth for 3–4 hours.

Trace the circumference of your tortilla press onto a sheet of baking paper, and cut out two circles per tortilla. Open the press and place one of the baking paper discs on the bottom. Place one ball of dough in the centre and place the other disc of paper on top. Gently close the press to form the tortilla, then open the press and remove the flattened dough (including the baking paper) — you now should have a tortilla pressed between two sheets of paper; the paper will help keep the shape of the tortilla, and keep it moist. Now continue until you have all the pressed tortilla shells you need.

Turn on your tortilla warmer, if you have one. Otherwise, partially fill a saucepan with water and bring to a simmer; line a bamboo steamer basket with a tea towel and set it over the simmering pan of water. Meanwhile, heat a chargrill pan or heavy-based frying pan over high heat.

When the chargrill pan is hot, peel the baking paper from one side of a tortilla and place in the hot pan, tortilla side down. Now carefully peel the paper off the back of the tortilla. Cook for about 30 seconds on each side — the tortilla should look lightly toasted; it's okay if a few air pockets form. Place the tortilla in your tortilla warmer or bamboo steamer to keep it warm. Continue this process until you've cooked all your tortillas.

Use immediately, or wrap well in plastic wrap and refrigerate for up to 2 days. To reheat them, you can warm the tortillas all at once in the steamer, or even zap them for a few seconds in a microwave.

BAMMY 101

PREPARATION: 30 MINUTES + 1 HOUR SOAKING // COOKING: 1¼ HOURS // MAKES 16

Here's how to make the basic bammy flatbreads, ready to top with your favourite tidbits (see our suggestions on pages 69–72).

Use a 15 cm (6 inch) pastry mould as a template to cut out 16 baking paper circles, to fit the mould interior. Set aside.

Peel the cassava, then grate it. Squeeze dry of any moisture and place in a mixing bowl. Add the salt and stir thoroughly, breaking up any lumps along the way. Divide the mixture into 40 g (1½ oz) balls the size of ping-pong balls and keep them underneath a damp paper towel until you have rolled them all out.

Set your pastry mould on a clean work surface. Place a cassava ball in the middle, place a baking paper disc on top, then press down with the back of a spoon to form a flat circle of even thickness. Repeat this process until you have flattened each ball of dough, stacking them between sheets of baking paper to stop them sticking together and to stop the dough drying out.

Pour the coconut milk into a plastic container that is deep enough to hold all the bammies.

Heat a heavy-based frying pan to medium–high heat and add a little vegetable oil. Place a bammy, dough side down, in the frying pan, and peel the baking paper off the top. Cook for 1–2 minutes, or until deep golden underneath — a slight char is good! — then flip it over and cook the other side for another 1–2 minutes, until golden. Add the bammy to the coconut milk. Repeat until all the bammies are bathing in coconut milk. Soak for at least 1 hour, or up to 24 hours, keeping them covered in the fridge.

When you've assembled your bammy fillings (see pages 69–72), you're ready to go. Fill a deep-fryer or large heavy-based saucepan one-third full of vegetable oil. Heat over medium heat until it reaches 180°C (350°F) when tested with a cooking thermometer, or until a cube of bread dropped into the oil turns golden brown in 15 seconds.

Working in batches of two or three, drain the bammies on paper towel, then deep-fry for 2 minutes, or until crisp on the outside, but still soft and chewy on the inside; test one if you're not sure. Drain on paper towel while cooking the remaining bammies.

While the bammies are still hot, but cool enough to handle, top them with your chosen fillings and serve.

600 g (1 lb 5 oz) cassava (see glossary)

1 teaspoon sea salt

2 x 400 ml (14 fl oz) tins of coconut milk

vegetable oil, for pan-frying and deep-frying

AREPA 101

PREPARATION: 20 MINUTES // COOKING: 10-20 MINUTES // MAKES ABOUT 12

A fresh arepa straight out of the pan will transport you to sunnier climes, for sure. We like to make these a tad thinner than the traditional recipe, so it's more about the filling and less about the dough. This approach makes them lighter too, which leaves room for... well, more arepas!

300 g (10½ oz/1 cup) pre-cooked
  yellow cornmeal (see glossary),
  such as the P.A.N. brand
vegetable oil, for brushing

Put the cornmeal in a large bowl. Add a good pinch of sea salt and make a well in the centre. Add 250 ml (9 fl oz/ 1 cup) water a little at a time, and gradually start to bring in the flour from the sides, mixing it with the water until a dough forms.

Knead the dough in the bowl for 2 minutes, ensuring everything is well combined, and adding a little more water if you see any cracking (meaning the dough needs a bit more moisture).

On a clean, lightly floured work surface, divide the dough into 12 portions. Roll out into rounds, about 1.5 cm (⅝ inch) thick, and about as wide as an English muffin. Cover the shaped arepas with a damp paper towel until ready to cook, so they don't dry out.

Heat a large heavy-based frying pan or barbecue flat plate to a medium heat.

Cooking them in batches if necessary, lightly oil both sides of each arepa and fry them for about 5 minutes on each side, or until golden.

Remove the arepas from the heat. Leave to cool slightly, then use a serrated knife to split them open, but not all the way through — leave a hinge on one side to keep the arepas together, like clamshells.

Add your chosen fillings (see pages 75–77) and serve.

These arepas are best eaten as quickly as possible, but any leftovers can be gently reheated in a low oven or under the grill (broiler) for 5–6 minutes.

BARBECUED CHICKEN TACOS
with MANGO SALSA

PREPARATION: 20 MINUTES + 3 HOURS MARINATING // COOKING: 10 MINUTES // SERVES 8–12

After about five minutes working around food establishments, I quickly discovered that a vast majority of people are afraid of anything 'new' or 'different'. Like, proper boogeyman scared-witless afraid. (Pork? I hate pork! Prawns? Eeew, aren't they the cockroaches of the sea? Pepper? Too spicy!)

If you know someone like that, this recipe is for them. This is a safe, friendly, reassuring taco that combines the familiar flavours of barbecued chicken, fresh mango and cooling lettuce to soothe sensitive dispositions. There you go, little baby. Hush now.

Put the chicken pieces in a large mixing bowl.

Place the achiote marinade ingredients in a blender and blitz to a smooth paste. Pour the marinade over the chicken, then use your hands to massage the marinade into the chicken. Cover with plastic wrap and marinate in the refrigerator for 3 hours.

When you're ready to serve, get your tortillas warming in a steamer or tortilla warmer (see page 56).

Meanwhile, heat a chargrill pan or barbecue to a medium–high heat. Grill the marinated chicken pieces for 3 minutes on each side, or until cooked through; aim for a few charred marks on the chicken, to give it a great smoky flavour.

Smear a little chipotle mayo over the middle of each warmed tortilla. Top with some shredded lettuce, then some chicken and mango salsa. Garnish with jalapeño slices and serve.

1 kg (2 lb 4 oz) whole boneless, skinless chicken thighs

ACHIOTE MARINADE
1½ tablespoons achiote paste (also called annatto; see glossary)
1 fresh jalapeño chilli, seeded and chopped
4 garlic cloves, chopped
1 teaspoon ground cumin
1 teaspoon smoked paprika
2 teaspoons dried oregano
juice of 1 large orange
60 ml (2 fl oz/¼ cup) red wine vinegar
60 ml (2 fl oz/¼ cup) olive oil
1½ teaspoons sea salt

TO SERVE
12 Real-deal corn tortillas (see page 56)
125 g (4½ fl oz/½ cup) Chipotle mayo (see page 271)
1 iceberg lettuce, finely shredded
½ quantity Mango salsa (see page 273)
2 fresh jalapeño chillies, sliced into thin rounds

BAJA FISH TACOS

PREPARATION: 20 MINUTES // COOKING: 15 MINUTES // SERVES 6-8

Let's get this chapter rolling with this Mexi–Californian taco classic. Wade out deep with some fried crispy fish, then add some fresh salsa and crunchy cabbage: it's the tastes of Venice Beach, folded into a small parcel for your mouth. Put on some rollerblades and get eating, Cali style.

With this dish, pay some attention to the frying of the fish — getting the coating super crispy is the key in getting this taco right.

On a plate or a flat dish, thoroughly combine the polenta, flour, salt, black pepper, cayenne pepper and garlic powder.

Crack the egg into a mixing bowl. Add 160 ml (5¼ fl oz) water and whisk together.

Get your tortillas warming in a steamer or tortilla warmer (see page 56) before you start cooking the fish. Heat up enough vegetable oil in a large heavy-based frying pan to fry the fish strips.

When you're all set, dip each fish strip into the egg mixture, then coat it in the polenta mixture, shaking off any excess. Add the fish to the hot oil and cook until golden — about 2–3 minutes on each side, depending on the thickness of the fish. Drain the fish pieces on a plate lined with paper towel.

To serve, pile some cabbage on each tortilla, then spoon the pico de gallo over. Add some fried fish and top with a squiggle of chipotle mayo and Mexican crema. Serve immediately, with lime cheeks for squeezing over.

150 g (5½ oz) polenta (cornmeal)

150 g (5½ oz/1 cup) plain (all-purpose) flour

½ teaspoon sea salt flakes

⅛ teaspoon freshly ground black pepper

¼ teaspoon cayenne pepper

¼ teaspoon garlic powder

1 egg

16 Real-deal corn tortillas (see page 56)

vegetable oil, for pan-frying

500 g (1 lb 2 oz) firm-fleshed white fish fillets, such as bream or latchet, cut into strips about 12 cm (4½ inches) long and 3 cm (1¼ inches) wide

TO SERVE

½ white or red cabbage, finely shaved

60 g (2¼ oz/¼ cup) Pico de gallo (see page 274)

60 g (2¼ oz/¼ cup) Chipotle mayo (see page 271)

60 g (2¼ oz/¼ cup) Mexican crema (see page 273)

2 limes, cut into cheeks or wedges

ASADO SHORT-RIB TACOS

PREPARATION: 20 MINUTES // COOKING: 15 MINUTES // SERVES 12

Whenever we go to LA, we eat way too many tacos at La Tehuana. Those guys work the grill like taco ninja bots. They sweat over a big pot of simmering meats, fish a slab out, whack it on a super-hot plate and dice it into caramelised chunks, while cooking your tortilla to order with their other hand. A thing of beauty, and all for about $1. Here is our version. You may need both hands for these ones.

2.5 kg (5 lb 8 oz) beef short ribs, cooked following the Short-rib nachos recipe on page 136, or 700–900 g (1 lb 9 oz–2 lb) left-over cooked short ribs

vegetable oil or lard, for pan-frying (if using left-over short ribs)

SLAW

¼ red cabbage, finely shaved

¼ Chinese cabbage (wong bok), finely shaved

6–8 small radishes, trimmed and grated

3–4 spring onions (scallions), thinly sliced

½ bunch (30 g/1 oz) coriander (cilantro), leaves picked

1 long red chilli, cut into thin rings and seeded if desired

2–3 limes, cut in half

1 tablespoon sesame oil

TO SERVE

12 Real-deal corn tortillas (see page 56)

sriracha hot chilli sauce (see glossary), for drizzling

2 teaspoons white sesame seeds, plus 2 teaspoons black sesame seeds, lightly toasted

125 g (4½ oz/½ cup) Sesame and garlic mayo (see page 276)

If using left-over short ribs from the night before, slice the rib meat into 2 cm (¾ inch) cubes. Pan-fry them in a little vegetable oil or lard, tossing them or shaking the pan for 3–4 minutes, or until they are crisp and caramelised all over, but still soft and melting in the middle. Set aside.

If you have cooked the short ribs from scratch for this recipe, ensure the finished meat has rested for at least 30 minutes, before slicing it into 2 cm (¾ inch) cubes. Set the meat aside (there is no need to pan-fry it).

Just before serving, make the slaw. Combine the cabbages, radish, spring onion, coriander and chilli in a mixing bowl. Squeeze the limes over to dress the slaw, then add the sesame oil and season with sea salt and freshly ground black pepper to taste. Mix thoroughly to combine.

TO SERVE

Get your tortillas warming in a steamer or tortilla warmer (see page 56).

Top them with some of the chopped rib meat, then some slaw. Finish with a drizzle of sriracha, a sprinkling of toasted sesame seeds and a dollop of sesame and garlic mayo. Start feasting straight away.

COFFEE and COLA-BRAISED BRISKET TACOS

PREPARATION: 40 MINUTES // COOKING: AT LEAST 6 HOURS FOR THE PORK +
15 MINUTES FOR THE CAPSICUMS // SERVES 12

Coffee, cola and beef may not sound like the best combination, but let this braise
stew down slowly and you'll end up with beef that is so sticky, rich and soft you'll
want to stuff a waterbed with it and float off into the taco astral planes.

Preheat the oven to its lowest setting; 90°C (195°F) is ideal.

Have your brisket rub ready in a mixing bowl and mix the cola through. Slather the mixture over both sides of the beef. Place in a large roasting tin and cover tightly with foil. Bake for at least 6 hours, or ideally overnight.

The brisket should pull apart easily with a fork — which is good, because you'll need a couple of forks and a few volunteers to help you shred the entire thing! So do that, now, and place the shredded meat in a great big bowl, discarding any fatty bits you don't like the look of.

Mix any juices from the roasting tin with the barbecue sauce, then mix it through the shredded meat. Set aside.

Char the whole capsicums on the open flame of a gas hob or barbecue for 8–10 minutes, or until the skins are blackened and blistered all over. (Alternatively, cut them into large flat chunks, place them skin side up on a grill tray and char the skins under a hot grill/broiler for 10–15 minutes.) Place in a bowl, cover with plastic wrap and leave to steam for 10–15 minutes. Peel off the charred skins, remove the seeds and membranes, then dice the flesh and set aside.

To make the slaw, combine the vegetables, coriander and chilli in a mixing bowl. Dress with the juice of 2 limes and a pinch of sea salt and leave for 2 minutes to let the lime juice work its magic and soften the cabbage a little. Now add more lime juice if you think it needs it.

Just before serving, thoroughly combine the coffee mayonnaise ingredients in a small bowl and set aside.

TO SERVE

Get your tortillas warming in a steamer or tortilla warmer (see page 56). On each warmed tortilla, place a small amount of the slaw. Top with some shredded brisket, then a dollop of coffee mayonnaise. Garnish with the roasted capsicum and a scattering of haloumi and serve.

1 quantity Brisket rub
  (from the Beef brisket recipe
  on page 110)
375 ml (13 fl oz/1½ cups) cola
4–5 kg (9–11 lb) side of beef
  brisket, trimmed of fat
250 ml (9 fl oz/1 cup) Barbecue
  sauce (see page 270)
2 red capsicums (peppers)

SLAW
¼ red cabbage, finely shaved
¼ white cabbage, finely shaved
6–8 small radishes, trimmed
  and grated
6–8 spring onions (scallions),
  thinly sliced
½ bunch (30 g/1 oz) coriander
  (cilantro), leaves picked
1 long red chilli, seeded and
  finely chopped
2–3 limes, cut in half

COFFEE MAYONNAISE
30 ml (1 fl oz) espresso coffee
250 g (9 oz/1 cup) whole-egg
  mayonnaise

TO SERVE
12 Real-deal corn tortillas
  (see page 56)
200 g (7 oz) haloumi cheese,
  finely grated

PORK BELLY TACOS

PREPARATION: 40 MINUTES + 2 HOURS COOLING
COOKING: 3-4 HOURS FOR THE PORK + 10 MINUTES FRYING // SERVES 6-10

We have reinvented and tweaked this taco a few times on a few different menus, but we always gravitate back to the original version. Basically it's small chunks of rich, fatty pork belly, some super-spicy mustard and a red cabbage slaw. It's hugely awesome and a nice break from braised-meat tacos.

Getting the pork right is all about balance: you want it to be juicy and rich — not too fatty and not too dry, our kind of just right.

THE PORK

1.5 kg (3 lb 5 oz) side of pork belly
1 tablespoon Chinese red pork seasoning (see glossary)
1 tablespoon Chinese cooking wine
60 ml (2 fl oz/¼ cup) dark soy sauce
80 ml (2½ fl oz/⅓ cup) light soy sauce
2 teaspoons white sugar
2 cm (¾ inch) knob of fresh ginger, sliced
1 bunch (60 g/2¼ oz) coriander (cilantro) stems and roots, thoroughly washed
2-3 star anise
½ cinnamon stick
1 dried red chilli
15 white peppercorns
1 litre (35 fl oz/4 cups) chicken stock

Preheat the oven to 170°C (325°F).

Place the pork in a roasting tin deep enough to accommodate it. Rub the pork on both sides with the red pork seasoning.

Put the cooking wine, soy sauces, sugar, ginger, coriander and spices in a mixing bowl. Pour in the stock and mix until thoroughly combined. Pour the mixture over the pork, then seal the roasting tin with foil. Transfer to the oven and bake for 3-4 hours, or until the pork is soft enough to fall away pretty easily when tested with a fork.

Remove from the oven and allow the pork to cool in the stock for a few hours.

JALAPEÑO MUSTARD

125 g (4½ oz/½ cup) American mustard
2 tablespoons pickled jalapeño chillies, drained

Blend the mustard and jalapeño chillies together and set aside, in a squeeze bottle if possible.

TO SERVE

vegetable oil, for pan-frying
½ red cabbage, thinly sliced
juice of 2 limes
18-20 Real-deal corn tortillas (see page 56)
125 ml (4 fl oz/½ cup) Barbecue sauce (see page 270)

Remove the cooled pork belly from the stock, discarding the stock. Slice the pork into 2.5 cm (1 inch) cubes.

Heat some vegetable oil in a heavy-based frying pan over medium–high heat. Fry the pork cubes for 4–5 minutes, or until crisp and caramelised on the outside. (Alternatively, you could deep-fry the buggers!)

Meanwhile, dress the cabbage with the lime juice and a good pinch of sea salt. Get your tortillas warming in a steamer or tortilla warmer (see page 56).

Take each warmed tortilla and squeeze a little barbecue sauce down the middle. Add a small pile of cabbage, then some fried pork belly. Finish with a squiggle of the jalapeño mustard and dig in!

CRUMBED AVOCADO TACOS
with TOMATILLO SALSA VERDE,
CHARRED CORN and HALOUMI

PREPARATION: 20 MINUTES // COOKING: 20 MINUTES // SERVES 8

You can get pretty sick of cooking the usual repertoire of eggplant (aubergine), mushrooms, not-bacon, near-meat and tofu for vegetarian buddies — so this taco is a little respite from such things, and the fried avocado works much better than you may think! Regardless of whether you're vego or not, this taco is a definite thumbs-up.

150 g (5½ oz/1 cup) plain (all-purpose) flour

120 g (4¼ oz/2 cups) panko (Japanese breadcrumbs; see glossary)

2 eggs

2 firm-ish avocados

Put the flour and breadcrumbs in separate bowls. In a third bowl, beat the eggs.

Now you want to cut each avocado into eight slices, and quickly crumb the slices so they don't oxidise and turn brown. To do this, cut one of the avocados in half lengthways, around the stone, and pull the two halves apart. Cut each half in half, then discard the stone. Cut each avocado quarter in half again, to give eight slices, and remove the peel. Quickly dust each avocado slice with flour, dip it in the beaten egg mixture, then coat in the panko crumbs.

Repeat with the remaining avocado and refrigerate until required.

CHARRED CORN

2 corn cobs, husks and silks removed

Bring a saucepan of lightly salted water to the boil. Add the corn cobs and cook for 7–8 minutes, or until tender. Drain and leave to cool.

Now use the open flame of a gas hob or a barbecue to slightly char the corn on each side for 2 minutes. (Alternatively, you could char them on a stovetop chargrill pan over medium heat.) Leave until cool enough to handle, then use a sharp knife to slice the kernels off the cob. Set aside.

TO SERVE

vegetable oil, for deep-frying

16 Real-deal corn tortillas (see page 56)

125 ml (4 fl oz/½ cup) Quick ranch dressing (see page 274)

1 iceberg lettuce, shredded

250 ml (9 fl oz/1 cup) Tomatillo salsa verde (see page 277)

250 g (9 oz) haloumi cheese, finely grated

Fill a deep-fryer or large heavy-based saucepan one-third full of vegetable oil. Heat over medium heat until it reaches 180°C (350°F) when tested with a cooking thermometer, or until a cube of bread dropped into the oil turns golden brown in 15 seconds.

Add the crumbed avocado slices in batches and cook for 2–3 minutes, or until golden. Remove with a slotted spoon and drain on paper towel.

Meanwhile, get your tortillas warming in a steamer or tortilla warmer (see page 56).

Squeeze a little ranch dressing down the centre of each warmed tortilla. Add a slice of crumbed avocado, a spoonful of barbecued corn kernels, some lettuce, and a drizzle of tomatillo salsa verde. Finish with a scattering of grated haloumi and serve.

JERK CHICKEN BAMMIES with QUICK WATERMELON SALSA

PREPARATION: 20 MINUTES + MARINATING // COOKING: 20 MINUTES // MAKES 12

Jerk chicken is always best cooked on a barbecue over glowing coals, but we're keeping things simple and grilling inside here. If you ever find yourself with a bit of left-over barbecued Jerk chicken (see page 108), you can always shred it up and use it in these bammies. The end result will be a little different, but not worse by any means!

Rub 2 tablespoons of the jerk paste over the chicken, and add a pinch of salt flakes for luck. Cover and leave to marinate in the fridge for a few hours, or overnight.

When you're ready to eat, get your chargrill pan nice and hot.

Meanwhile, put all the watermelon salsa ingredients in a bowl. Mix together and add a pinch of salt flakes.

Mix the remaining jerk paste through the mayonnaise and set aside.

TO SERVE

Following the Bammy 101 recipe on page 57, remove your bammies from their coconut milk bath and deep-fry them as instructed.

While they're draining on paper towel, cook the chicken thighs for 2–3 minutes on each side; getting a little black crust on the thigh is always good. Let the chicken rest on a plate for a few minutes, before cutting it into thin slices.

Add a teaspoon of the jerk mayo to each bammy. Top with the chicken, then the watermelon salsa, and serve them straightaway.

12 x 150 g (5½ oz) boneless, skinless chicken thigh fillets
3 tablespoons Jerk paste (see page 273)
sea salt flakes, for seasoning
60 g (2¼ oz/¼ cup) whole-egg mayonnaise
12 Bammies (see page 57), ready to be deep-fried

QUICK WATERMELON SALSA
200 g (7 oz) watermelon flesh (no seeds), cut into 5 mm (¼ inch) cubes
1 teaspoon chopped dill
3-4 sliced pickled jalapeño chillies (see glossary), finely chopped
zest and juice of 1 lime
2 tablespoons extra virgin olive oil

PORK BAMMIES with PINEAPPLE SALSA

PREPARATION: 20 MINUTES // COOKING: 20 MINUTES // MAKES 16

'I hate pulled pork…' said nobody, EVER. Okay, more like nobody we know (we respect diversity). Anyway, we love pulled pork. It's the dish that defines the southern USA, and we salute those dudes. Combine it with a little taste of Jamaica, and that's our kind of snack.

This recipe makes tasty work out of pulled-pork leftovers; otherwise make the pulled pork from scratch following the recipe on page 114, though you might want to reduce the quantity somewhat. The pineapple salsa is best made immediately prior to serving, as the pineapple will begin to ferment very quickly.

Combine the pineapple salsa ingredients in a mixing bowl. Add a pinch of sea salt and stir thoroughly. Set aside.

Following the Bammy 101 recipe on page 57, remove your bammies from their coconut milk bath and deep-fry them as instructed.

While they're draining on paper towel, thoroughly mix together the thinly sliced cabbage and jerk mayo, to make a simple slaw.

Just before serving, gently reheat or warm up your pulled pork. Place a spoonful of slaw on each bammy. Top with a generous pile of pork, finish with a spoonful of pineapple salsa and serve.

16 Bammies (see page 57), ready to be deep-fried

½ small red cabbage, very thinly sliced

2–3 tablespoons Jerk mayo (see page 272)

800 g (1 lb 12 oz) Puerto Rican pulled pork (see page 114)

PINEAPPLE SALSA

½ pineapple, peeled and cored, then very finely diced

½ red onion, very finely diced

juice of 2 limes

4 tablespoons finely chopped coriander (cilantro) stems and leaves

60 ml (2 fl oz/¼ cup) extra virgin olive oil

PRAWN BAMMIES

PREPARATION: 15 MINUTES // COOKING: 20 MINUTES // MAKES 16

A sure-as-sure-can-be crowd pleaser, this is the simplest and daintiest of the taco bunch. Just grab the best-quality prawns you can find or afford, then barbecue and build. Pair these beauties with a cold beer, some sunglasses and a deck chair and you have your weekend/life sorted.

16 Bammies (see page 57),
   ready to be deep-fried
16 giant raw prawns (shrimp),
   peeled and deveined, tails
   removed
125 ml (4 fl oz/½ cup) fruity,
   hot barbecue sauce (we like
   Walkerswood ginger mango
   hot sauce)
½ quantity Mango salsa
   (see page 273)
16 coriander (cilantro) sprigs,
   to garnish
35 g (1¼ oz/½ cup) lightly
   toasted shredded coconut,
   to serve

Following the Bammy 101 recipe on page 57, remove your bammies from their coconut milk bath and deep-fry them as instructed.

Meanwhile, heat a chargrill pan or barbecue to a medium–high heat, then cook the prawns for 2–3 minutes, so that they pick up a little char and are cooked through.

Place a dollop of hot sauce on each bammy. Add a prawn, then some mango salsa. Garnish with a coriander sprig and a small mound of coconut and serve.

SOFT-SHELL CRAB AREPAS

PREPARATION: 20 MINUTES // COOKING: 15 MINUTES // SERVES 12

Not much can improve a piece of deep-fried soft-shell crab. Not a burger bun, or even a taco. We've tried nearly every version out there, and they're never as good as you think they're going to be… until now!

For some reason the texture and flavour of the arepa and the freshness of charred corn works really well here with the fried soft-shell crab, so we're converted. The flavours in this dish are a confused mix of Thai and South American, but don't let that stop you: it's as tasty as.

Fill a deep-fryer or large heavy-based saucepan one-third full of vegetable oil. Heat over medium heat until it reaches 180°C (350°F) when tested with a cooking thermometer, or until a cube of bread dropped into the oil turns golden brown in 15 seconds.

Pour the rice flour onto a dinner plate. Dredge each crab with the flour, evenly coating it. Dust off the excess flour, then dip each crab into the tempura batter.

Gently lower each crab into the hot oil, leaving plenty of space between them; depending on the size of your deep-fryer, you may need to cook them in several batches. Give the pieces a little jiggle to stop them sticking together, then don't touch them for 2–3 minutes. Jiggle again, then cook for a further 2–3 minutes, or until the coating on the crabs is nice and crisp. Remove from the hot oil and drain on paper towel. Sprinkle immediately with a pinch of salt flakes.

Meanwhile, in a mixing bowl, combine the coriander, mint, chilli and lime juice. Season with a pinch of salt flakes.

Use a serrated knife to split the warm arepas open, but not all the way through — leave a hinge on one side to keep the arepas together.

Into each arepa, squeeze a little chipotle mayo. Insert a piece of crab and some of the fresh herb salad. Finish with a few drops of sriracha and serve.

vegetable oil, for deep-frying

175 g (6 oz/1 cup) rice flour, for dredging

3 small frozen soft-shell crabs, thawed, cleaned, patted dry and cut into quarters

1 quantity Tempura batter (see page 277)

salt flakes, for seasoning

1 bunch (60 g/2¼ oz) coriander (cilantro), leaves picked

1 bunch (60 g/2¼ oz) mint, leaves picked

1 long red chilli, seeded and thinly sliced

juice of 1 lime

TO SERVE

12 Arepas (see page 58), warmed

125 g (4½ oz/½ cup) Chipotle mayo (see page 271)

sriracha hot chilli sauce (see glossary), for drizzling

POPCORN PRAWN AREPAS
with BANANA KETCHUP

PREPARATION: 40 MINUTES // COOKING: 1 HOUR // SERVES 12

The banana ketchup recipe makes more than you'll need, but once you've tasted it, you'll slather it on everything, from fish to chicken to steaks. It can be made way ahead of time as it'll last for a good few weeks in the fridge.

vegetable oil, for deep-frying

20 g (¾ oz) shop-bought, ready-to-eat salted popcorn

salt flakes, for seasoning

125 g (4½ oz/1 cup) cornflour (cornstarch)

12 extra-large raw prawns (shrimp), peeled and deveined, leaving the tails intact

2 egg whites, lightly beaten

3 tablespoons Banana ketchup (see below)

12 Arepas (see page 58), warmed

BANANA KETCHUP

2 tablespoons canola oil

¾ teaspoon achiote paste (see glossary)

1 small yellow onion, chopped

2 garlic cloves, crushed

2 red bird's eye chillies, chopped

1 generous tablespoon tomato paste (concentrated purée)

2 large ripe bananas, mashed

125 ml (4 fl oz/½ cup) apple cider vinegar

2 firmly packed tablespoons dark brown sugar

½ teaspoon freshly ground black pepper

pinch of sea salt

pinch of ground cloves

1 teaspoon soy sauce

1 bay leaf

To make the banana ketchup, combine the canola oil and achiote paste in a saucepan. Place over low heat and leave to gently sizzle for 2 minutes. Turn the heat up to medium, add the onion and cook, stirring often, for 5–7 minutes, or until soft and translucent. Add the garlic and chilli and sauté for 1–2 minutes, until aromatic. Now add the tomato paste and cook, stirring often, until the mixture is a reddish orange and the tomato paste is no longer visible.

Stir in the mashed bananas, combining well. Stir in 60 ml (2 fl oz/¼ cup) water, along with the vinegar, sugar, pepper, salt, cloves, soy sauce and bay leaf. Bring to the boil, then reduce the heat to a simmer. Partially cover with a lid, then simmer for 20–30 minutes, or until the mixture is thick — like ketchup! Remove from the heat and leave to cool for 10 minutes. Discard the bay leaf.

Purée the mixture using a hand-held stick blender. Taste, then adjust as needed by adding water to thin it, sugar to sweeten it, or vinegar for a bit more tartness. Transfer to a clean jar and keep in the fridge for up to 3 weeks.

TO SERVE

Fill a deep-fryer or large heavy-based saucepan one-third full of vegetable oil. Heat over medium heat until it reaches 170°C (325°F) when tested with a cooking thermometer, or until a cube of bread dropped into the oil turns golden brown in 20 seconds.

Blend or smash the popcorn with a rolling pin until it has a breadcrumb consistency. Place in a bowl, then mix the cornflour and a pinch of salt flakes through.

Place the prawns in a large bowl, add the egg whites and gently mix until coated all over. Holding them by the tail, dip each one into the cornflour mixture, then add them to the hot oil in batches of four or five. Cook for 2 minutes, then drain on paper towel and sprinkle with salt flakes.

Place a prawn on each arepa, top with a teaspoon of the banana ketchup and eat straightaway.

CHEESE AREPAS

PREPARATION: 15 MINUTES // COOKING: 5 MINUTES // SERVES 12

This arepa is so cute we want to invite it out on a date, make it a mix tape,
buy it a steak dinner and lay it down on a bed of rose petals.

Heat a large heavy-based frying pan or barbecue flat plate to a medium heat.

Add a little vegetable oil and cook the haloumi for 1–2 minutes on each side, or until golden and crisp.

Meanwhile, use a serrated knife to split the warm arepas open, but not all the way through — leave a hinge on one side to keep the arepas together.

Into each arepa, squeeze a small amount of salsa roja. Insert a piece of fried haloumi and as much corn salsa as you can jam in there. Enjoy hot.

vegetable oil, for pan-frying
250 g (9 oz) block of haloumi
  cheese, cut into 12 slices
12 Arepas (see page 58), warmed
125 ml (4 fl oz/½ cup) Salsa roja
  (see page 274)
½ quantity Corn salsa
  (see page 272)

DUCK BINGS

PREPARATION: 40 MINUTES + OVERNIGHT MARINATING // COOKING: 1¼ HOURS // SERVES 12-16

We've eaten so many duck pancakes at our favourite late-night Chinese restaurant at 2 am we've lost count. This is our ode to their pancake radness, but with a slightly American-style barbecue sauce twist. Some people might call this blasphemy; we call it delicious.

Wash the duck thoroughly inside and out with cold water. Pat dry with paper towel. In a mixing bowl, combine the sugar, star anise, ginger and spring onion, along with a good few pinches of sea salt. Stuff this mixture into the cavity of the duck. Use a bamboo skewer, or a needle and thread, to close up the cavity, then place the duck in a colander in the sink.

In a small bowl, mix the maltose with 2 tablespoons of the vinegar.

Boil a full kettle of water. Pour the boiling water into a large jug, then pour in the remaining vinegar. Pour this vinegar and hot water mixture over the duck, ensuring all the skin comes in contact with the boiling water. Pat dry with paper towel.

Place the duck in a roasting tin and smear the maltose vinegar mixture over the skin, ensuring it is evenly coated. Place the roasting tin, uncovered, in the fridge overnight.

The next day, remove the duck from the refrigerator and allow it to come to room temperature.

Preheat the oven to 180°C (350°F). Cover the duck with foil and roast for 30 minutes.

Turn the heat up to 200°C (400°F). Remove the foil and roast the duck for a further 30 minutes, or until the duck is cooked through, golden brown and crisp.

Remove from the oven and immediately carve the duck, making sure that each piece of skin has a little meat attached to it.

To serve, warm the pancakes according to the packet instructions, then keep them covered with a tea towel (dish towel) to stop them drying out.

In a small bowl, combine the hoisin and barbecue sauce. Smear some of the mixture over each warmed pancake. Add some cucumber batons, then top with the duck pieces, making sure each serve has a little skin and meat.

Garnish with the spring onion, sesame seeds and chilli strips and serve.

1.8-2 kg (4 lb-4 lb 8 oz) duck

75 g (2½ oz/⅓ cup) caster (superfine) sugar

3 star anise

3 cm (1¼ inch) knob of fresh ginger, peeled and coarsely chopped

8-10 spring onions (scallions), coarsely chopped

1 tablespoon maltose or honey

60 ml (2 fl oz/¼ cup) red wine vinegar

TO SERVE

12-16 ready-made Chinese pancakes (see glossary)

125 ml (4 fl oz/½ cup) hoisin sauce

125 ml (4 fl oz/½ cup) Barbecue sauce (see page 270)

2 Lebanese (short) cucumbers, sliced into batons

8 spring onions (scallions), green part only, cut into long, thin strips

2 tablespoons white sesame seeds, lightly toasted

2 long red chillies, cut into long, thin strips

STIR-FRIED PORK BINGS with PEANUT SAUCE and LIME

PREPARATION: 40 MINUTES + 3 HOURS MARINATING // COOKING: 20 MINUTES // SERVES 6

Here the flavours of South-East Asia bring out all the piggy goodness from a prime piece of pork belly. When cooking the pork belly, hot and fast is the rule — and do let it rest a little before you serve it up, so it's meltingly tender.

500 g (1 lb 2 oz) boneless
   pork belly, cut into 2 cm
   (¾ inch) chunks
12 ready-made Chinese pancakes
   (see glossary)
¼ head iceberg lettuce, very
   thinly sliced
3–4 tablespoons chopped coriander
   (cilantro), to serve
2–3 limes, cut into wedges

PINEAPPLE & CHILLI MARINADE
2 tablespoons fish sauce
2 tablespoons light soy sauce
2 tablespoons pineapple juice
125 ml (4 fl oz/½ cup) coconut milk
1 tablespoon palm sugar (jaggery)
1 tablespoon sambal chilli sauce
2 garlic cloves, crushed

PEANUT SAUCE
1 lemongrass stem, pale part
   only, very finely chopped
2 garlic cloves, crushed
½ teaspoon grated fresh ginger
2 teaspoons canola oil
2 teaspoons kecap manis
   (Indonesian sweet soy sauce)
125 ml (4 fl oz/½ cup) coconut milk
2 teaspoons sugar
2 teaspoons sambal chilli sauce
juice of 1 lime
125 g (4½ oz/½ cup) peanut butter

Combine all the marinade ingredients in a bowl, mixing well to dissolve the sugar. Add the pork and toss to coat on all sides, then cover and marinate in the refrigerator for at least 3 hours, or overnight for a more flavoursome result.

When you're nearly ready to serve, make the peanut sauce. Add the lemongrass, garlic and ginger to a food processor or blender and purée with a splash of water until you have a paste.

Add the spice paste to a small saucepan and gently cook off the raw flavours, stirring over low heat for 5 minutes. Stir in the remaining peanut sauce ingredients and bring to a simmer, then remove from the heat and leave to cool while cooking the pork.

Drain the marinade off the pork. Heat a frying pan or wok over very high heat. When the pan is VERY hot, add the pork and stir-fry quickly for 2–3 minutes. This is pork belly, so it will have a little 'bite', but once it is cooked, let it rest on a warmed plate for 5 minutes and it will be nice and tender.

Meanwhile, warm the pancakes according to the packet instructions, then keep them covered with a tea towel (dish towel) to stop them drying out.

Add a little lettuce to each pancake, then top with a good spoonful of the stir-fried pork. Drizzle with the peanut sauce and sprinkle with the coriander. Serve with lime wedges, for squeezing over.

SALT and PEPPER TOFU BINGS

PREPARATION: 30 MINUTES // COOKING: 15 MINUTES // SERVES 8

Another version of a classic Chinese dish. It's really the combination of crispy, spiced crust, soft tofu, fresh salad and spicy sauce that makes this recipe so much more than the sum of its parts. A true king of bings.

Put the salt and pepper mix in a mixing bowl. Add the flour and cornflour and mix until thoroughly combined.

In another mixing bowl, combine the cabbage and radish salad ingredients. Season with a pinch of sea salt.

Fill a deep-fryer or large heavy-based saucepan one-third full of vegetable oil. Heat over medium heat until it reaches 180°C (350°F) when tested with a cooking thermometer, or until a cube of bread dropped into the oil turns golden brown in 15 seconds.

Pat the tofu cubes dry with paper towel. Gently toss half the tofu through the seasoned flour mixture, then immediately add to the hot oil and cook for 5 minutes, or until the coating is crisp. Drain on paper towel and repeat with the remaining tofu cubes.

Meanwhile, warm the pancakes according to the packet instructions, then keep them covered with a tea towel (dish towel) to stop them drying out.

Place a little of the cabbage and radish salad on each warmed pancake, followed by a few fried tofu cubes. Add a squiggle of the red pepper dressing, then the sesame and garlic mayo. Garnish with the spring onion and serve.

1 quantity Salt and pepper mix (see page 275)

2 tablespoons plain (all-purpose) flour

2 tablespoons cornflour (cornstarch)

300 g (10½ oz) block of silken tofu, cut into 1.5 cm (⅝ inch) cubes

vegetable oil, for deep-frying

CABBAGE & RADISH SALAD
¼ red cabbage, thinly sliced

¼ Chinese cabbage (wong bok), thinly sliced

1 bunch (60 g/2¼ oz) coriander (cilantro), leaves picked

4-6 radishes, trimmed and chopped into very thin matchsticks

juice of 1 lime

TO SERVE
12 ready-made Chinese pancakes (see glossary)

125 ml (4 fl oz/½ cup) Korean red pepper dressing (see page 273)

125 g (4½ oz/½ cup) Sesame and garlic mayo (see page 276)

8 spring onions (scallions), green part only, thinly sliced

KUNG PAO CHICKEN BINGS

PREPARATION: 30 MINUTES + 1 HOUR MARINATING // COOKING: 15 MINUTES
SERVES 6–8

Kung pao chicken: it's become about as bastardised as Western–Chinese
food can get. So we decided to kick it up a notch and deep-fry ours,
in keeping with our reputation for taking something good and
making it... more trashy. In a good way.

500 g (1 lb 2 oz) boneless,
  skinless chicken thighs, cut
  into 1.5 cm (⅝ inch) cubes
3 teaspoons Chinese rice wine
2 teaspoons sesame oil
2 tablespoons light soy sauce
3 tablespoons sichuan peppercorns
125 g (4½ oz/1 cup) cornflour
  (cornstarch)
1 tablespoon sea salt
¼ red cabbage, thinly sliced
¼ Chinese cabbage (wong bok),
  thinly sliced
juice of 1 lime
vegetable oil, for deep-frying

TO SERVE
12 ready-made Chinese pancakes
  (see glossary)
125 ml (4 fl oz/½ cup) hoisin
  sauce
125 ml (4 fl oz/½ cup) Barbecue
  sauce (see page 270)
thin spring onion (scallion)
  strips, to garnish
70 g (2½ oz/½ cup) roasted
  peanuts, crushed
sriracha hot chilli sauce
  (see glossary), for drizzling

Place the chicken in a mixing bowl. Drizzle with the rice wine, sesame oil and soy sauce, then toss to coat all over. Cover with plastic wrap and marinate in the fridge for 1 hour.

Toast the sichuan peppercorns in a small dry frying pan over medium heat for 3–5 minutes, or until fragrant, tossing frequently so they don't burn. Finely grind them using a mortar and pestle (or tip them onto a clean chopping board and finely crush them with a rolling pin). Transfer to a mixing bowl, add the cornflour and salt and thoroughly mix together.

In a mixing bowl, toss together the cabbages and lime juice. Season with a pinch of sea salt and set aside.

Fill a deep-fryer or large heavy-based saucepan one-third full of vegetable oil. Heat over medium–low heat until it reaches 160°C (315°F) when tested with a cooking thermometer, or until a cube of bread dropped into the oil turns golden brown in 30–35 seconds.

Shake off any excess marinade from the chicken pieces, then dredge them through the seasoned cornflour. Working in batches if necessary, add them to the hot oil and cook for 5 minutes, or until golden and crisp. Drain on paper towel.

Meanwhile, warm the pancakes according to the packet instructions, then keep them covered with a tea towel (dish towel) to stop them drying out.

In a small bowl, combine the hoisin and barbecue sauce. Top each warmed pancake with a little dressed cabbage, followed by the fried chicken and a drizzle of the hoisin sauce mixture. Garnish with spring onion, sprinkle with the peanuts, drizzle with a few drops of sriracha and serve.

BREAD
OR ALIVE

Burgers are a big deal the world over. Everyone seems to have an opinion on what one is, where to get it and what should or shouldn't be in one. We'd rather steer clear of the argument altogether and just keep going about doing our own thing; collectively we've eaten enough of them to hopefully have a clue.

If you ask us…

THE BUN should be the softest one you can find. Treat it nice. Treat it kind — don't overstuff it.

THE FILLINGS: a beef patty, pickle, tomato sauce and melted cheese is the simplest route to burger alchemy, but this is a whole chapter on burgers and stuff you find between two pieces of bread (hello, hot dog)… so there are clearly a few other options that work.

Go with your burger instincts, and chop and change recipes for sauces and fillings as you like, but do us a favour: DON'T EVER PUT CHICKEN WITH BEEF. It just doesn't work.

So what are you waiting for? Let's get carb loading.

HOT DOG ROLLS

PREPARATION: 30 MINUTES + UP TO 2 HOURS RISING // COOKING: 30 MINUTES
MAKES 12

Sure, you can always buy in your hot dog rolls, but you'll get extra brownie points if you make 'em yourself. You can finish the rolls with a sprinkling of sesame seeds, nigella seeds or poppy seeds if you're feeling a little fancy.

2 teaspoons dried yeast

1½ teaspoons caster (superfine) sugar

120 ml (4 fl oz) warm water

950 g (2 lb 2 oz) plain (all-purpose) flour, sifted twice, plus extra for dusting

1 teaspoon sea salt

2 large eggs

120 ml (4 fl oz) warm milk

45 g (1½ oz) unsalted butter, melted, plus extra for greasing

TO FINISH

3 egg yolks, lightly beaten with 2 teaspoons water

seeds, for sprinkling (optional)

In the bowl of an electric mixer, combine the yeast, sugar and half the warm water. Let stand for 5–10 minutes, until the mixture becomes frothy.

Add the flour and salt to the yeast mixture. In a separate bowl, lightly beat the eggs with the milk, then add to the flour mixture with the melted butter.

Attach the dough hook to the mixer, and have the remaining warm water at the ready.

Turn the mixer onto medium–low, adding the remaining warm water to the flour mixture until a soft dough has formed. Now knead for 5 minutes in the mixer, or if you're feeling strong, a good 8–10 minutes by hand.

Shape the dough into a ball, then place in a lightly greased bowl. Cover with plastic wrap and leave the bowl somewhere warmish for an hour or so, until the dough has doubled in size.

Punch the dough back by gently sticking your fist in the middle. Now divide the dough into 12 equal portions. Gently roll each one out into a hot dog–shaped roll, about 18–20 cm (7–8 inches) long. Place on a lightly greased baking tray, then leave for another 30–45 minutes in the same place you proved the dough the first time round.

Preheat the oven to 170°C (325°F). When you're happy your hot dog rolls have proved long enough, gently brush them all over with the egg wash. If you wanted to garnish with seeds, now is the time…

Bake the rolls for 25–30 minutes, or until they have turned a nice, dark golden brown. Turn out onto a wire rack and leave to cool.

These buns really rock when they've been lightly steamed for 2 minutes before using, or even zapped for 5–10 seconds on high in a microwave.

SOFT BURGER BUNS

PREPARATION: 30 MINUTES + ABOUT 2 HOURS RISING // COOKING: 20 MINUTES
MAKES 10–12

Asian bakeries are a great place to start if you're looking to channel a fast food–style sugary bun, but in case you feel like having a crack at it yourself, we reckon this recipe is pretty on the money.

Add the milk, sugar, yeast, egg and melted butter to a small jug. Stir well and set aside for 8–10 minutes, or until the yeast has become foamy.

Place the flour in the bowl of an electric mixer, fitted with a dough hook. Add the salt to one side of the bowl, and the yeast mixture to the other. On a low setting, gently mix the flour into the yeast mixture for 4–5 minutes, until everything is well combined. The mixture will be sticky, creating burgers that are soft, rather than dense.

Scrape the dough out onto a lightly floured work surface and knead with the heel of your hand for a good 8–10 minutes. You'll know the dough is ready when you gently press two fingers into the dough, and it slowly springs back, leaving no trace of the fingerprints in the dough.

Place the dough in an oiled bowl. Leave to rise in a draught-free place for at least 1 hour, or until it has doubled in size.

Gently punch the dough down with your closed fist to remove excess air bubbles. Divide the dough into 10–12 equal portions, depending on how big you'd like your burgers. Leave the dough to rest for another 10 minutes; this will help with forming the buns.

Shape the dough into burger buns (or into hot dog rolls if you like). Place on lightly floured baking trays. Cover with plastic wrap and leave to rise in a warm place for another 45 minutes to 1 hour, or until doubled in size again.

Preheat the oven to 190°C (375°F). Brush the buns with the egg wash and sprinkle with the sesame seeds. Bake for about 20 minutes, or until golden brown.

Remove from the oven and cover with a clean tea towel (dish towel); this will help keep the buns soft, as they'll gently steam as they cool. Once cooled, store them in an airtight container; they'll be fine for 2–3 days. To soften them up again before using, just zap them in a microwave on high for 5–10 seconds.

375 ml (13 fl oz/1½ cups) warm milk
2 tablespoons caster (superfine) sugar
1 tablespoon dried yeast
1 large egg
60 g (2¼ oz) butter, melted
600 g (1 lb 5 oz/4 cups) plain (all-purpose) flour
1 teaspoon sea salt

TO FINISH
1 egg, beaten with 2 tablespoons water
1 tablespoon sesame seeds, approximately

FRIED CHICKEN BURGERS with SALSA ROJA and CORN SALSA

PREPARATION: 25 MINUTES + OVERNIGHT MARINATING // COOKING: 30 MINUTES // SERVES 6

The very first fried chicken burger we put on one of our menus was a blatant attempt to rip off an almost godly burger sold by a big American fried-chicken franchise. We've travelled a long way since then. Of all the versions of a fried chicken burger we've come up with, this one is our favourite.

12 large boneless, skinless chicken thighs, about 150 g (5½ oz) each

1 tablespoon sea salt

500 ml (17 fl oz/2 cups) buttermilk

vegetable oil, for deep-frying

½ red cabbage, thinly sliced

juice of 1 lime

Chipotle mayo (see page 271), for dressing

HERB & CHILLI FLOUR

300 g (10½ oz/2 cups) plain (all-purpose) flour

1 tablespoon onion powder

1 tablespoon garlic powder

1 tablespoon dried oregano

1 tablespoon dried sage

1 tablespoon chilli powder

1 tablespoon sweet paprika

TO SERVE

6 brioche burger buns, or Soft burger buns (see page 87)

Chipotle mayo (see page 271), for drizzling

½ quantity of Corn salsa (see page 272)

Salsa roja (see page 274), for dolloping

Place the chicken thighs in a container. Sprinkle with the salt, then pour the buttermilk over. Pop the lid on, give it a good shake to combine, then marinate in the refrigerator overnight.

When you're ready to cook, fill a deep-fryer or large heavy-based saucepan one-third full of vegetable oil. Heat over medium–low heat until it reaches 155°C (310°F) when tested with a cooking thermometer, or until a cube of bread dropped into the oil turns golden brown in 35–40 seconds.

Meanwhile, toss the herb and chilli flour ingredients together in a mixing bowl, ensuring they are thoroughly combined. Once well mixed, place in a large zip-lock bag.

Remove the chicken from the buttermilk, allowing any excess buttermilk to drip off. Add the chicken pieces to the bag of spiced flour, seal the bag and shake it like crazy.

Working in batches to prevent sticking or reducing the oil temperature, remove the floured chicken from the bag and carefully drop into the hot oil. Fry for 6–7 minutes, or until the chicken is cooked through. Don't worry if the batter looks quite dark — the paprika and chilli powder will darken the crust as it cooks. Remove from the oil and drain on paper towel while cooking the remaining chicken.

While the chicken is cooking, toss the cabbage in a mixing bowl with the lime juice and a pinch of sea salt. Add enough chipotle mayo to coat the cabbage to create a lightly dressed slaw.

TO ASSEMBLE

Split and toast the buns. Add a little more chipotle mayo to the bottom buns, followed by a good pile of the slaw, two pieces of the fried chicken, a heaped tablespoon of corn salsa and a dollop of salsa roja. Squirt some more chipotle mayo on the cut side of the top buns if you like things messy. Slap the bun lids on top and enjoy straightaway.

HICKORY BEEF BURGERS

PREPARATION: 20 MINUTES // COOKING: 20 MINUTES // SERVES 6

We love the great nation that is the USA; we've done a lot of time there (though not the kind that involves wearing orange and not dropping the soap).

This recipe is a homage to what we believe to be one of the world's best burgers, from the Apple Pan, in Los Angeles. The Apple Pan is a proper old-school diner: no ordering system, no plates, no cutlery, no cups, and you're in and out in seven minutes. It is run by the most efficient 60-year-old dudes on the planet, cooking patties to order. It's a special thing to witness, and this burger is a special thing to put in your face because it reminds us of them.

Heat a barbecue flat plate or large heavy-based frying pan to a medium–high heat. Add a little vegetable oil. Meanwhile, preheat the grill (broiler) to medium–high.

Cook the bacon on the barbecue or in the frying pan and leave to drain on paper towel.

Put the beef, salt, pepper, mustard and liquid smoke in a mixing bowl and mix with your hands until well combined. Divide the mixture into 12 even patties (we like 'em thin, like the Golden Arches do). Cook to your liking — we suggest medium-rare, so that the middle is still a little pink: about 2 minutes on each side.

When your patties are cooked to your liking, top with the cheese and melt under the grill.

TO ASSEMBLE

Split and toast the buns. Smear a heaped teaspoon of special sauce on the bottom buns. Add some lettuce, a beef patty, then a bacon rasher. Top with another beef patty, then some dill pickle slices.

Squiggle a generous amount of mustard and ketchup on the top buns, put the lids on, squeeze those babies together and serve immediately, with a pile of hot chips on the side.

vegetable oil, for frying

6 bacon rashers, rind removed

1.5 kg (3 lb 5 oz) of the best-quality minced (ground) beef you can afford; ideally, an 80% meat/20% fat combo

3 teaspoons salt flakes

½ teaspoon freshly ground black pepper

3 teaspoons dijon mustard

60 ml (2 fl oz/¼ cup) liquid smoke (see glossary)

12 slices American cheese (the yellow, highly processed stuff, individually wrapped in plastic) — or 24 slices if you like your burgers extra cheesy!

TO SERVE

6 hamburger buns

Special sauce (see page 276), for slathering

½ iceberg lettuce, finely shredded

3 dill pickles, sliced into rounds

American mustard, for drizzling

ketchup (tomato sauce), for drizzling

hot crinkle-cut chips, to serve

LUXURY TOFU BURGERS

PREPARATION: 20 MINUTES // COOKING: 20 MINUTES // SERVES 6

Tofu alone isn't anything to write home about. Deep-fried tofu, however, is LUXURY tofu. We wanted to create a special tofu dish that all our vegetarian friends (and everyone else) would love. And what's not to love about luxury?

THE SLAW
¼ Chinese cabbage (wong bok), finely shredded
1 long red chilli, finely diced
6-8 radishes, trimmed and cut into matchsticks
½ bunch (30 g/1 oz) coriander (cilantro), leaves picked
juice of 1 lime
1 teaspoon sesame oil

SRIRACHA MAYONNAISE
1½ tablespoons sriracha hot chilli sauce (see glossary)
125 g (4½ oz/½ cup) whole-egg mayonnaise

TEMPURA TOFU
vegetable oil, for deep-frying
175 g (6 oz/1 cup) rice flour
1 heaped tablespoon Salt and pepper mix (see page 275)
300 g (10½ oz) block of medium-firm silken tofu, cut into 6 slices
1 quantity Tempura batter (see page 277)
salt flakes, for seasoning
1 tablespoon sesame seeds

THE REST
6 brioche burger buns, or Soft burger buns (see page 87)
Salt and pepper mix (see page 275), for sprinkling

In a mixing bowl, toss together the slaw ingredients. Season to taste with sea salt and set aside.

Combine the sriracha mayonnaise ingredients in a small bowl and set aside.

To prepare the tofu, fill a deep-fryer or large heavy-based saucepan one-third full of vegetable oil. Heat over medium heat until it reaches 180°C (350°F) when tested with a cooking thermometer, or until a cube of bread dropped into the oil turns golden brown in 15 seconds.

On a plate, sift together the rice flour and salt and pepper mix. You'll want to cook no more than two tofu slices at a time, to prevent overcrowding the fryer, so gently dust the first two tofu slices with the seasoned flour, then dip them into the tempura batter. Gently drop them into the hot oil and deep-fry for 3 minutes, or until the batter has turned golden brown. Remove from the oil and drain on paper towel, sprinkling each piece with a few salt flakes and a pinch of sesame seeds.

Repeat with the remaining tofu slices.

TO ASSEMBLE
Split and toast the buns. Spread a little sriracha mayonnaise on the cut side of each bun.

Top the bottom buns with the slaw, then sit the tofu on top. Sprinkle with a pinch of salt and pepper mix, stick the lids on and eat.

7–HOUR LAMB SANDWICHES

PREPARATION: 25 MINUTES // COOKING: 7½ HOURS // SERVES 6–10

This sandwich is really about lamb. Slowly braised, melt-in-your-mouth lamb.
This one has been around since our first menu line-up, and is still going strong.
Its beauty is in the magical thing that happens when you braise lamb slowly,
and understand that sometimes the simplest dishes are the best.
Eat this and become a better person.

Preheat the oven to 100°C (200°F), or set a slow cooker
to the same temperature.

Heat a large heavy-based frying pan over medium–high
heat. Add a little olive oil, then brown the lamb for about
10 minutes, so all sides are a little golden. Transfer the
lamb to a deep braising dish (one with a tight-fitting lid)
or the slow cooker.

In the same frying pan, heat a little more olive oil.
Add the onion, carrot, bay leaves and thyme. Cook, stirring,
for a few minutes, then add the mixture to the lamb.

Pour in 250 ml (9 fl oz/1 cup) water. Seal the braising
dish with the tight-fitting lid, or pop the lid on your slow
cooker. Cook the lamb for 7 hours — the goal is low
and slow here.

After your 7 hours is up, carefully remove the lamb
from the braising dish or slow cooker and set aside
until cool enough to handle.

Strain the liquid through a fine-mesh sieve and pour it
into a small saucepan. Turn the heat up and stir in the gravy
powder until no lumps remain, adding salt flakes and freshly
ground black pepper to taste. Simmer for 5–10 minutes,
or until the sauce has thickened into a nice gravy.

Coarsely shred the lamb, into a mixing bowl, and season
with salt and pepper.

TO ASSEMBLE

In a bowl, mix together the spiced yoghurt ingredients.

Split and toast the rolls. Spread a little mayonnaise on
the bottom half of each roll. Place a handful of lettuce
on top, then some of the lamb, followed by a dollop of
the spiced yoghurt. Top with a handful of alfalfa and
pop the lids on.

You've waited long enough to consume these ones,
so tuck in straightaway!

olive oil, for pan-frying
1 kg (2 lb 4 oz) lamb neck
   fillet, or 1.5 kg (3 lb 5 oz)
   lamb shoulder
1 brown onion, halved
1 carrot, halved lengthways
2 bay leaves
a few thyme sprigs
2 tablespoons gravy powder
salt flakes, for seasoning

SPICED YOGHURT
150 g (5½ oz) Greek-style yoghurt
1 tablespoon whole-egg mayonnaise
1 teaspoon ground cumin

TO SERVE
6-10 soft bread rolls
60 g (2¼ oz/¼ cup) whole-egg
   mayonnaise
½ iceberg lettuce, finely shredded
250 g (9 oz) alfalfa sprouts

KONFUSION KLUB SANDWICHES

PREPARATION: 30 MINUTES // COOKING: 25 MINUTES // SERVES 6

It is an urban myth that the club sandwich was invented in a casino in Saratoga Springs, New York. It was actually invented in Seoul, Korea, and this is the original recipe. Okay, so maybe not — but once you taste it, you won't want it any other way.

6 boneless, skinless chicken breasts

Korean red pepper dressing (see page 273), for brushing

12 bacon rashers, rind removed

vegetable oil, for pan-frying

6 free-range eggs

1 tablespoon sesame seeds, lightly toasted

salt flakes, for seasoning

TO SERVE

18 slices of soft white bread (3 slices per sandwich)

Sesame and garlic mayo (see page 276), for slathering

1 butter lettuce, leaves separated, washed and dried

honey mustard (store-bought is fine), for dolloping

Korean red pepper dressing (see page 273), for drizzling

300 g (10½ oz) packet of your favourite potato crisps

Heat a chargrill pan or barbecue to a medium–high heat.

Working with one portion at a time, place the chicken breasts between two sheets of plastic wrap and flatten them slightly using a meat mallet, rolling pin or wine bottle. Now use a sharp knife to slice each breast in half, lengthways.

Brush the chicken pieces with the red pepper dressing, then place on the hot grill, along with the bacon. (If using a frying pan, you can cook the bacon under a hot grill/broiler.)

Cook the chicken for 3–4 minutes on each side, or until cooked through, basting regularly with more red pepper dressing. Once the chicken is cooked and the bacon is crisp, remove them from the heat. Set aside, covered with foil to keep warm.

Heat a frying pan over medium–high heat. Add a little vegetable oil, then crack the eggs into the pan. Fry for 2 minutes on each side, seasoning them with the sesame seeds and a small pinch of sea salt. You want the yolks to be soft in the centre, and not too runny — unless you can handle yolk running down your arm while you eat…

TO ASSEMBLE

While everything else is happening, toast the bread slices and start building your triple-decker sandwiches.

Spread each toasted bread slice with some sesame and garlic mayo. Layer the sandwiches however you like, adding the grilled chicken, bacon, lettuce, a bit more sesame and garlic mayo, honey mustard, fried egg, along with a little red pepper dressing, in any which way you like — just remember to stick a toasted bread layer in the middle somewhere, adding some more squiggles of red pepper dressing as you go.

When you're done, top with a final bread layer, then stick two toothpicks in each sandwich, so that they'll hold together when you cut them in half.

Serve with a bowl of slaw on the side, and a handful of potato crisps.

MEDIA NOCHE

PREPARATION: 30 MINUTES // COOKING: 20 MINUTES // SERVES 4-6

Apparently the story behind the creation of the original media noche (which means 'midnight' in Spanish) was that when Cubans would come home from a hard night of burning up the dance floor, they'd go straight to the kitchen and make this. So it's kind of like the official Cuban midnight snack.

Our version incorporates three kinds of pork product, making it a real heart-starter (or stopper, depending on who you are). It's a monster, so share it. Or don't, if you're a Hungry Hungry Hippo.

This recipe is more a set of assembly instructions — but after a night of burning up the dance floor, who has time to cook? If you're really organised, these little snacks can even be pre-made, wrapped in plastic wrap and kept in the fridge for a day or two, until you're ready to heat and eat.

Right, so dig out 16 toothpicks or small wooden skewers, each about 10 cm (4 inches) long.

Lay two of the bread slices on a clean work surface. Using a butter knife, smear one-quarter of the mayonnaise and mustard over each one. Top each slice with one-quarter of the Swiss cheese, then one-quarter of the smoked pork, ham, jamón and sliced pickles.

Top each portion with another slice of bread, then spread each slice with the remaining mayonnaise and mustard. Layer with the remaining cheese, meats and pickles, then pop the lids on.

Using a heated sandwich press — or a large heavy-based frying pan set over medium–low heat, and another pan to press the sandwiches down — toast your wickedly delicious midnight snacks until the bread is golden and the cheese has melted.

Using a sharp serrated knife, slice each toasted sandwich into eight bits, giving 16 portions all up. Skewer a chunk of dill pickle onto each toothpick, then secure each toasted bread portion and have a defibrillator at the ready.

1 loaf of white bread, cut lengthways into 6 even slices

60 g (2¼ oz/¼ cup) whole-egg mayonnaise

60 g (2¼ oz/¼ cup) dijon mustard

24 slices Swiss cheese

500 g (1 lb 2 oz) Smoked pork loin (see page 160), sliced, or use sliced pork from a deli

12 slices of the best ham you can afford

12 goodly large slices of jamón serrano (or good prosciutto, at a pinch)

4 large dill pickles, each cut into four thin slices, plus 16 extra chunks to garnish

CHILLI DAWGS

PREPARATION: 1 HOUR IF SMOKING THE FRANKFURTERS + AN EXTRA 20 MINUTES
COOKING: ABOUT 15 MINUTES // SERVES 6

Chilli dogs are pretty self-explanatory. They're very basic, really: chilli (con carne) on a bun, with a frankfurter and some cheese and jalapeño…

Sometimes, though, the easiest things need a little 'splaining. Steam the bun for maximum softness, get that chilli beef recipe on point — and, if you can, smoke the frank (not 100% necessary, but a nice point of difference in flavour).

For us, the authentic American touch comes in the form of spray cheese — we love it! We make our dawgs double size, just because we can, but they work just as well as single ones.

1 handful of wood chips, suitable for smoking, soaked in water for at least 30 minutes (optional)

6 skinless frankfurters

100 g (3½ oz) pickled jalapeño chillies, finely chopped

1 brown onion, finely diced

6 Hot dog rolls (see page 86)

500 g (1 lb 2 oz) Chilli mince (see page 271), warmed

225 g (8 oz) spray cheese (Mexican nacho flavour, if available); you can use spreadable cheese instead

If smoking your franks, the easiest way to do this is using a kettle barbecue or hooded barbecue. Prepare your barbecue for smoking. Light the coals, wait for the heat to die down, then add your soaked wood chips to the coals. Place your franks on the grill and close the lid for 10 minutes to allow the maximum amount of smoke penetration. Turn the dogs to ensure they're evenly grilled. (Google ways to smoke meat in an oven — you can smoke the franks the same way, too!)

Alternatively, warm a chargrill pan or barbecue to a medium heat. Cook the franks for 4–5 minutes, or until heated through, turning them now and then. Keep warm.

Meanwhile, in a mixing bowl, combine the jalapeño chilli and onion and set aside.

Split the buns and steam them until soft and warm — either in a microwave for 10 seconds on high, or in a large bamboo steamer set over a saucepan of simmering water.

Place the grilled franks in the steamed buns. Top with a generous spoonful of chilli mince, then add a good squiggle of spray cheese. Top the lot with the jalapeño mixture and serve.

REUBEN DAWGS

PREPARATION: 20 MINUTES // COOKING: 15 MINUTES // SERVES 6

A Reuben sandwich walks into a pub. So does a hot dog. The inevitable happens and they have a love child. This is the love child.

Put it in your mouth. Swallow it. Love it.

Warm a chargrill pan or barbecue to a medium heat. Cook the franks for 4–5 minutes, or until heated through, turning them now and then. Keep warm.

Meanwhile, pour about 2.5 cm (1 inch) water into a saucepan and bring to a simmer on the stove.

Take each hot dog roll and split it along the middle. Tear up the cheese slices and place them inside the rolls. Add the franks, along with the pastrami, then place the rolls in a bamboo steamer. Set the steamer over the saucepan of simmering water and steam the dawgs for about 5 minutes, or until the cheese starts to melt.

Remove from the steamer and top the dawgs with the sauerkraut, pickles and a squiggle of mustard. Sprinkle with poppy seeds and serve.

6 skinless frankfurters
6 Hot dog rolls (see page 86)
12 slices Swiss cheese
300 g (10½ oz) sliced pastrami, the best quality you can find
250 g (9 oz) jar of sauerkraut
crinkle-cut bread and butter pickles, to serve
60 g (2¼ oz/¼ cup) dijon mustard, in a squeeze bottle if possible
poppy seeds, for sprinkling

CHILLI DAWGS

REUBEN DAWGS

DRAGON DAWGS

DRAGON DAWGS

PREPARATION: 30 MINUTES // COOKING: 2½ HOURS // SERVES 6-8

Look, we'll admit this hot dog looks pretty medieval. Some would even say unappealing, but trust us, it's a total taste sensation. It's octopus wrapped in bacon: two titans of taste thrown together. A lot of our customers didn't really get this one, but that's the thing about people, they don't get things.

When you're making this, take some time with the octopus, or the texture can end up more 'shoe sole' than you may like. Cooking occy is a lot like sex. It should be quick and hot, or long and slow. Anything else is just awkward.

1 kg (2 lb 4 oz) large octopus
  tentacles

vegetable oil, for deep-frying

12 bacon rashers, rind removed

salt flakes, for seasoning

TO SERVE

6-8 Hot dog rolls (see page 86)

¼ red cabbage, finely shredded

¼ white cabbage, finely shredded

juice of ½ lime

salt flakes, for seasoning

125 g (4½ oz/½ cup) Chipotle
  mayo (see page 271)

125 g (4½ oz/½ cup) Pico de
  gallo (see page 274)

10 pickled jalapeño chillies,
  finely chopped

coriander (cilantro) leaves,
  to garnish

Bring a saucepan of water to a simmer. Check with a thermometer that the water is around 75°C (165°F), then pop the octopus in and let it cook for about 2 hours — just try and keep the temperature around the 75°C (165°F) mark and you should be fine.

After 2 hours, drop the octopus into some iced water to shock it cold, then leave it under cold running water for 5 minutes.

TO SERVE

Fill a deep-fryer or large heavy-based saucepan one-third full of vegetable oil. Heat over medium heat until it reaches 180°C (350°F) when tested with a cooking thermometer, or until a cube of bread dropped into the oil turns golden brown in 15 seconds.

Separate each octopus tentacle and pat dry with paper towel. Wrap each tentacle with a bacon strip. Gently lower a few into the hot oil and fry in batches for 2–3 minutes, or until golden. Remove and drain on paper towel, sprinkling immediately with salt flakes.

Meanwhile, pour about 2.5 cm (1 inch) water into a saucepan and bring to a simmer on the stove. While the octopus is cooling slightly, steam the buns in a bamboo steamer over the pan of simmering water for about 5 minutes, or until soft and warm.

In a mixing bowl, combine the cabbages with a squeeze of lime juice and a pinch of salt flakes.

Partially split the warm buns and spoon in a little chipotle mayo. Add the crispy octopus tentacles, followed by the cabbage and a little pico de gallo. Garnish with the jalapeño chilli and coriander leaves and serve.

CHEEZUS DAWGS

PREPARATION: 20 MINUTES // COOKING: 15 MINUTES // MAKES 6

Visualise a corn dog. Visualise a hot dog. Combine those two things in your mind.
Hold that thought. Now follow these steps and you'll get the real thing.
This is heart-stopping white-trash fast-food at its finest.

Fill a deep-fryer or large heavy-based saucepan one-third full of vegetable oil. Heat over medium heat until it reaches 180°C (350°F) when tested with a cooking thermometer, or until a cube of bread dropped into the oil turns golden brown in 15 seconds.

To make the corn dog batter, crack the eggs into a bowl, add the milk and lightly beat together. Stir in the canola oil. In a separate bowl, mix all the dry ingredients together. Now mix the wet ingredients into the dry ingredients and whisk until you have a smooth, thick batter.

Place a wooden skewer lengthways inside each frankfurter, so you have six dog 'lollipops'; this will make them easier to handle during deep-frying. Now roll each dog in a little extra flour, to help the batter stick to them.

Roll the dogs in the batter, making sure they're coated all the way around, and from top to bottom. Let the batter run off a little by holding the dogs upside down.

Gently place in the hot oil and cook for 3–5 minutes, or until the batter is golden; depending on the size of your fryer, you may need to cook them in batches.

Meanwhile, warm your hot dog rolls in a steamer for 2 minutes, or zap them in a microwave for 5–10 seconds on high to soften them.

TO SERVE

Split the rolls down the middle and place a dawg in each one, removing the skewers for serving. Squiggle the nacho cheese from top to bottom. Do the same with the tomato sauce, filling in the lines where the cheese didn't go. Now eat these straightaway!

vegetable oil, for deep-frying
6 skinless frankfurters
6 Hot dog rolls (see page 86)
225 g (8 oz) spray cheese (Mexican nacho flavour, if available); you can use spreadable cheese instead
tomato sauce (ketchup), for drizzling

CORN DOG BATTER

2 eggs
250 ml (9 fl oz/1 cup) low-fat milk
60 ml (2 fl oz/¼ cup) canola oil
2 tablespoons sugar
1 teaspoon sea salt
2 teaspoons baking powder
200 g (7 oz/1⅓ cups) corn meal (see glossary)
100 g (3½ oz/⅔ cup) plain (all-purpose) flour, plus a little extra for dusting the dogs

50 SHADES OF BEIGE, BABY

Here are some of the stupider creations we've come up with. They ventured deep into dude-food land, never to return. Most of them jumped straight out of the deep-fryer and onto the plate. Some of these dishes worked, and some were unmitigated disasters. You decide!

FRIED LOBSTER DONUT

FRIED BANANA TACO

TRADIE DAWG

FATBOY BURGER

SAUSAGE & CLAM PIZZA

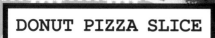

DONUT PIZZA SLICE

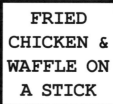

FRIED CHICKEN & WAFFLE ON A STICK

MEAT PIE BURGER & FRIES

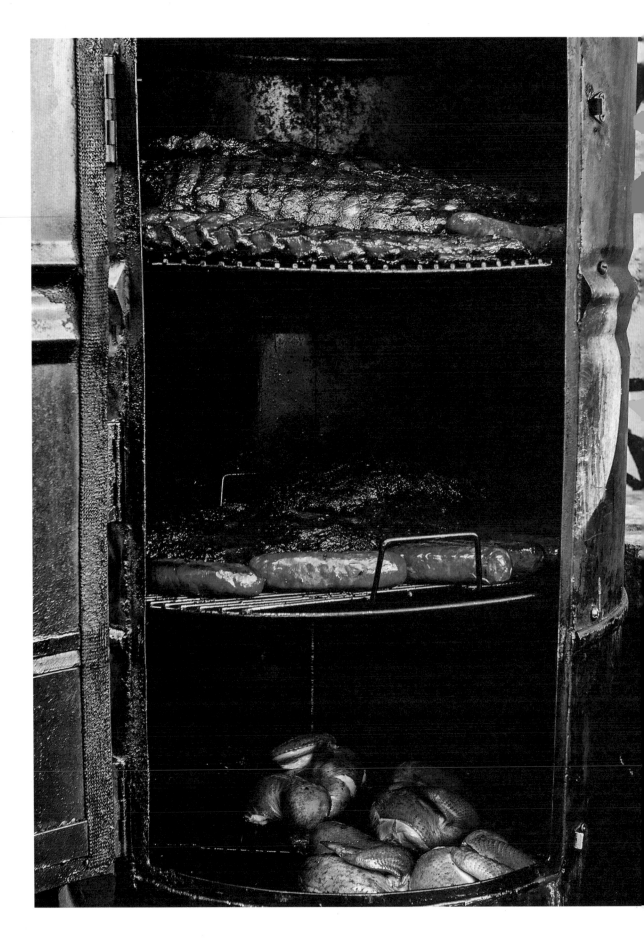

★GROUP LOVE★

It's a sunny Sunday. Grab some mates, fire up the barbecue, play a game of backyard cricket, down a couple of dozen cold ones and get cooking these real (large) crowd pleasers.

This is food for backyard feasting of epic proportions. Barbecue blazing, smokers… errr… smoking, pots boiling, Cypress Hill playing, strangers meeting, paper plates piling high, cups overflowing: it's about people you know and like having a good time. Big serves, big flavours, big fun.

Meat is usually the star of this show, so all of these recipes require giving your proteins a little love and attention. The upside is that most of the work is preparation, allowing you to be part of the party, rather than a slave to it. Mix these meaty numbers with a few fresh numbers from the Salads chapter on pages 186–201 and you're really on to something.

JERK CHICKEN

PREPARATION: 30 MINUTES + OVERNIGHT BRINING // COOKING: 40 MINUTES // SERVES 8

This is THE classic Jamaican barbecue dish that will bring a tropical vibe to any backyard gathering, guaranteed. The flavours are zesty, aromatic and heady. Mix that with a bit of smoky barbecue goodness and you're home.

In Jamaica, this dish is traditionally cooked by the roadside on a converted 44-gallon drum grill. Our version embodies the spirit of the original, but taking into account that you probably don't have one of those hanging about in your garage.

2 x 1.3 kg (3 lb) chickens, cut into 8 pieces each (the two breasts cut into four, and the two leg portions into four — or ask your friendly local butcher to do this for you)

3–4 tablespoons Jerk paste (see page 273), plus extra for basting

vegetable oil, for brushing

BRINE

230 g (8 oz/1 cup, firmly packed) light brown sugar

630 g (1 lb 6 oz/2 cups) coarse cooking salt

2 allspice berries

2 dried chillies

TO SERVE

Quick slaw (see page 274)

lemon wedges

Dirty rice (see page 176); optional

Combine the brine ingredients in a saucepan and pour in 1 litre (35 fl oz/4 cups) water. Bring to a simmer over low heat and stir until the sugar and salt have completely dissolved. Set aside until completely cool.

Place the chicken pieces in a plastic container that is large enough to hold them all, as well as an additional 4 litres (140 fl oz/16 cups) of liquid. Pour the brine over the chicken, plus an extra 3 litres (105 fl oz/12 cups) water. Place the lid on the container and leave to brine in the refrigerator overnight. The brine will help the chicken stay juicy during the cooking process.

When you're ready to cook, fire up the barbecue. A charcoal version is best, but using the grill on a gas barbecue is an acceptable substitute.

Remove the chicken pieces from the brine and pat dry with paper towel. Place in a bowl and season with sea salt and freshly ground black pepper. Spoon the jerk paste onto the chicken. Using clean hands (gloves are also a good idea!), massage the paste into the chicken.

When the coals have started to ash, oil the grill and add the chicken pieces, skin side down. Cook for 20–30 minutes, or until the chicken is cooked through, turning the pieces over halfway through, and basting with more jerk paste if you'd like it really spicy! The chicken should have a dark, aromatic crust, but the interior should still be tender and juicy.

Remove the chicken from the heat and set aside to rest for 10 minutes. Serve with the slaw and lemon wedges, and a big bowl of dirty rice if desired.

BEEF BRISKET

PREPARATION: 40 MINUTES + 3 HOURS SOAKING + 1–3 HOURS RESTING
COOKING: 10–16 HOURS // SERVES 8–12

Perfecting brisket is a life-long pursuit, so you better get started right away. People spend their lives chasing the ultimate pink 'smoke ring' beneath the 'bark', or surface crust — and there really is so much you can learn about how to transform this relatively cheap and fatty cut into the king of barbecue meats.

Take your time, this is a weekend job: follow the steps to the letter, and you'll be rewarded with a slab of molten brisket gold.

When it comes to brisket, our tip — as with any meat — is don't skimp on quality. Even the best brisket in the world will still cost less than fillet. Choose one with an even layer of fat — or even better, one where you can see the marbling (the layers of intramuscular fat going all through the meat). It's this fat that will slowly break down and internally baste your meat, giving it an amazing flavour and texture. A charcoal barbecue with a lid is the best tool for the job, and a digital meat thermometer is crucial; these are cheap as chips and a good investment, as you can use them to check the temperature of all kinds of meats, whether roasted, barbecued or grilled.

This recipe can be used in all manner of ways. It is glorious as it is, served with slaw on the side; or shred it down and use it for tacos, nachos, rolls, or even as a topping for a Hillbilly barbecue pizza (see page 143).

1 side of beef brisket, weighing 4–5 kg (9–11 lb)

1 kg (2 lb 4 oz) wood chips, suitable for smoking (pecan or walnut work well for beef), soaked in water for about 3 hours

BRISKET RUB

50 g (1¾ oz/⅔ cup) freshly ground coffee

85 g (3 oz/⅓ cup) sea salt

80 g (2¾ oz/⅓ cup, firmly packed) dark brown sugar

2 tablespoons smoked paprika

2 tablespoons chilli powder (preferably from ancho or pasilla chillies; you'll find these Mexican chilli varieties in spice shops and fine food stores)

1 tablespoon garlic powder

1 tablespoon onion powder

2 teaspoons ground cumin

2 teaspoons freshly ground black pepper

If you're thinking of eating in the late afternoon, say from 4 pm onwards, then this is the recipe for you! You'll need to wake up early to start preparing this dish, but it's worth it — so get up and get out of bed, you have work to do…

Around 4 am, light the coals in a hooded barbecue and allow them to burn through until they start to ash. The internal temperature when you eventually place the brisket on to cook should be around 130°C (265°F), dropping to 110°C (230°F) for the remainder of the cooking time — which can take anywhere from 10 to 16 hours. Controlling the temperature all comes down to regulating the amount of oxygen the fire is getting. Cutting the oxygen off (by closing the air holes on your barbecue) will bring the temperature down; opening them up will raise the temperature. Getting the temperature perfect doesn't happen instantly, and will take some practice, so have a play with your barbecue.

Pat the beef dry with paper towel. You can trim some of the fat off the top of the brisket; there's a hundred YouTube videos to help you with this. In a mixing bowl, thoroughly combine all the brisket rub ingredients. Tip the mixture onto the beef and massage it in on all sides. Set aside until the barbecue has reached the right temperature.

When the internal temperature of the barbecue has reached 130°C (265°F), move the coals to the sides of the barbecue, as you only want indirect heat when cooking the beef. Sprinkle the soaked wood chips onto the coals, place the grill on top, and place your beef on the barbecue.

Close the lid and allow the barbecue temperature to drop to 110°C (230°F). You'll need to keep an eye on the temperature, and add additional charcoal and wood chips to keep the temperature more or less constant for at least 10 hours.

Around the 8–10 hour mark, use a meat thermometer to check the internal temperature of the beef. You're aiming for 85°C (185°F). If in doubt, ask Uncle YouTube how beef brisket should look when it's done.

This next bit is super important: LET IT REST. You might have heard all those TV chefs talk about resting meat, but on this occasion it's vital. You don't want to have gotten up early and cooked the meat for 10 hours, only to fall down at this final hurdle! So, wrap the brisket loosely in foil or baking paper and leave it somewhere warmish — in an oven inside on its lowest setting (no more than 50°C/120°F) is ideal. The longer you rest the brisket the better; anywhere from 1 hour to 3 hours will be good.

When you're ready to serve, remove the foil or baking paper and place the beef down on a large chopping board.

Now you need to work out which way the grain of the meat is running — you'll see fibres or 'lines' running across the meat. Take a really sharp knife and slice the meat in the OPPOSITE direction, into slices about 5 mm (¼ inch) thick; cutting meat *against* the grain gives you far more tender slices than cutting the meat with the grain. Now kick back and enjoy the fruits of your labours.

BLACK

BEEF BRISKET

PUERTO RICAN PULLED PORK

**PREPARATION: 24 HOURS BRINING + 2 HOURS SOAKING + 1 HOUR RESTING THE PORK
COOKING: 4–5 HOURS // SERVES 10 + LEFTOVERS**

Suckling pig is delicious in any language or culture. In Puerto Rico, it's known as 'lechon'. A mixture of onion, coriander (cilantro), aji chillies and other ingredients are blended with salt and used to cure the pig for two days, before it is trussed on a spit and cooked over coals, so it's glossy and crisp on the outside, and tender inside.

We take this idea and mash it up with American barbecue sensibilities. On the day of serving, all you'll need to do is sit back with a piña colada and occasionally stoke the coals until the pork is ready.

TO BRINE THE PORK

230 g (8 oz/1 cup, firmly packed)
  light brown sugar

65 g (2¼ oz/½ cup) sea salt flakes

4 bay leaves

1 x 4 kg (9 lb) piece of pork shoulder,
  bone in, skin removed if possible
  (ask your butcher to do this)

Put the sugar, salt flakes and bay leaves in a saucepan and pour in 500 ml (17 fl oz/2 cups) water. Bring to a simmer over low heat and stir until the salt and sugar have completely dissolved.

Remove the brine from the heat, pour in 1 litre (35 fl oz/4 cups) cold water and set aside until it has cooled completely.

Place the pork shoulder in a very large container that has a lid. Pour the brine over. Pop the lid on and refrigerate the pork in the brine for 24 hours.

THE RUB

1½ teaspoons Caribbean spice mix,
  such as Sazón seasoning (see glossary)

2 teaspoons dried oregano

2 teaspoons garlic powder

2 teaspoons smoked paprika

zest of 1 orange

Thoroughly combine the rub ingredients in a bowl. Remove the pork shoulder from the brine and pat dry with paper towel, making sure it is completely dry. Massage the rub mixture into the pork, ensuring an even coating.

FOR SMOKING

500 g (1 lb 2 oz) wood chips suitable
  for smoking, soaked in water for at
  least 2 hours

TO SERVE

Quick slaw (see page 274)
Tostones (see page 14)
Barbecue sauce (see page 270)

Light the coals in a hooded barbecue and allow the heat to come down to 110°C (230°C). Move the coals to the sides of the barbecue, scatter a handful of soaked wood chips on the coals and place the grill on top.

Place the pork on the barbecue and close the lid. Barbecue the pork at a constant 100–110°C (200–225°F) for 4–5 hours. You'll need to add a small amount of charcoal and wood chips occasionally to maintain the temperature and keep the smoke flowing.

After 4 hours, use a meat thermometer to start checking the internal temperature of the pork. The meat should be around 90°C (195°F), and should lift away from the bone easily; continue cooking if the pork is not quite there.

Once done, remove the pork from the heat, cover it in foil and set aside to cool and rest for 30 minutes, or up to 1 hour.

Just before serving, use a couple of forks to shred the pork meat from the bone, reserving any juices that leached out during the resting process, and pouring these back over the meat.

Serve up your pulled pork with slaw, tostones and barbecue sauce.

CAJUN SNOW CRAB BOIL

PREPARATION: 30 MINUTES // COOKING: 35 MINUTES //SERVES 6

A crab boil — or any other seafood boil — is one of the greatest American traditions outside of the barbecue. The name is pretty self-explanatory: it's basically boiled seafood, thrown in a bag and tossed around with a buttery sauce. Once tossed, all you need to do is fish out the seafood and eat it with your hands.

Snow crab is our go-to crustacean as it has a good meat-to-shell ratio, making the payoff that much sweeter. Then all you need, aside from great seafood, is a pile of bibs and a bucket filled with water and lemon slices to clean yo-self after.

Snow crab and king crab legs are sold at most fish markets. They are cooked at sea, then frozen, so it's just a case of thawing them, boiling for a few minutes and coating them in a sauce. If you wanted to cook fresh crab, mud crabs, blue swimmers and spanner crabs are all great options.

To truly recreate the boil, it's awesome to serve the crab (or other seafood) in individual bags. We use thick, heavy-duty ones, about 30 x 45 cm (12 x 18 inches) in size, used for vacuum-sealing food. Any good hospitality store will have them, but do buy decent-quality ones. The last thing you need is the bags bursting!

To make the Cajun butter sauce, melt the butter in a saucepan over medium–low heat. Add the onion and garlic and cook for 20–30 minutes, or until the onion is soft, but not coloured. Sprinkle with the Cajun seasoning and cayenne pepper and cook for a further 5 minutes, or until fragrant. Season to taste with salt flakes and keep warm.

Meanwhile, get the boil happening. Take the largest pot you can find and fill it with water. Add the Old Bay Seasoning, cayenne pepper, onions, lemons and bay leaves. Bring the water to the boil and leave to bubble away for 10 minutes.

Drop the crab pieces into the boiling water and leave for 5 minutes. Remove from the water, drain briefly, then toss in the warm Cajun butter sauce.

You can then recreate the 'boil' by dividing the crab among six individual 30 x 45 cm (12 x 18 inch) vacuum-seal bags with plenty of the Cajun butter sauce; this can be a bit tricky to do on your own, so you may need someone to hold the bag open for you, roll the top of the bag up and secure each one with a clothes peg.

Have some implements ready for diners to extract the juicy goodness from the crabs — crab-shell crackers, pliers, small hammers. Serve up the crab boil, with crusty baguettes on the side.

3 kg (6 lb 12 oz) snow crab
  or king crab legs
crusty baguettes, to serve

CAJUN BUTTER SAUCE
250 g (9 oz) salted butter
3 brown onions, finely diced
5 garlic cloves, crushed
2 tablespoons Cajun seasoning
1 teaspoon cayenne pepper
salt flakes, for seasoning

THE BOIL
4 tablespoons Old Bay Seasoning
  (an American spice mix; see
  glossary)
1 tablespoon cayenne pepper
2 brown onions, halved
2 lemons, halved
10 fresh bay leaves

MEXICAN PRAWN BOIL

PREPARATION: 45 MINUTES // COOKING: 1 HOUR // SERVES 6

Continuing on the seafood boil-up train, this recipe channels all the powers of all the gods of old El Paso. This boil combines big, juicy prawns with Tex–Mex sauciness: another frankenfood dish, taking things we like from the Southern US and South of the Border and smashing them together.

MEXICAN SAUCE

125 g (4½ oz) unsalted butter

3 brown onions, sliced

3 garlic cloves, thinly sliced

35 g (1¼ oz/⅓ cup) ground cumin

¾ teaspoon ground cinnamon

1 tablespoon sweet paprika

1 tablespoon ground coriander

125 g (4½ oz/½ cup) tomato paste (concentrated purée)

125 g (4½ oz/½ cup) chipotle chillies in adobo sauce (see glossary)

250 ml (9 fl oz/1 cup) Mexican-style hot chilli sauce, such as Tapatío or Cholula

3 coriander (cilantro) roots, washed and roughly chopped

2 teaspoons raw (demerara) sugar

salt flakes, for seasoning

Melt the butter in a large heavy-based saucepan over low heat. Add the onion and garlic and cook slowly for 15–20 minutes, until the onion is completely soft and starting to caramelise.

Add the spices and cook for a further 5 minutes, before adding the tomato paste, chipotle chillies and all their adobo sauce, as well as your chosen hot sauce. Stir until well combined. Bring the heat up to medium, then reduce the heat and gently simmer for 10 minutes, or until the sauce has thickened.

Add the coriander root, sugar and a good pinch of salt flakes. Stir to combine, then leave to bubble away for 5 minutes. Remove from the heat.

Use a hand-held stick blender to blitz the sauce until smooth. Set aside and keep warm.

THE REST

1 handful salt

3 heaped tablespoons Old Bay Seasoning (an American spice mix; see glossary)

4 kg (9 lb) extra large raw prawns (shrimp); ask your fishmonger for 'U6' prawns (which means you'll get about 6 prawns per pound), or 'jumbo' prawns

4 limes, cut into wedges

2 baguettes, sliced and warmed

When your Mexican sauce is almost ready, dig out your largest saucepan, fill it with water and bring to the boil. Throw in the salt and Old Bay Seasoning.

Add the prawns to the boiling water and cook for 4–5 minutes, or until just opaque — if your pan isn't large enough to hold them all, just cook the prawns in batches.

Scoop out the prawns using a sieve, shake off the excess water and place in a large mixing bowl. Once all the prawns are cooked, pour a few ladlefuls of your warm Mexican sauce over the top and mix to evenly coat the prawns.

Divide the prawns among six individual vacuum-seal bags, each measuring 30 x 45 cm (12 x 18 inches) or thereabouts, securing each bag with a clothes peg.

Serve hot, with the lime wedges for squeezing and warm baguette slices.

ASADO BEEF SKEWERS

PREPARATION: 40 MINUTES + 20 MINUTES MARINATING + 10 MINUTES RESTING
COOKING: 10 MINUTES // SERVES 4

Those Brazilians have worked out a thing or two about beef. Here, coffee and brown sugar bring out rich, caramelised beef flavours, and when cut with the sharp, acidic chimichurri sauce, the result is highly addictive. Rump cap, also known as tri-tip, is the usual beef cut for this dish, and is relatively inexpensive. Rump cap is the triangular-shaped cut of meat that sits on top of the rump. It is readily available from most good butchers these days.

Light the coals in your barbecue. Heat the barbecue to a high heat. Get yourself some really big metal skewers — ideally ones about 30–40 cm (12–16 inches) long — and keep them handy.

While the barbecue is heating up, combine the asado rub ingredients in a large mixing bowl. Leaving the fat on the beef, cut the meat into 100 g (3½ oz) chunks (about 5 cm/2 inches square), using a sharp knife. Place them in the asado rub, massaging it in thoroughly. Leave to marinate for 20 minutes, but no longer than 30 minutes, or the rub mixture will start to 'cook' the beef.

While the beef is marinating, make the chimichurri sauce. Add the herbs, cumin, paprika, garlic and onion to a blender. Turn the blender on and pour in the vinegar. Now pour in the olive oil in a slow, steady stream, until all the ingredients are combined into a coarse paste. Season with salt flakes and set aside.

Thread the beef pieces onto your metal skewers. By now your grill should be hot, so oil it to stop the beef sticking to it. Place the skewers on the grill and season each one with a generous pinch of salt flakes. Grill for 4–5 minutes, or until the beef is cooked to medium-rare, turning halfway through. Remove the skewers from the heat, cover them in foil and allow to rest for 10 minutes.

Place the skewers on a serving plate, pouring any juices that have collected from resting back over the meat. Lightly sprinkle with more salt flakes, then drizzle the chimichurri sauce all over. Serve with the lemon wedges for squeezing.

1.2 kg (2 lb 10 oz) rump cap
   (ask for the fat to be kept on)
vegetable oil, for brushing
salt flakes, for seasoning
2 lemons, cut into wedges

ASADO RUB

460 g (1 lb/2 cups firmly packed)
   light brown sugar
½ teaspoon ground cumin
45 g (1½ oz/½ cup) freshly
   ground coffee
2 teaspoons table salt

CHIMICHURRI SAUCE

2 bunches flat-leaf (Italian)
   parsley, about 80 g (2¾ oz)
   each, chopped
1 bunch (80 g/2¾ oz) mint,
   chopped
1 bunch (60 g/2¾ oz) oregano,
   leaves picked
2 teaspoons ground cumin
2 teaspoons smoked paprika
5 garlic cloves, peeled
1 small red onion, diced
80 ml (2½ fl oz/⅓ cup) red wine
   vinegar
80 ml (2½ fl oz/⅓ cup) extra
   virgin olive oil
salt flakes, for seasoning

HELLSHIRE FISH

PREPARATION: 25 MINUTES // COOKING: 1 HOUR // SERVES 4-6

Fried fish for two looks way less boring when it's deep-fried and sitting upright, swimming right towards you.

Hellshire is the name of a beach in Jamaica. We imagine sitting at a table next to the beach, eating this dish with your hands, sand between your toes...

To make the rundown sauce, heat a little vegetable oil in a heavy-based saucepan over medium heat. Fry the onion and garlic for 3 minutes, or until the onion has softened and become translucent.

Stir in the capsicum, chilli and curry powder, then the coconut cream, tomatoes and 250 ml (9 fl oz/1 cup) water. Bring the mixture to a simmer and cook for 40 minutes, or until the sauce has thickened enough that it coats the back of a spoon. Whisk in the butter, set aside and keep warm.

Using a sharp knife, make three long diagonal slashes on both sides of the fish, all the way to the bone. Use bamboo skewers to open out the fins by pinning them back. Wedge a toothpick or two into the cavity of the fish so that it will sit upright (this is for the final presentation).

Fill a deep-fryer or large heavy-based saucepan one-third full of vegetable oil. Heat over medium heat until it reaches 170°C (325°F) when tested with a cooking thermometer, or until a cube of bread dropped into the oil turns golden brown in 20 seconds.

Pat the fish dry inside and out with paper towel. Carefully lower the fish into the hot oil. Deep-fry for 8–10 minutes, or until the fish is cooked through and the skin is nice and crisp.

Carefully remove from the oil and drain on paper towel. Season immediately with salt flakes and freshly ground black pepper.

Serve the fish sitting upright, drizzled with some of the rundown sauce, with the dirty rice, lime halves and remaining rundown sauce on the side.

1 x 800 g (1 lb 12 oz) whole sweet-fleshed white fish, such as red snapper or baby barramundi, cleaned and scaled

vegetable oil, for deep-frying

salt flakes, for seasoning

Dirty rice (see page 176), to serve

lime halves, to serve

RUNDOWN SAUCE

vegetable oil, for pan-frying

1 brown onion, finely diced

2 garlic cloves, crushed

1 red capsicum (pepper), diced

½ habanero chilli (see glossary), seeded and finely chopped (wear gloves while doing this!)

½ teaspoon curry powder

400 ml (14 fl oz) tin coconut cream

4 roma (plum) tomatoes, diced

50 g (1¾ oz) butter, diced

WHOLE STUFFED TROUT with SOBRASADA, FENNEL, RADISH and CHILLI

PREPARATION: 35 MINUTES // COOKING: 20 MINUTES // SERVES 2

Okay, so a whole cooked fish never elicits as much of a response as a hulking great piece of meat at a carnivorous gathering, but you have to have options — and this is one your healthy friends will love. We've baked the fish in the oven, but you can also wrap it in a layer of baking paper, then a layer of foil, and cook it over a charcoal barbecue.

The richness of the trout works well with spicy sobrasada — that addictive soft, spreadable salami the Spanish are so proud of. You'll find sobrasada in Spanish delicatessens and fine food and charcuterie stores. Add fennel to the party (fish's best mate), and you're on, Donkey Kong!

700 g (1 lb 9 oz) whole rainbow
   trout, cleaned
100 g (3½ oz) sobrasada (soft,
   cured spreadable spicy Spanish
   salami; see glossary)
green tips from 2 large fennel
   bulbs (from the salad below)
1 tablespoon olive oil
salt flakes, for seasoning
1 orange or lemon, cut into chunks

FENNEL, RADISH & CHILLI SALAD
2 large fennel bulbs
8 radishes
2 zucchini (courgettes)
1 long red chilli, seeded and
   finely chopped
½ bunch (30 g/1 oz) dill,
   leaves picked
juice of 1 lemon
2 tablespoons extra virgin
   olive oil
salt flakes, for seasoning

Pat the fish dry with paper towel. Using a sharp knife, make six evenly spaced slits along the top of the fish. Take the sobrasada and stuff each slit with as much as you can fit in there. Flip the fish over and repeat on the other side.

Cut the green heads off the fennel and stuff them inside the cavity of the fish, along with a generous pinch of sea salt. Refrigerate the fish until 30 minutes before you are ready to cook it.

Meanwhile, preheat the oven to 220°C (425°F) while you make the salad.

Using a mandoline, finely shave the fennel bulbs. Do the same with the radishes and zucchini until you have a pile of beautifully thin, crunchy vegetables. Place the vegetables in a salad bowl, along with the chilli and dill. Dress with the lemon juice, olive oil and a generous pinch of salt flakes and freshly ground black pepper. Mix to combine, then set aside.

Return now to the fish. Line a roasting tin with baking paper. Rub the outside of the fish with the olive oil and sprinkle with salt flakes. Place the fish in the roasting tin, add the orange chunks and roast for 15–20 minutes, or until the flesh of the fish flakes easily when tested with a fork.

Transfer the fish to a serving plate. Pour any juices from the roasting tin back over the fish. Serve with the salad, and the roasted orange chunks for squeezing over.

* COUCH * CRUISING

This chapter is all about your next big night IN. You know those kind of nights. Maybe it's the night after a big night out. Normally it's a Sunday. Sometimes a Monday. The rain is falling, the TV is on, and so are the trackie pants.

Whatever the night, these are comfort dishes, designed to repair your spirit, nourish your soul and whisper sweet sounds into your ears to make it all better: *Come on. We can get through this together. Let's make it feel alright...*

These are dishes to cook instead of ordering takeaway or defrosting frozen fish fingers. In short, these recipes are all sure-fire party starters — if by party you mean being at home alone, sitting next to the heater and watching trashy television.

EMPANADA FLOATER

PREPARATION: 1 HOUR // COOKING: ABOUT 3 HOURS // SERVES 8

If there's one thing we like, it's appropriating the food traditions
of other cultures and making them our own. This dish steals the English
'pie floater', and the Spanish empanada, and we've smashed them
both together. Jolly good/Olé!

PIE FILLING

2 tablespoons vegetable oil

250 g (9 oz) chuck steak, cut into
2 cm (¾ inch) chunks

1½ tablespoons plain (all-purpose) flour,
plus extra for dusting

500 g (1 lb 2 oz) minced (ground) beef

1 brown onion, finely diced

2 garlic cloves, chopped

180 g (6 oz/2 cups) sliced button
mushrooms

375 ml (13 fl oz/1½ cups) beef stock

1 tablespoon tomato paste (concentrated
purée)

1 tablespoon gravy powder (optional)

a dash of worcestershire sauce

a dash of HP Sauce, or other brown sauce

Heat the vegetable oil in a heavy-based saucepan over medium–high heat. Dust the steak cubes with the flour, then brown them for about 5 minutes, turning occasionally, until evenly browned on all sides. Remove from the pan and set aside.

Add the minced beef and onion to the pan and cook for 5–8 minutes, or until the beef is nicely browned, breaking up any clumps with a wooden spoon. Add the garlic, mushrooms, stock and tomato paste, then use a wooden spoon to scrape loose as much of the crusty browned goodness from the bottom of the pan as possible.

Return the steak to the pan and reduce the heat to a gentle simmer. Place the lid on, leaving a small gap to allow a little steam to escape. Leave to simmer for 2 hours, or until the steak cubes are tender. If the stew is still a little too liquid at this point, gradually whisk in some of the gravy

powder, a little at a time, to thicken it, stopping when you reach the desired consistency; you want a rich, thick gravy, not a kindergarten paste.

Season the stew with a dash each of worcestershire and HP sauce, as well as freshly cracked black pepper to taste. Remove from the heat and set aside to cool.

POTATO MASH

2 kg (4 lb 8 oz) Dutch cream potatoes,
or any other good mashing variety

60 ml (2 fl oz/¼ cup) hot milk or cream

150 g (5½ oz) cold butter, diced

salt flakes, for seasoning

ground white pepper, for seasoning

Near serving time, bring a large saucepan of water to the boil. Meanwhile, peel the potatoes and cut them into large chunks.

Add the potatoes to the pan and cook for 15–20 minutes, or until tender. Drain the potatoes in a colander, then cover the colander with a tea towel (dish towel) and leave for 5 minutes.

Place the potatoes in a ricer, or mash the potatoes thoroughly in a mixing bowl. Add the hot milk and, using a whisk, begin to beat in the butter, a few cubes at a time. Season to taste with salt flakes and white pepper. Keep warm.

MUSHY PEAS

500 g (1 lb 2 oz) frozen baby peas

20 g (¾ oz) butter

100 ml (3½ fl oz) hot vegetable stock
or water

1 handful mint leaves

salt flakes, for seasoning

CONTINUED OVER ➤

◄ **CONTINUED FROM PREVIOUS PAGE**

While the potatoes are cooking, bring another large saucepan of water to the boil. Add the frozen peas and cook for 1 minute.

Drain the peas, then return them to the pan. Add the butter, stock, mint leaves and a good pinch of salt flakes and freshly ground black pepper. Use a hand-held stick blender to blitz the peas, retaining a little texture — don't go for a smooth purée. Keep warm.

GRAVY
```
500 ml (17 fl oz/2 cups) ready-made gravy
  (reconstituted from powder - go ahead,
  we won't tell!)
50 g (1¾ oz) sobrasada (soft, cured,
  spreadable spicy Spanish salami;
  see glossary)
```

Just before serving time, heat the gravy in a small saucepan, then stir the sobrasada through until a uniform consistency is achieved. Keep warm.

THE REST
```
8 sheets frozen puff pastry, thawed
1 egg, lightly beaten
```

Preheat the oven to 190°C (375°F). Line a baking tray with baking paper.

While the oven is heating up, gently warm your pie filling (from the previous page).

Using a 15 cm (6 inch) cutter or a small plate as a guide, cut out eight rounds from the pastry. Spoon as much of the filling as you can onto one half of each round, making sure you'll still be able to fold the other half over and seal the empanadas. Use a little water to dampen the pastry edges, then fold the other pastry half over, to make a half-moon. Gently crimp the sealed edges using a fork, then use a pastry brush to glaze the empanadas with the beaten egg.

Place the empanadas on the baking tray and bake for 15–20 minutes, or until the pastry is deeply golden.

To serve, spoon a mound of the buttery mash onto each serving plate, then top with a hot empanada. Add a nice mound of mushy peas, drizzle with the gravy and serve.

CURRY GOAT

PREPARATION: 30 MINUTES + OVERNIGHT STEEPING // COOKING: 2½ HOURS // SERVES 6

Curry goat is a Caribbean thing — and yes, they call it 'curry goat', not 'goat curry'. It's huge in the United Kingdom, where there's a healthy population of ex-pats and a healthy appreciation for what makes Britain great: the cultural contribution of its many residents originally from somewhere else.

Our executive chef, Jamie Thomas, is a Brit who now lives in Australia. So this take on curry goat, like many things we do, may not be as authentic as it is tasty. Plus, goat is… #thegoat.

CURRY GOAT

1.5 kg (3 lb 5 oz) goat shoulder, on the bone, cut into 3–4 cm (1¼–1½ inch) chunks by your butcher

1 tablespoon ground turmeric

salt flakes, for seasoning

1 brown onion, roughly chopped

10 garlic cloves, chopped

4 cm (1½ inch) knob of fresh ginger, roughly chopped

2 tablespoons fennel seeds

150 g (5½ oz/1 cup) plain (all-purpose) flour

olive oil, for pan-frying

1 teaspoon ground allspice

2 teaspoons chilli powder

1 cinnamon stick

10 fresh curry leaves

1 red chilli, split lengthways

500 ml (17 fl oz/2 cups) chicken stock

250 ml (9 fl oz/1 cup) coconut cream

TO SERVE

½ bunch (30 g/1 oz) coriander (cilantro), leaves picked

1 long red chilli, seeded and finely diced

1 lime, cut into 6 wedges

Dirty rice (see page 176)

Put the goat pieces in a large bowl. Rub thoroughly with the turmeric and a good sprinkling of salt flakes and freshly ground black pepper.

In a food processor, blend the onion, garlic and ginger to a coarse paste. Set aside.

In a dry frying pan over medium heat, cook the fennel seeds for 1–2 minutes, or until fragrant. Transfer the seeds to a mortar and pestle or a spice grinder, then bash or whiz to a fine consistency.

Dust the goat pieces with the flour. Heat a little olive oil in a large heavy-based saucepan over medium–high heat, then brown the goat in batches for about 5 minutes on each side. Remove from the pan and set aside.

Pour a little more olive oil into the same saucepan, then add your onion and ginger paste. Stirring continuously so it doesn't stick too much to the pan, cook the paste for 5 minutes, or until fragrant.

Add your freshly ground fennel seeds, along with the allspice, chilli powder, cinnamon stick, curry leaves and chilli, stirring to combine. Return the browned goat pieces to the pan, then pour in the stock and coconut cream.

Bring the contents to a gentle simmer. Stirring occasionally to stop the curry sticking to the bottom, cook, uncovered, for 1–2 hours, or until the sauce has reduced to a nice thick consistency and the meat is tender.

Set aside and allow to cool. Decant the curry into a lidded container, place in the refrigerator and leave it there overnight, to help develop those luscious flavours — curries are always better the next day!

When you're ready to serve, gently reheat the curry. Transfer to a serving dish, then garnish with the coriander and chilli. Serve hot, with the lime wedges and dirty rice.

PARMAGGEDON

PREPARATION: 45 MINUTES // COOKING: 1 HOUR // SERVES 6

When the ice caps have melted, the carbon credits have been spent and meteors are falling from the sky, this is the schnitzel we'll be eating. The parmigiana to end all parmigianas: chicken, ham, cheese, sauce and sobrasada colliding together, ending all hope of getting that belt back on when you're done.

SCHNITZELS

6 x 200 g (7 oz) boneless,
  skinless chicken breasts
225 g (8 oz/1½ cups) plain
  (all-purpose) flour
3 free-range eggs, lightly beaten
  with a drop of milk
120 g (4¼ oz/2 cups) panko
  (Japanese breadcrumbs)

NAPOLI(ISH) SAUCE

1 tablespoon olive oil
1 small red onion, finely diced
1 garlic clove, finely chopped
2 capsicums (peppers), one red
  and one yellow, finely diced
2 x 400 g (14 oz) tins chopped
  tomatoes
2 bay leaves
a few lemon thyme sprigs
1 teaspoon raw (demerara) sugar

TO SERVE

vegetable oil, for deep-frying
200 g (7 oz/2 cups) grated
  cheddar cheese
65 g (2½ oz/½ cup) grated
  mozzarella cheese
150 g (5½ oz) sobrasada (soft,
  cured, spreadable spicy Spanish
  salami; see glossary)
finely shredded flat-leaf (Italian)
  parsley, to garnish
Quick slaw (see page 274)
hot fries (see pages 144–151);
  optional

To make the schnitzels, lay a chicken breast on a chopping board, ready to 'butterfly' it. Using a steady hand, hold a long, sharp knife along the side of the chicken. Without cutting all the way through, use a sawing action to cut the chicken almost all the way through to the other side, leaving a 'hinge' attached. Open the chicken out, place a sheet of plastic wrap on top, then lightly bash the chicken with a rolling pin to flatten it as evenly as possible, to a 1–1.5 cm (½–⅝ inch) thickness. Repeat with the remaining chicken.

Dust the flattened chicken breasts with the flour, dip each fillet into the beaten egg mixture, then dip into the panko crumbs. Set aside, covered with plastic wrap, on a tray in the refrigerator until ready to fry; the schnitzels can be crumbed up to 1 day ahead.

To make the sauce, heat the olive oil in a heavy-based saucepan over medium–low heat. Gently sweat the onion and garlic for 3 minutes, or until the onion is translucent and soft. Add the capsicums and cook for 5 minutes, or until softened. Stir in the tomatoes, bay leaves, thyme sprigs and sugar. Season with a good pinch of sea salt and freshly ground black pepper, then simmer for 30 minutes, or until reduced and thickened to a sauce consistency.

When the sauce is nearly ready, fill a deep-fryer or large heavy-based saucepan one-third full of vegetable oil. Heat over medium heat until it reaches 180°C (350°F) when tested with a cooking thermometer, or until a cube of bread dropped into the oil turns golden brown in 15 seconds.

Meanwhile, preheat the grill (broiler) to medium–high.

Remove the crumbed chicken pieces from the fridge. Working in batches, gently lower the schnitzels into the hot oil and fry each batch for 5–6 minutes, or until golden and cooked through. Remove and drain on paper towel.

Arrange all the fried chicken schnitzels on a baking tray. Top each one with some Napoli(ish) sauce, a handful of the grated cheeses and a few blobs of sobrasada. Grill for 6–8 minutes, or until the cheese has melted and started to bubble. Serve hot, garnished with parsley, with the slaw on the side, and hot fries if desired.

HAWAII
pineapple, bacon, cheese

WORLD OF SCHNITZELS

Imagine if planet Earth was a schnitzel, the countries of the globe were toppings, and your tongue had a first-class round-the-world plane ticket. Welcome to Schnitzel Earth. Every pub needs a schnitzel (or four), so you can imagine we've come up with a few since opening our various venues.

Just top your basic schnitty (see Parmageddon recipe, page 130) with flavours from your favourite country and it's happy days.

MEXICO
slow-cooked beans, Chilli mince
(page 271), peppers, sour cream

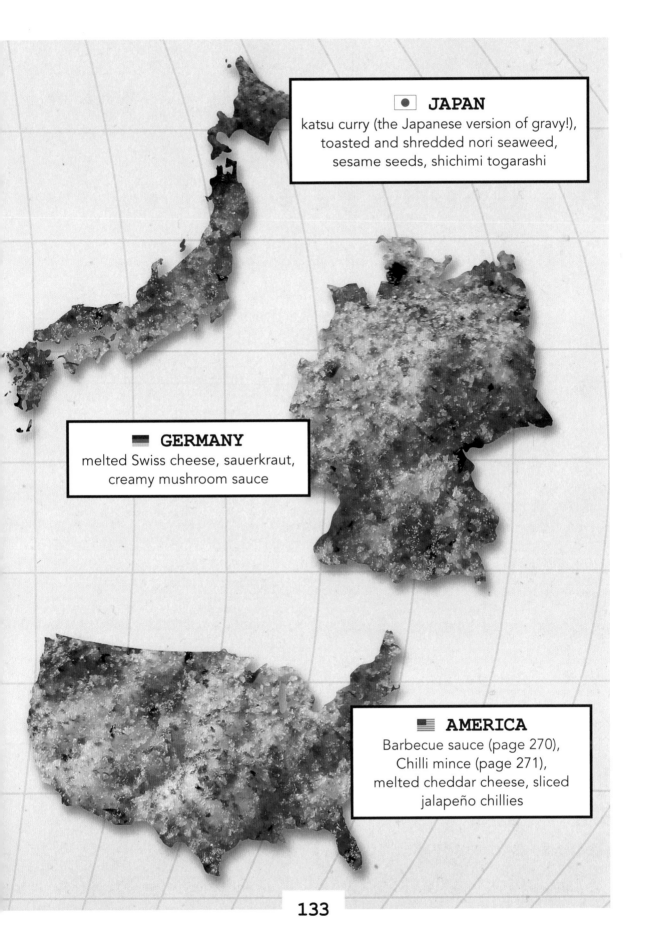

🇯🇵 JAPAN
katsu curry (the Japanese version of gravy!),
toasted and shredded nori seaweed,
sesame seeds, shichimi togarashi

🇩🇪 GERMANY
melted Swiss cheese, sauerkraut,
creamy mushroom sauce

🇺🇸 AMERICA
Barbecue sauce (page 270),
Chilli mince (page 271),
melted cheddar cheese, sliced
jalapeño chillies

VEGO NACHOS

PREPARATION: 40 MINUTES + 10 MINUTES FOR THE TORTILLA CHIPS
COOKING: 1¼ HOURS + 15 MINUTES FOR THE TORTILLA CHIPS // SERVES 6–10

Be honest. There aren't many instances where 'meat free' is better than the 'with meat' option. But when you do find a dish that is complete without meat, it's worth celebrating — and making! In fact, we reckon this vego nachos quite often trumps its meaty sibling.

This is Tex–Mex at its best: sour cream, guacamole, beans, crunchy corn chips, melty cheese: yes, yep, check, yeah and ohhh yeah.

THE BEANS

olive oil, for pan-frying
2 brown onions, thinly sliced
1 garlic clove, finely chopped
2 teaspoons ground cumin
2 teaspoons sweet paprika
generous pinch of ground cinnamon
1 teaspoon chilli powder
2 x 400 g (14 oz) tins chopped tomatoes
2 x 400 g (14 oz) tins Mexican bean mix, drained and rinsed
400 g (14 oz) tin red kidney beans, drained and rinsed
2 teaspoons salt flakes
2 bay leaves
1 bunch (60 g/2¼ oz) coriander (cilantro), leaves and stems coarsely chopped

Heat a little olive oil in a heavy-based saucepan over medium–low heat. Gently cook the onion and garlic for 3–4 minutes, or until translucent and slightly coloured. Add the spices and cook for a further 5 minutes, or until they become fragrant.

Add the tomatoes and their liquid, along with the beans, salt and bay leaves. Stir to combine. Bring to the boil, then reduce the heat to low. Allow the beans to simmer for 40 minutes, or until the sauce has reduced and thickened.

Stir in the coriander, remove from the heat and set aside. The bean mixture will keep in the fridge in an airtight container for 2–3 days.

GUACAMOLE

4 ripe avocados
2 long red chillies, finely chopped
juice of 2 limes
1 red onion, finely diced
½ bunch (30 g/1 oz) coriander (cilantro), stems and leaves finely chopped
salt flakes, for seasoning

Cut the avocados in half. Remove the stones, then scoop the flesh into a bowl. Add the remaining ingredients and mash together with a fork, keeping some of the texture in the avocado.

Place a layer of plastic wrap directly over the top of the guacamole, to stop oxygen getting in and turning the avocado black.

The guacamole is best used same day, but will keep for up to 2 days in the fridge.

TORTILLA CHIPS

230 g (8 oz) packet of blue corn
    tortillas (see glossary); if you
    prefer, you can use blue or white
    corn chips instead, and omit the
    deep-frying step
vegetable oil, for deep-frying
1 teaspoon salt flakes
½ teaspoon sweet paprika

We like a bit of fancy now and then, so we like
to fry up some tortillas into chips and serve them
with the nachos. Cut your tortillas, if using, into
triangles roughly the size of a corn chip.

Fill a deep-fryer or large heavy-based saucepan
one-third full of vegetable oil. Heat over medium
heat until it reaches 170°C (325°F) when tested
with a cooking thermometer, or until a cube of
bread dropped into the oil turns golden brown
in 20 seconds.

Fry the tortillas in batches for 1–2 minutes, or
until crisp. Drain the tortilla chips on paper towel
and immediately season with salt flakes and a
sprinkling of the paprika.

The tortilla chips can be cooked a few hours
ahead, but are best used same day.

FOR TOPPING

185 g (6½ oz/1½ cups) grated cheddar
    cheese
150 g (5½ oz/1 cup) grated mozzarella
    cheese
pickled jalapeño chillies, drained
    and sliced into rings
125 g (4½ oz/½ cup) sour cream
Pico de gallo (see page 274)
½ bunch (30 g/1 oz) coriander
    (cilantro), leaves picked

When you're ready to serve, preheat the grill
(broiler) to medium–high.

Arrange your fried tortilla chips or corn
chips in a baking dish. Top with a good ladleful
or two of the bean mix (you may not need to use
it all; freeze any leftovers in an airtight container
for another day).

Scatter all the cheese over the top and bake
for 5–8 minutes, or until the cheese has melted
and starts to bubble.

Add the remaining toppings and serve hot.

SHORT-RIB NACHOS

PREPARATION: 45 MINUTES // COOKING: 4 HOURS // SERVES 8–10

It is a scientific fact that nobody hates nachos. It's basically the perfect combination of fat, flavour and texture. This version takes things to a fancy new level, using cola-braised short ribs instead of minced (ground) meat. For an extra wow factor, use BLUE corn chips instead of regular ones (insert 'ooohs' and 'aaaahs' here)...

THE SHORT RIBS

2.5 kg (5 lb 8 oz) beef short ribs

salt flakes, for seasoning

olive oil, for pan-frying

1 brown onion, roughly chopped

5 garlic cloves, chopped

2 dried chipotle chillies

2 teaspoons dried oregano

2 teaspoons ground cumin

2 teaspoons ground coriander

400 g (14 oz) tin chopped tomatoes

1 tablespoon tomato paste
   (concentrated purée)

375 ml (13 fl oz/1½ cups) cola

Preheat the oven to 160°C (315°F). Season the ribs with some salt flakes and freshly ground black pepper and set aside.

Heat some olive oil in a heavy-based saucepan over medium heat. Sauté the onion and garlic for about 3 minutes, then stir in the chillies, oregano, spices, tomatoes and tomato paste until combined. Bring the mixture to a simmer, then add the cola. Stir thoroughly and bring back to the boil.

Heat some more olive oil in a large heavy-based saucepan over medium–high heat. Working in batches, brown the ribs for 3–4 minutes on each side, adding each batch to a roasting tin.

Once all the ribs are in the roasting tin, pour the simmering sauce over, then cover tightly with foil. Bake for 3 hours, or until the meat comes away easily from the bone. Remove from the oven and set aside.

When the ribs are cool enough to handle, remove and discard the bones. Shred the meat and set aside.

Returning to the sauce, skim off any excess fat that has floated to the top and strain out the solids. Pour the strained sauce into a saucepan

and simmer over medium heat for 15–20 minutes, or until reduced to a thick, rich sauce. Season with salt flakes and freshly ground black pepper. Add the shredded rib meat and stir to combine.

TO SERVE

100 g (3½ oz) unsalted corn chips
   per person

125 g (4½ oz/1 cup) grated cheddar cheese

150 g (5½ oz/1 cup) grated mozzarella
   cheese

4 ripe avocados

2 limes, halved

250 g (9 oz/1 cup) sour cream

Corn salsa (see page 272)

Pico de gallo (see page 274)

½ bunch (30 g/1 oz) coriander (cilantro)
   leaves and stems, finely chopped

60 g (2¼ oz/1 cup) pickled jalapeño
   chillies, drained and chopped

Preheat the grill (broiler) to medium–high.

Divide the chips among small heatproof serving dishes, of about 250 ml (9 fl oz/1 cup) capacity. Top with a generous amount of the saucy short rib mixture and scatter all the grated cheese over the top. Place under the grill and cook for 3–5 minutes, or until the cheese has melted and is starting to bubble. Remove from the heat.

Halve the avocados, remove the stones and cut the flesh into small chunks. Drizzle with the juice of the limes, then spoon the diced avocado evenly around the nachos. Add a dollop of sour cream and spoon the corn salsa around too.

Drizzle the pico de gallo over the top. Garnish the lot with a sprinkling of coriander and chopped jalapeño chillies and serve.

STEAK FRITES with KIMCHI BÉARNAISE

PREPARATION: 30 MINUTES // COOKING: 30 MINUTES // SERVES 6

For this heart-warming steak dish, you can choose whatever steak tickles your belly, but we like rump — or even better, a hanger steak, if you can get it. The hanger's fat content and texture is just right: rich, and with a good amount of chew. Plus you only get one per cow, and there's something kind of ballin' about that. The tweaked-out béarnaise sauce adds extra bold flavours and takes a simple weeknight steak to more luxurious places.

To make the kimchi béarnaise, drain the kimchi, reserving 50 ml (1¾ fl oz) of the pickling liquid. Place the kimchi in a blender, blitz to a smooth purée and set aside.

Heat a saucepan over medium heat. Add the reserved kimchi liquid, along with the shallot, tarragon, peppercorns, star anise and vinegar. Simmer for 5–7 minutes, or until the liquid has reduced to about 80 ml (2½ fl oz/⅓ cup). Remove from the heat and set aside to cool.

Set up another saucepan by pouring in about 500 ml (17 fl oz/2 cups) water and bringing the heat up so the water is just simmering. Take a heatproof glass mixing bowl that fits on top of the saucepan; strain in the cooled vinegar, then whisk in the egg yolks. Place the bowl over the barely simmering pan of water and start whisking. The mixture will start to thicken and double or triple in volume.

Once the sauce has started to thicken, whisk in the butter, a few cubes at a time, until all the butter is incorporated. Remove from the heat and whisk in the kimchi purée to taste. The sauce will keep for an hour or so while you're getting everything else ready; keep it somewhere near the stove, ideally a little warmer than room temperature.

Season the steaks with salt flakes and freshly ground black pepper. Cook them to your preferred degree of doneness — as a rule, medium-rare is best for flavour and texture, just sayin'. You'll know you're getting close to medium-rare when blood just starts to pool on the top of the steak. Remove from the heat, cover the steaks loosely with foil and set aside to rest for 5 minutes.

Meanwhile, cook the fries according to the packet instructions. Drain on paper towel and immediately season with salt flakes.

Serve the steaks with a good dollop of kimchi béarnaise, with the hot fries and remaining béarnaise on the side.

KIMCHI BÉARNAISE

100 g (3½ oz/1 cup) kimchi (Korean pickle; see glossary)
2 French shallots, finely chopped
2 tarragon sprigs
5 black peppercorns
1 star anise
200 ml (7 fl oz) white wine vinegar
3 free-range egg yolks
250 g (9 oz) unsalted butter, at room temperature, diced

TO SERVE

6 steaks, of your preferred cut and weight, at room temperature
salt flakes, for seasoning
frozen shoestring fries
vegetable oil, for deep-frying (optional)

KICK TANG CHICKEN

PREPARATION: 30 MINUTES + 2 HOURS MARINATING // COOKING: 45 MINUTES // SERVES 4-8

If you drive down Pico Boulevard from Santa Monica to Downtown Los Angeles, you'll eventually come across Dino's Chicken & Burgers. It's the ultimate option in ghetto fast food. We always joked that the owner was a Greek guy in a Mexican part of town trying to cook Portuguese chicken — at least that's what it tastes like. It has loads of vinegar tang, looks like it came out of a tandoori oven, and is served with a life-changing sloppy-as rice in a styrofoam box.

This is our ode to Dino, the world's best takeout chicken. We serve ours with either hot shoestring fries or our Dirty rice.

1 tablespoon achiote paste
   (see glossary)
60 ml (2 fl oz/¼ cup) orange juice
60 ml (2 fl oz/¼ cup) olive oil
5 garlic cloves, chopped
2 tablespoons roughly chopped
   rosemary leaves
1.3 kg (3 lb) free-range chicken,
   cut into 4-8 pieces

KICK TANG SAUCE
250 ml (9 fl oz/1 cup) Tapatío
   hot sauce, or other Mexican-
   style hot chilli sauce
juice of 1 lime
2 garlic cloves, crushed
½ teaspoon dried oregano
2 teaspoons achiote paste
   (see glossary)
salt flakes, for seasoning

TO SERVE
500 g (1 lb 2 oz) frozen
   shoestring fries (optional)
vegetable oil, for deep-frying
   (optional)
salt flakes, for seasoning
Dirty rice (page 176); optional
12 flour tortillas, about 15 cm
   (6 inches) in size, warmed
Quick slaw (see page 274)
lime halves

In a mixing bowl, thoroughly combine the achiote paste, orange juice, olive oil, garlic and rosemary. Add all the chicken, ensuring that each piece is thoroughly coated in the mixture. Cover with plastic wrap and marinate in the refrigerator for at least 2 hours.

Put all the kick tang sauce ingredients in a blender and blitz together, then adjust the seasoning with a little more lime juice or salt flakes if needed. Set aside.

When you're ready to eat, fire up the barbecue to a medium heat. Meanwhile, remove the chicken from the fridge to take the chill off it.

Grill the chicken for 10–15 minutes on each side, until slightly charred on the outside and cooked through, basting the chicken with some of the kick tang sauce during the last 10 minutes of cooking.

Remove the chicken from the heat, give it another generous basting of kick tang sauce, then set aside to rest for 5 minutes.

Meanwhile, if serving the chicken with hot fries, cook them according to the packet instructions. Drain on paper towel and immediately sprinkle with salt flakes.

Serve the chicken with your choice of hot fries or dirty rice, with a stack of warmed tortillas and a pile of slaw on the side, and some lime halves for squeezing over.

From here, you can build your own ghetto burrito, or use the tortillas and fries or rice to mop up all the juices. Your call.

ADOBO MEATBALLS

PREPARATION: 45 MINUTES // COOKING: 1¼ HOURS
MAKES ABOUT 25 (ENOUGH FOR 4–6 PEOPLE)

The meatball game is all about a density preference. Want 'em big and soft?
Pad the recipe out with breadcrumbs or flour. A more solid structure?
More killer (that's meat, Bob), less filler.

We prefer ours the latter — smaller, firmer and chock-full of meaty goodness.
Make sure your minced meat isn't too lean, or you'll end up with hockey pucks:
fat equals flavour and a more tender result.

MEATBALLS
3 large carrots
500 g (1 lb 2 oz) minced
   (ground) pork
500 g (1 lb 2 oz) minced
   (ground) chicken
1 teaspoon smoked paprika
3 teaspoons salt flakes
pinch of chilli powder
240 g (8½ oz/3 cups, lightly
   packed) fresh breadcrumbs

ADOBO & TOMATO SAUCE
olive oil, for pan-frying
2 brown onions, finely diced
2 garlic cloves, finely diced
½ teaspoon ground cumin
½ teaspoon dried oregano
250 ml (9 fl oz/1 cup)
   chicken stock
2 x 400 g (14 oz) tins
   chopped tomatoes
2 x 400 g (14 oz) tins chipotle
   chillies in adobo sauce
   (see glossary)
1 teaspoon salt flakes

TO SERVE
½ bunch (40 g/1½ oz) flat-leaf
   (Italian) parsley, chopped
50 g (1¾ oz/½ cup) finely grated
   parmesan cheese

To make the meatballs, peel and coarsely grate the carrots, then steam for 3–5 minutes, or until tender. Leave to cool, then place in a large mixing bowl. Add the remaining meatball ingredients and mix until thoroughly combined. Roll the mixture into 50 g (1¾ oz) balls, about the size of golf balls. Place them on a lined tray and refrigerate until ready to cook; the meatballs can be made up to 24 hours ahead of time.

To make the adobo and tomato sauce, heat a little olive oil in a heavy-based saucepan over medium heat. Sweat the onion for 3 minutes, or until soft and translucent. Add the garlic, cumin and oregano and cook for a further 5 minutes.

Stir in the stock, tomatoes, and the chillies and their adobo sauce. Bring the mixture to a simmer and leave to bubble away for 30 minutes. The sauce should be nice and thick and saucy at this point — if it is still too liquid, continue simmering until the sauce is further reduced. Add the salt flakes, to taste.

Once the sauce has reached its desired thickness, use a hand-held stick blender to blitz the sauce to a uniform texture. Add the meatballs to the simmering sauce, cover and simmer for a further 30 minutes, or until the meatballs are cooked through.

Transfer the meatballs and sauce to a serving dish. Scatter with the parsley and parmesan and serve.

HILLBILLY BARBECUE PIZZA

PREPARATION: 30 MINUTES // COOKING: 5 MINUTES + 15-20 MINUTES PER PIZZA BATCH
SERVES 8-10

The Italians may have invented pizza, but the Americans took the ball and ran with it. We've kept the thinner, Italian-style base, but topped it with decidedly in-your-face American toppings. Some may consider it sacrilege, but there's no denying that barbecue sauce on a pizza does something pretty magical when it meets mouths. Besides, we ain't no purists here.

This is an excellent recipe for using up left-over barbecued or braised meats, so plan this as your 'day after the night before' go-to.

Preheat the oven to 220°C (425°F). If you have a pizza baking stone, heat it up in the oven for at least 30 minutes prior to using. Alternatively, line four baking trays with baking paper (or use two baking trays and bake the pizzas in two batches).

Divide the pizza dough into four balls and roll them out as thinly as you can.

Heat a frying pan over medium heat. Brown the bacon for 4–5 minutes, or until crisp and golden. Remove from the pan and drain on paper towel.

Generously smear your Napoli(ish) sauce over the pizza bases, almost to the edges. Evenly distribute the bacon, meat, pepperoni and corn over the bases. Sprinkle a good handful of the cheeses on each pizza.

Bake on the pizza stone or pizza trays for 15–20 minutes, or until the dough is golden and cooked through.

Squiggle some barbecue sauce over each pizza, cut into pieces and serve.

1 quantity Pizza dough (from the Korean barbecued pizza recipe on page 36)

8 bacon rashers, rind removed, finely diced

500 ml (17 fl oz/2 cups) Napoli(ish) sauce (from the Parmageddon recipe on page 130)

200 g (7 oz) left-over pulled pork (see page 114), braised short rib meat (see page 136) or barbecued chicken

200 g (7 oz) hot pepperoni, thinly sliced

300 g (10½ oz) tin corn kernels, drained and rinsed (or use Corn salsa; see page 272)

250 g (9 oz/2 cups) grated cheddar cheese

300 g (10½ oz/2 cups) grated mozzarella cheese

250 ml (9 fl oz/1 cup) Barbecue sauce (see page 270)

FRIES

Nothing says 'awesome night in' like frying off a truckload of fries and working your way through them while eyeballing some heavy-duty television.

We are fans of fries of all shapes and sizes. From hand-cut to sweet potato, frozen-aisle section, shoestring and thick-cut, you really can't go wrong.

They can get a whole lot more right though, with the right seasonings or toppings. Here are a few of our favourites.

SALTY LANGUAGE

The simplest way to transform fries is with seasoning. Mix different spices with salt and pepper and fries can go from simple to downright spectacular. Each of our pubs has a signature seasoning — here are some we love the most.

CURRY SALT

2½ teaspoons sea salt
½ teaspoon curry powder

Combine the ingredients and store in an airtight container in the pantry until needed.

This one is great sprinkled over anything deep-fried, and is especially good with plantains or sweet potato chips and fried chicken.

PAPRIKA SALT

1 tablespoon coriander seeds
1 tablespoon cumin seeds
2 tablespoons smoked paprika
¼ teaspoon cayenne pepper
1½ tablespoons sea salt

In a dry frying pan over medium heat, toast the coriander and cumin seeds for a few minutes, until they become fragrant.

Grind the toasted seeds using a spice grinder or a mortar and pestle, then combine with the remaining ingredients. Store in an airtight container in the pantry until needed.

The paprika salt is terrific sprinkled over plain chips or fried calamari.

NORFOLK SALT

¼ teaspoon ground star anise
¼ teaspoon ground cardamom
¼ teaspoon ground cinnamon
2 tablespoons chilli powder
3 tablespoons ground sichuan peppercorns
65 g (2¼ oz/½ cup) sea salt

Combine all the ingredients and store in an airtight container in the pantry until needed.

We really only sprinkle this one on fries — but we're sure you'll find other uses for it…

LOBSTER FRIES

PREPARATION: 45 MINUTES // COOKING: 1½ HOURS // SERVES 4–6

To really get you in the mood, listen to sea shanties while making these fries. Here the Australian/British favourite of chips and gravy is elevated to new heights — with lobster gravy, no less! Add cheese and chives to those fries and it's a 'umami' punch in the face.

A note on pricey crustaceans such as crabs, crayfish or lobsters: whenever you splash out on them, make the most of them by storing the shells in the freezer until you have enough to make a stock or sauce. Now that's stretching luxury. Otherwise, ask your local fishmonger if you can buy their spare shells… they'll probably give them to you for nix.

The lobster sauce makes about 1 litre (35 fl oz/4 cups) — more than you'll need for this recipe. It freezes really well, so seal the left-over sauce in an airtight container and stash it in the freezer for next time. It will easily keep for a month.

LOBSTER SAUCE

20 g (¾ oz) butter

1 brown onion, roughly chopped

2 garlic cloves, finely chopped

1 fennel bulb, roughly sliced

1 celery stalk, roughly chopped

1 carrot, roughly chopped

2 kg (4 lb 8 oz) lobster or crab shells

60 g (2¼ oz/¼ cup) tomato paste (concentrated purée)

2 teaspoons Old Bay Seasoning (an American spice mix; see glossary)

2 roma (plum) tomatoes, chopped

2 shots pastis or dry vermouth, such as Pernod or Noilly Prat

1 litre (35 fl oz/4 cups) tomato juice or Clamato juice (see glossary)

THE REST

3 bacon rashers, rind removed, cut into thin strips

2 corn cobs, husks and silks removed

vegetable oil, for deep-frying (optional)

1 kg (2 lb 4 oz) frozen shoestring fries

salt flakes, for seasoning

125 g (4½ oz/1 cup) grated cheddar cheese

150 g (5½ oz/1 cup) grated mozzarella cheese

4 tablespoons finely chopped chives

To make the lobster sauce, melt the butter in a heavy-based saucepan over medium heat. Sauté the onion and garlic for 3–4 minutes, or until the onion is soft and translucent. Add the fennel, celery and carrot and sauté for a further 2–3 minutes.

Meanwhile, place the lobster shells in a plastic bag. Give them a really good bashing with a rolling pin to break the pieces down as small as you can.

Returning to the pan, stir the tomato paste and Old Bay Seasoning through the onion mixture. Continue stirring and cooking out the seasoning for another few minutes. Stir in the tomato, pastis and tomato juice. Bring to the boil, then add the smashed lobster shells. Pour in enough water to just cover the shells, then reduce the heat and simmer the sauce for 1 hour.

Remove the sauce from the heat. Being careful of hot splashes, gradually pour it into a blender or liquidiser, shells and all. Blitz the sauce until it is as shiny and smooth as you can get it.

Pass the sauce through a fine-mesh sieve to filter out any bits of shell you've missed. Season with sea salt and freshly ground black pepper. Set aside and keep warm.

Right, now you've got your sauce ready, it's time to get all the other bits together. Heat a frying pan over medium–high heat. Brown the bacon for 3–4 minutes, or until crisp. Remove from the pan and drain on paper towel.

Bring a saucepan of water to the boil. Add the corn cobs and blanch for 30 seconds, then drain and leave until cool enough to handle. Cut the kernels from the cobs and set aside.

Cook the fries according to the packet instructions. Drain on paper towel and season immediately with salt flakes and freshly ground black pepper.

Meanwhile, preheat the grill (broiler) to medium–high.

Divide the hot fries among heatproof serving plates. Top with a few spoonfuls of the hot lobster sauce, then scatter the corn, bacon and all the grated cheese over the top. Place under the grill and cook for 3–4 minutes, or until the cheese has melted and has started to bubble.

Garnish with the chives and serve.

CHILLI FRIES

LOBSTER FRIES

SAFARI FRIES

3-BIT FRIES

CHILLI FRIES

PREPARATION: 15 MINUTES // COOKING: 20 MINUTES // SERVES 4-6

If we've said it once, we've said it a thousand times. That Chilli mince recipe is one flexible friend. While great on nachos and Chilli dawgs (see page 98), it's also amazing on fries as the chips soak up all the flavours.

vegetable oil, for deep-frying

1 kg (2 lb 4 oz) 13 mm (⅝ inch)
   crinkle-cut frozen fries

500 g (1 lb 2 oz/2 cups) Chilli
   mince (see page 271), warmed

Mexican nacho-flavoured spray
   cheese, for squirting

pickled jalapeño chillies,
   chopped, to serve

coriander (cilantro) sprigs,
   to garnish

Preheat the oven to 190°C (375°F).

Fill a deep-fryer or large heavy-based saucepan one-third full of vegetable oil. Heat over medium heat until it reaches 180°C (350°F) when tested with a cooking thermometer, or until a cube of bread dropped into the oil turns golden brown in 15 seconds. Add the fries and cook according to the packet instructions. Drain on paper towel.

Place the fries on a baking tray lined with baking paper, or a heatproof serving dish. Top with the chilli mince and bake for 6–8 minutes, or until the beef is warmed through.

Add a good squiggle of the spray cheese, top with the jalapeño, garnish with coriander and serve.

3-BIT FRIES

PREPARATION: 15 MINUTES // COOKING: 15 MINUTES //SERVES 4-6

This recipe is a fairly accurate representation of what is (or should be) in the fridge at home at any given time. Bacon, sriracha sauce, spring onion and sour cream? Surely these things go together... it's okay, they do!

vegetable oil, for deep-frying

1 kg (2 lb 4 oz) 13 mm (⅝ inch)
   crinkle-cut frozen fries

4 bacon rashers, rind removed,
   finely chopped

125 g (4½ oz/½ cup) sour cream

2-3 spring onions (scallions),
   finely chopped

sriracha hot chilli sauce
   (see glossary), to serve

Fill a deep-fryer or large heavy-based saucepan one-third full of vegetable oil. Heat over medium heat until it reaches 180°C (350°F) when tested with a cooking thermometer, or until a cube of bread dropped into the oil turns golden brown in 15 seconds. Add the fries and cook according to the packet instructions. Drain on paper towel.

Meanwhile, heat a frying pan over medium–high heat. Fry the bacon for 3–4 minutes, or until crisp and browned.

Divide the hot fries among serving dishes and toss the bacon through. Add a dollop of sour cream and garnish with the spring onion. Drizzle with the chilli sauce and serve.

SAFARI FRIES

PREPARATION: 15 MINUTES // COOKING: 25 MINUTES // SERVES 4–6

Our tribute to an LA legend: In-N-Out Burger's famous animal-style fries. Whoever thought to mix cocktail sauce with fries ought to be congratulated, awarded and promoted.

Preheat the oven to 190°C (375°F). Line a baking tray with baking paper.

Fill a deep-fryer or large heavy-based saucepan one-third full of vegetable oil. Heat over medium heat until it reaches 180°C (350°F) when tested with a cooking thermometer, or until a cube of bread dropped into the oil turns golden brown in 15 seconds. Add the fries and cook according to the packet instructions. Drain on paper towel.

Meanwhile, melt the butter in a frying pan over medium–high heat. Sauté the onion for 3–4 minutes, or until golden. Remove from the heat and set aside.

Spread the fried chips on the baking tray and season with salt flakes. Top with the sautéed onion, then scatter the grated cheese over. Bake for 6–8 minutes, or until the cheese has melted and has started to bubble.

Divide among serving dishes, then drizzle with the special sauce. Sprinkle with the smoked paprika, garnish with parsley and dig right in.

vegetable oil, for deep-frying
1 kg (2 lb 4 oz) 1 cm (½ inch) straight-cut frozen chips
20 g (¾ inch) butter
1 large brown onion, diced
salt flakes, for seasoning
125 g (4½ oz/1 cup) grated cheddar or monterey jack cheese
375 ml (13 fl oz/1½ cups) Special sauce (see page 276)
½ teaspoon smoked paprika
thinly sliced flat-leaf (Italian) parsley, to garnish

* FANCY *
SCHMANCY

This chapter is as fancy as it's getting, guys. This is the top. How's the view? These recipes are all about kicking it up a notch. They're for impressing the missus, the mister, your friends, your enemies… or even yourself.

Our version of fancy recommends no square plates, spheres, schmears or foams. You might say that it's the least-fancy fine food you will ever cook, which is the point. These dishes are meant to be cooked — not looked at on the page and never tried for fear of abject failure. These recipes really are the pick of the litter, in terms of containing a touch more finesse than the dishes in the more relaxed chapters.

The intention? A cracking night in, to rival any you'd have out.

MORCILLA-STUFFED SQUID
with DIABLO SAUCE

PREPARATION: 45 MINUTES // COOKING: 50 MINUTES // SERVES 4

By now, you'll be well versed with the fact that we're disciples of the school of 'so wrong, it's right'. At our Spanish-inspired digs, The Carrington, we had the idea to create a dish consisting of a seafood sausage of some kind. This notion eventually evolved into a take on the very classic Spanish pairing of morcilla (blood sausage), stuffed inside squid, and served with a rich, aromatic and spicy diablo sauce. It remains one of the most popular dishes on the menu, so you see — there is sometimes method to our madness!

This recipe relies on finding both the best-quality morcilla and Spanish paprika. It will make all the difference between good and really great.

DIABLO SAUCE

2 red capsicums (peppers)

2 yellow capsicums (peppers)

1 red onion

5 garlic cloves, peeled

100 ml (3½ fl oz) olive oil

1 tablespoon sweet Spanish paprika

1 teaspoon cayenne pepper

1 teaspoon caster (superfine) sugar

2 x 400 g (14 oz) tins roma (plum) tomatoes

good pinch of sea salt flakes

Cut the capsicums into halves or quarters and remove all the seeds and white membranes. Finely dice the flesh, into 5 mm (¼ inch) pieces; you'll need about 500 g (1 lb 2 oz) of diced capsicum all up. Do the same with the onion, then thinly slice the garlic.

Heat the olive oil in a heavy-based saucepan over medium heat. When the oil is getting hot, add the onion and cook for 4–5 minutes, or until soft. Add the garlic and cook for a further 2–3 minutes, to cook the garlic off a little.

Add the diced capsicum, paprika and cayenne pepper, stirring well. Cook gently for a bit, being careful not to burn the spices — but it does help to cook the spices out a little, to take away their raw

spice flavour. Add the sugar and stir for another minute or two, until the mixture starts to stick a little on the bottom of the pan.

When all the ingredients look like they've got to know each other, add the tomatoes and salt flakes. If the tomatoes are whole, just bash them a little with your spoon to break them up a bit; the cooking process will sort them out, and a few chunks here and there is fine. Leave the sauce on a very gentle simmer for 10–15 minutes.

Remove from the heat, then cover until ready to serve; the sauce can now sit happily for a few hours. If you wanted to make it the day before and gently reheat it, this works even better.

THE SQUID

60 ml (2 fl oz/¼ cup) olive oil

1 brown onion, finely diced

2 garlic cloves, chopped

1 teaspoon ground fennel

2 teaspoons ground cumin

1 tablespoon smoked Spanish paprika

1 tablespoon sweet Spanish paprika

½ teaspoon hot Spanish paprika (or cayenne pepper, if you can't find it)

2 morcilla sausages (see glossary), weighing about 320 g (11¼ oz) in total

pinch of sea salt flakes (optional)

4-6 whole cleaned squid tubes, with tentacles, weighing about 150 g (5½ oz) each

Heat the olive oil in a heavy-based frying pan over medium heat. Gently cook the onion for 2 minutes, or until the onion is translucent and soft, but not coloured. Add the garlic and spices, mixing well for another 2 minutes. Set aside to cool.

Dice the sausages, then place in a food processor and blitz for 2–3 seconds, just to break them up; the mixture should resemble coarsely ground beef. Tip into a mixing bowl and stir in the cooled onion and garlic mixture, mixing it in well. Adjust the seasoning with a small pinch of salt flakes if you think it needs it — the morcilla will already have been seasoned when it was made, so we generally don't add much more salt.

Spoon the mixture directly into the cavity of each squid, or place it in a disposable piping (icing) bag, cut about 2.5 cm (1 inch) off the bottom of the bag and pipe the mixture into each squid cavity. Take care not to overfill the squid, as the mixture will expand when cooked. Using toothpicks, seal up the ends of each squid to hold them in shape, and to attach the head and tentacles at the same time.

POACHING & GRILLING THE SQUID

The next step involves poaching the stuffed squid in a saucepan of boiling water, just before serving time. If you have access to a Cryovac machine, seal each squid in a plastic bag. Otherwise, use a generous amount of plastic wrap to wrap each squid tightly so that the water will not penetrate the plastic during poaching.

Fill a saucepan with water and place it over medium heat. When the water has just started to simmer (about 85°C/185°F), poach the wrapped squid for 5 minutes, or until you see the oils start to release from the morcilla. Remove from the water and set aside for a few minutes until you're ready to serve.

While the squid is poaching, heat a barbecue grill or chargrill pan to a medium–high heat. Once the grill is hot, unwrap the squid. Work out which bit is the top of each squid; if you see two 'flaps' on the squid, this is the bottom end. Grill the top side for 2 minutes — just enough to get some nice grill marks happening.

TO SERVE

Transfer your grilled squid to a chopping board. Remove the toothpicks. Using a sharp knife, cut five incisions across the body of each squid, cutting only about two-thirds of the way through.

Spoon some warm diablo sauce onto your serving plates, lay the squid on top and serve.

JERK HANGER STEAK

JERK HANGER STEAK with PINEAPPLE FRITTERS and SALSA HOOCH

PREPARATION: 1 HOUR + OVERNIGHT MARINATING
COOKING: 20 MINUTES + 20 MINUTES RESTING // SERVES 4-6

Ask any chef who likes steak and they will tell you that hanger is basically the best thing going. There's only one per animal, so it's almost as rare as hen's teeth, but better tasting, with a great texture and a rich, luxurious beefiness. It's the ultimate in simple pleasures, and any good butcher will be able to find it for you. Paired with pineapple fritters and salsa hooch, it's a holiday to Hawaii in your dining room, complete with vintage smoking jacket and ukulele.

1 kg (2 lb 4 oz) piece of hanger steak

JERK PASTE RUB
6-10 fresh habanero chillies
   (see glossary)
1 brown onion, finely chopped
3-4 spring onions (scallions),
   finely chopped
1 garlic clove, finely chopped
1 tablespoon fresh thyme leaves
2 teaspoons salt flakes
1 teaspoon freshly ground black pepper
1 teaspoon sugar
1 teaspoon ground allspice
½ teaspoon ground cinnamon
¼ teaspoon freshly grated nutmeg

Start by making the jerk paste rub. Wearing a pair of disposable gloves, finely chop the chillies (don't rub your eyes, these mothers are hot). Scrape the chillies into a food processor, add the remaining rub ingredients and blend together to form a paste.

Rub the mixture thoroughly all over both sides of the steak. Cover with plastic wrap and refrigerate overnight.

SALSA HOOCH
1 bunch (75 g/2½ oz) mint, leaves picked
1 bunch (75 g/2½ oz) coriander
   (cilantro), leaves picked
2 large French shallots, peeled
1 long red chilli, seeded and roughly
   chopped
2 garlic cloves, peeled
juice of 1 lime
100 ml (3½ fl oz) extra virgin olive oil
salt flakes, for seasoning

Place the herbs, shallots, chilli, garlic cloves and lime juice in a food processor. With the motor running, add the olive oil in a thin stream, until all the ingredients are incorporated and the mixture looks like a salsa verde. Taste and season with salt flakes and freshly ground black pepper.

Cover and set aside until required; the salsa can happily sit for up to 5–6 hours; after that it will start to change colour due to its acid content, but will still be fine to use.

CURRIED MAYO SLAW

¼ red cabbage, thinly sliced

¼ white cabbage, thinly sliced

4-5 radishes, thinly sliced

2 spring onions (scallions), chopped

juice of 1 lime

250 g (9 oz/1 cup) whole-egg mayonnaise

2 teaspoons curry powder

pinch of ground turmeric

4 tablespoons finely chopped coriander
  (cilantro) stems and leaves

Put all the cabbage in a bowl. Add the radish, spring onion and lime juice and toss together.

In a small bowl, combine the mayonnaise, curry powder, turmeric and coriander and mix to make a mayo. Toss enough of the curried mayo through the salad to nicely coat the ingredients. Season to taste.

The slaw can be made 3–4 hours ahead, in which case keep it refrigerated with a damp cloth on top and dressed at the last minute.

TO SERVE

Pineapple fritters (see page 185)

15 g (½ oz/¼ cup) shredded coconut,
  lightly toasted

2 limes, quartered

When you're ready to eat, remove the steak from the fridge and bring it to room temperature.

Heat a barbecue grill or chargrill pan to a medium–high heat. Grill the steak for 4–6 minutes on each side, or until the internal temperature of the steak registers 55–60°C (130–140°F) on a meat thermometer. Remove from the grill, cover loosely with foil and set aside to rest for 15–20 minutes.

Meanwhile, prepare the pineapple fritters as directed on page 185.

Slice the steak and arrange on a platter or tray, then arrange the pineapple fritters and slaw alongside. Garnish with the shredded coconut. Pour the salsa hooch into a bowl and serve on the side, with the lime quarters for squeezing over.

SMOKED PORK LOIN with FRIED MUSSELS and MANGO SALSA

PREPARATION: 1 HOUR // COOKING: 3 HOURS // SERVES 6

There are dishes you love... and then there are death-row dinners — the ones you dream about and would be content to hoe into as your last meal in this life. It's a huge call, but this dish, which combines elements of surf'n'turf, smoke, texture, bold flavours and pork, just might be our favourite in this whole book.

TO SMOKE THE PORK

a good handful of wood chips, suitable for smoking

2 kg (4 lb 8 oz) piece of pork loin, skin off, silver skin removed; the skin is great for the Pork chips on page 18!

olive oil, for coating

salt flakes, for seasoning

Leave the wood chips to soak in a bowl of water for at least 30 minutes. Meanwhile, light the coals in a kettle barbecue or hooded barbecue and allow the heat to die down to 120°C (250°F).

Coat the pork loin with a slug of olive oil. Season with salt flakes and freshly ground black pepper and rub in thoroughly.

Move the coals to the edges of the barbecue and sprinkle the soaked wood chips over them. Place the pork in the middle of the grill and close the lid. Smoke the pork for about 2 hours, or until the internal temperature reaches 66°C (151°F) when tested with a meat thermometer.

Remove the pork from the grill, then wrap it in foil. Set aside to rest while preparing the remaining ingredients.

MANGO SALSA

3 ripe but firm mangoes, peeled and stoned, flesh finely diced

3 long red chillies, seeded and finely chopped

½ red onion, finely diced

2 garlic cloves, finely chopped

4 tablespoons finely chopped coriander (cilantro) stems and leaves

juice of 1 lime

150 ml (5 fl oz) extra virgin olive oil

1 teaspoon salt flakes

Combine all the salsa ingredients in a mixing bowl. Taste and adjust the seasoning, then cover and set aside until you're ready to serve. This salsa is best used within an hour or two of making.

THE MUSSELS

1 kg (2 lb 4 oz) mussels (or enough
   to end up with 36 perfectly cooked
   mussels), scrubbed well, hairy
   beards removed

150 g (5½ oz/1 cup) plain (all-purpose)
   flour

2 free-range eggs

1 teaspoon milk

120 g (4¼ oz/2 cups) panko (Japanese
   breadcrumbs; see glossary)

vegetable oil, for deep-frying

In a large saucepan, bring about 250 ml (9 fl oz/ 1 cup) water to a simmer over medium–high heat. Add the mussels and place the lid on. Steam for 3–4 minutes, or until the mussels start to open.

Remove the mussels from the saucepan and set aside to cool. Discard any mussels that haven't opened at least partially. Once cool enough to handle, carefully remove the meat from the shells. Discard the shells, reserving the meat.

Spread the flour on a plate. In a bowl, whisk together the eggs and the milk. Spread the panko crumbs on another plate.

Fill a deep-fryer or large heavy-based saucepan one-third full of vegetable oil. Heat over medium heat until it reaches 180°C (350°F) when tested with a cooking thermometer, or until a cube of bread dropped into the oil turns golden brown in 15 seconds.

Working in small batches, lightly dust a few mussels with the flour, then dip them into the egg mixture, then the breadcrumbs. Add them to the hot oil and cook for 2–3 minutes, or until golden and crisp. Drain on paper towel.

TO SERVE

1 bunch (60 g/2¼ oz) coriander
   (cilantro), leaves picked

6 radishes, sliced into thin rounds

salt flakes, for seasoning

Remove the rested pork from the foil and carve it on the diagonal, using a sharp knife. Arrange on six warmed serving plates.

Spoon the mango salsa over and around each plate, then arrange six fried mussels on top. Garnish with the coriander and radish and finish the whole thing with a generous pinch of salt flakes.

KINGFISH, SMOKED EGGPLANT AND ESCOVITCH PEPPERS

KINGFISH, SMOKED EGGPLANT and ESCOVITCH PEPPERS

PREPARATION: 45 MINUTES // COOKING: 45 MINUTES // SERVES 6

Escovitch, escabeche, escoveech, escabecio... call it what you like. Almost every Latin/Mediterranean/Caribbean country has a version, but they are all basically dishes in which a quick-pickling liquid gives a supercharged acidic, mega-tangy flavour to vegetables or fish. In our case, we use the Jamaican version to pickle capsicum (peppers).

This dish is really simple. It relies on the beauty of a simple piece of barbecued fish, the smokiness of a baba ghanoush–style eggplant purée, and those delicious pickled bits of goodness to do the talking.

SMOKED EGGPLANT PURÉE

2 eggplants (aubergines)

1 tablespoon plain yoghurt

good pinch of ground allspice

juice of ½ lemon

salt flakes, for seasoning

Prick the eggplants a few times with a fork. Over an open flame (a gas hob or a barbecue are perfect), char the eggplants evenly until blackened all over and very soft to the touch. This will take about 20 minutes all up — about 5 minutes on each side, turning each eggplant four times.

Place in a bowl, cover with plastic wrap and set aside to steam for 10 minutes.

Once cool enough to handle, halve the eggplants and scoop out the soft, smoky flesh. Place the eggplant flesh in a blender along with the remaining purée ingredients, seasoning with salt flakes and freshly ground black pepper to taste. Blitz until a smooth paste forms.

Transfer to a bowl, cover and set aside at room temperature until needed; alternatively, the purée can be made a day ahead and gently heated before serving to take the fridge chill off.

ESCOVITCH PEPPERS

1 yellow capsicum (pepper), cut in half

1 red capsicum (pepper), cut in half

2 carrots, peeled

3-4 red Asian shallots, peeled

1 teaspoon sugar

250 ml (9 fl oz/1 cup) vinegar

1 teaspoon fennel seeds

5 whole allspice berries (if you can't get these, just leave them out)

1 teaspoon black peppercorns

1 long red chilli, seeded and thinly sliced

170 ml (5½ fl oz/⅔ cup) extra virgin olive oil

2 tablespoons chopped flat-leaf (Italian) parsley

good pinch of salt flakes

Start by removing the seeds and any of the white membranes from inside the capsicums. Cut the flesh as thinly as possible into strips.

Run a fork down the length of the carrots, pressing quite hard so you score some grooves into them. Now slice the carrots as thinly as possible, into rounds, so you end up with some pretty-looking slices; a Japanese-style mandoline is great for this.

Slice the shallots into the thinnest possible rounds, then set aside with the other vegetables.

In a stainless steel saucepan, combine the sugar, vinegar, fennel seeds, allspice berries, peppercorns and chilli. Warm over medium heat until the sugar has dissolved, then bring the mixture up to a boil.

Add the capsicum, carrot and shallot. Take the pan straight off the heat and leave the vegetables in the pan to cool. Once cooled, stir in the olive oil, parsley and salt.

The vegetables can be pickled a few days ahead. Store them in their pickling liquid and refrigerate until needed; bring back to room temperature for serving.

THE REST

6 x 180 g (6½ oz) kingfish fillets, or
  any other firm-fleshed white fish fillets,
  skin on

olive oil, for brushing

salt flakes, for seasoning

Heat a barbecue or chargrill pan to a medium–high heat. Oil the fish on both sides and season with salt flakes and freshly ground black pepper.

Grill the fish, skin side down, for 2–3 minutes, then repeat on the other side. The fish should be just cooked; it will be opaque in the middle.

TO SERVE

Place a dollop of the smoked eggplant purée on each serving plate, and top with a piece of grilled fish. Scatter the escovitch peppers over and around the plate, along with a little of the pickling liquid, and you're ready to get stuck straight in.

JERK LAMB NECK
with EGGPLANT RUNDOWN

PREPARATION: 45 MINUTES + 30 MINUTES MARINATING
COOKING: 1½ HOURS // SERVES 6

We first served this dish as part of a Bob Marley birthday dinner we hosted at one of our venues. We liked it so much that we quickly added it to the regular menu. Lamb neck is one of the best 'bang for your buck' lamb cuts out there. When treated right, it's tender and juicy, but still retains its meaty texture. It's slow-cooking gold.

THE EGGPLANT RUNDOWN

2-3 eggplants (aubergines), cut into 2.5 cm (1 inch) dice; all up you'll need about 700 g (1 lb 9 oz) diced eggplant

150 ml (5 fl oz) olive oil, approximately

1 large onion, cut into 1 cm (½ inch) dice

1 celery stalk, cut into 1 cm (½ inch) dice

4 garlic cloves, thinly sliced

1 knob of fresh ginger (about 20 g/ ¾ oz), peeled and finely grated

1 long red chilli, sliced into thin rounds

1 teaspoon curry powder

1 teaspoon ground allspice

1 teaspoon ground turmeric

400 g (14 oz) tin chopped roma (plum) tomatoes

Unless you have a mega-large frying pan, it's best to fry the eggplant in two or three batches. The eggplant will sponge up all the oil, so it's best to fry it up in a few goes and to not crowd the pan.

Heat some of the olive oil in a large frying pan over high heat. When the oil is hot, add as much of the eggplant as you feel happy with and cook for 4–5 minutes, or until golden brown; you may feel the need to add a drop more oil as you go. Once you have a batch ready, drain it on paper towel while you fry up the rest of the eggplant.

Place a saucepan over medium heat and add another splash of olive oil. Cook your onion and celery for 2–3 minutes, until soft and golden, then add your garlic, ginger and chilli and cook for another minute or two.

Stir in the spices and cook gently for another minute. Now add your cooked eggplant and the tomatoes and bring to a simmer — the mixture should resemble the famous French dish ratatouille at this stage. Leave to gently cook for a further 5–10 minutes, making sure it doesn't stick to the bottom of the pan.

Take the mixture off the heat and set aside until needed; the eggplant rundown can be prepared a day ahead and stored in an airtight container in the fridge, then gently reheated for serving.

THE LAMB

4 lamb neck fillets, about 350 g (12 oz) each

2 teaspoons Jerk paste (see page 273)

Trim the lamb of any visible sinew. Rub the lamb thoroughly with the jerk paste and set aside at room temperature for 30 minutes.

Meanwhile, fire up the barbecue and get the coals going; you're looking for a medium heat, anywhere around 140–160°C (285–320°F).

Spread the coals out on your barbecue, so you won't be cooking over a direct heat. Place the lamb in a spot where it's not going to burn. Leave to gently cook for about 40 minutes.

(If you'd prefer to cook the lamb in the oven, you can simply brown it in a frying pan, place it in a roasting tin and gently cook in a preheated 130°C/250°F oven for 40 minutes.)

Remove the lamb from the barbecue or oven, loosely cover with foil and allow to rest for 20 minutes while assembling the rest of the dish.

THE REST

150 g (5½ oz) plain yoghurt

a couple of pinches of curry powder

salt flakes, for seasoning

125 ml (4 fl oz/½ cup) vegetable oil

4-5 red Asian shallots, sliced into
   thin rings

75 g (2½ oz/½ cup) plain (all-purpose)
   flour

a few fresh curry leaf sprigs (optional)

extra virgin olive oil, for drizzling
   (optional)

In a small bowl, mix together the yoghurt and curry powder. Season to taste with salt flakes and freshly ground black pepper and set aside.

Heat a frying pan over medium heat and add the vegetable oil. Separate the shallot rings and dust them lightly with the flour. Drop them into the hot oil and fry for 3–4 minutes, or until golden and cooked through. Drain on paper towel.

Heat the oil up again, and quickly fry off your curry leaves, if using; drain on paper towel.

TO SERVE

Spoon equal amounts of the eggplant rundown onto your six plates. Carve the lamb against the grain into slices about 1 cm (½ inch) thick, then arrange evenly over the eggplant.

Add a few small dollops of the curry yoghurt here and there, then scatter your shallot rings and any curry leaves, if using, around to make it look fancy. Give each plate an extra pinch of salt flakes, and a little drizzle of extra virgin olive oil if you'd like. Serve immediately.

BEEF CHEEKS WITH CARROT, COFFEE AND PRUNES

BEEF CHEEKS with CARROT, COFFEE and PRUNES

PREPARATION: 1 HOUR // COOKING: 5½ HOURS // SERVES 6

Beef cheeks are a perfect cut for a slow braise such as this. They cook right down, and the result is so soft you can't believe it's not butter. The coffee-soaked prunes add a tart contrast to the richness of the beef, while the carrot purée brings it all together. This is a really delicious combination of flavours, and best of all, the hard work is done ahead of time, so you can kick back and rake in the compliments. If you want some green in your life, some hot buttered kale or spinach goes great here too.

A good one for cold nights and hot company.

THE CHEEKS

6 evenly sized beef cheeks, silver skin removed (you can ask your butcher to do this)

salt flakes, for seasoning

125 ml (4 fl oz/½ cup) extra virgin olive oil

3 large carrots, roughly chopped

1 garlic bulb, halved (you can leave on any fine papery skins)

1 brown onion, chopped

250 ml (9 fl oz/1 cup) red wine

1.5 litres (52 fl oz/6 cups) beef stock

3 bay leaves

10 thyme sprigs, leaves picked

1 teaspoon fine sea salt

Check over the beef cheeks, trimming off any excess sinew. Place them in a bowl and season with salt flakes and freshly ground black pepper.

Heat a little of the olive oil in a heavy-based saucepan over medium–high heat. Working in batches, brown the beef for at least 5–6 minutes on each side, making sure you get a good colour. Remove from the pan and set aside.

In the same saucepan, heat the remaining olive oil. Sauté the carrot, garlic bulb halves and onion for 12–15 minutes, or until the onion and garlic are nicely browned.

Return the beef to the pan, along with the remaining ingredients. Reduce the heat to the lowest possible setting, cover with a lid and gently braise for 3–4 hours, or until the cheeks are so tender they start to fall apart when prodded with a knife.

Remove from the heat and set aside.

PRUNES

18 prunes, pitted

750 ml (26 fl oz/3 cups) strong, hot black coffee

While the cheeks are doing their thing, place the prunes in a mixing bowl and pour the hot coffee over. Set aside for about 1 hour, or until the prunes have plumped up.

CARROT PURÉE

500 g (1 lb 2 oz) carrots, chopped

salt flakes, for seasoning

40 g (1½ oz) cold butter

When you're nearly ready to serve, place the carrots in a saucepan and add just enough water to cover. Add a pinch of salt flakes and gently cook for about 10 minutes, or until nice and tender. Once you're happy the carrots are soft, strain them, reserving the cooking water.

Add the carrots to a blender, along with the butter. Purée until silky smooth, adding as much of the reserved carrot water as needed to achieve a smooth texture.

Set aside and keep warm.

BUTTERED SPINACH

600 g (1 lb 5 oz) baby spinach leaves
30 g (1 oz) butter
salt flakes, for seasoning

Just before serving, put the spinach in a large saucepan and place over low heat. Add the butter and a pinch of salt flakes, pop the lid on and cook for 3–5 minutes, or until the spinach has just wilted. Keep warm.

TO SERVE

Remove the beef cheeks from the braising liquid and set aside somewhere warm.

Strain the braising liquid and pour it back into the pan. Place over medium heat and cook for about 20 minutes, or until the liquid has reduced by half, and forms a sauce thick enough to coat the back of a spoon. Stir in the prunes and the black coffee and season to taste.

When ready to serve, gently reheat the cheeks in the reduced braising sauce.

Place a dollop of carrot purée in the middle of each warmed serving plate. Place a beef cheek on top, then artfully spoon a few prunes and reduced braising liquid over the dish.

Add a nice mound of buttered spinach alongside, then prepare for high praise from all those gathered round.

BRAISED BEEF SHORT RIBS
with CHIMICHURRI

PREPARATION: 40 MINUTES // COOKING: 4¼ HOURS // SERVES 6

The Japanese and Koreans understood the beauties of short ribs long before the Western world's recent obsession with them. There is so much to love about short ribs: they're rich, take on flavour really well, and cook down into meltingly tender, fiendishly evil mouthfuls of deliciousness. We find the smallest of excuses to put them on our menus — from braised and barbecued on the bone, to shredded and loaded into tacos and quesadillas, they're tops.

To cut the richness, zesty chimichurri sauce comes to the rescue and balances out all the decadence.

Do your braising the evening before so you can play host, rather than chef, on the night.

THE BRAISE

2 tablespoons olive oil

6 single beef short ribs; ask your butcher to cut these for you

salt flakes, for seasoning

2 brown onions, roughly chopped

2 celery stalks, roughly chopped

2 carrots, roughly chopped

250 ml (9 fl oz/1 cup) Pedro Ximénez sherry (see glossary)

500 ml (17 fl oz/2 cups) beef stock

2 fresh bay leaves

20 thyme sprigs

5 black peppercorns

Preheat the oven to 130°C (250°F).

Heat 1 tablespoon of the olive oil in a heavy-based frying pan over medium–high heat. Season the ribs with salt flakes and freshly ground black pepper. Add half the ribs and brown them for 5–6 minutes on each side, ensuring all the sides are nicely coloured. Remove to a plate while browning the remaining ribs.

Heat the remaining olive oil in the same hot frying pan, then sauté the onion, celery and carrot until coloured all over.

Arrange the sautéed vegetables in a roasting tin, then place the ribs on top, drizzling them with any of the resting juices.

Place the frying pan back on the heat. Pour in the sherry and let it simmer for 2 minutes, before pouring in the stock. Use a wooden spoon to scrape any bits from the bottom of the pan. Once the liquid has begun to simmer, pour it over the vegetables and ribs in the roasting tin. Add the bay leaves, thyme and peppercorns.

Seal the roasting tin tightly with foil, transfer to the oven and bake for 3 hours, or until the ribs are tender, and the meat comes away easily from the bone when prodded with a fork. Set aside to cool in the liquid.

CAULIFLOWER PURÉE

1 large cauliflower, chopped into florets;
   you'll need about 650 g (1 lb 7 oz)
   florets
100 g (3½ oz) cold butter, cut into
   2.5 cm (1 inch) cubes
salt flakes, for seasoning

We actually smoke the cauliflower before we cook it, but this isn't essential… just super dooper if you can be bothered!

Add the cauliflower florets to a medium saucepan and pour in just enough water to cover. Bring to a simmer and cook for 8–10 minutes, or until nice and tender.

Drain the cauliflower, reserving the cooking liquid. Place the cauliflower in a blender, along with the butter. Purée until smooth, adding some of the reserved cooking liquid if you think it needs a little help along.

Season with salt flakes and freshly ground black pepper to taste. Set aside and keep warm.

TO SERVE

Chimichurri sauce (see Asado beef
   skewers recipe on page 119)

Remove the ribs from the cooled braising liquid and set aside.

Strain the liquid and pour it into a saucepan. Bring to the boil, skimming off any fat or debris that comes to the surface. Cook for 20–30 minutes, or until the liquid has reduced and thickened into a sauce. Season with salt and pepper to taste.

Meanwhile, heat the grill (broiler) to medium. Place the ribs on a grill tray lined with foil and heat under the grill until warmed through.

To serve, place a spoonful of the cauliflower purée onto each warmed serving plate. Place a rib on top, then drizzle some of the reduced braising sauce over the rib and around the plate. Finish with a dollop of chimichurri sauce.

* BREAK IT *
ALL UP

The best leading actor is nothing without an excellent supporting cast. In this chapter, you'll find a bunch of little dishes perfect for passing around at your next dinner party. Sides are designed to complement the main attractions and balance out the mood a little, so mix and match according to what seems like a good idea — it usually is!

ISLAND SLAW

PREPARATION: 20 MINUTES // SERVES 6-8

You can judge a pub on the quality of its slaw: that's the law. Each of our venues has a version of a classic slaw — it's basically the 'fried chicken' of salads. This semi-tropical version works well with anything vaguely Jamaican, and in particular anything grilled on the barbecue.

½ red cabbage
½ white cabbage
8 radishes, trimmed
1 tablespoon Jerk paste
  (see page 273)
250 g (9 oz/1 cup) whole-egg
  mayonnaise
1 bunch (60 g/2¼ oz) coriander
  (cilantro), stems and leaves
  finely chopped
salt flakes, for seasoning

Using a mandoline or a food processor, slice the cabbages and radishes as thinly as you possibly can.

In a large mixing bowl, thoroughly combine the jerk paste and mayonnaise. Add the cabbage, radish and coriander and mix everything together until the salad ingredients are evenly coated in the jerk mayo.

Season to taste with salt flakes and freshly ground black pepper. This slaw is best made just prior to serving.

DIRTY RICE

PREPARATION: 15 MINUTES // COOKING: 20 MINUTES // SERVES 6-10

Dirty rice's natural habitat is next to a scorching serve of Jerk chicken (see page 108), but this fragrant side will go nicely with just about anything. Heady allspice, coriander and mint give it a wildly aromatic edge and its signature 'dirty' look. This one works a treat in a rice cooker, if you have one. Potpourri for the soul.

400 g (14 oz/2 cups) long-grain
  white rice
1 bunch (60 g/2¼ oz) coriander
  (cilantro), stems and leaves
  finely chopped
1 bunch (80 g/2¾ oz) mint, leaves
  picked and chopped
6-8 spring onions (scallions),
  finely chopped
2 teaspoons ground allspice
50 g (1¾ oz) butter, at room
  temperature
1 teaspoon salt flakes

Put the rice in a colander and rinse under cold running water until the water runs clear.

Tip the rice into a large saucepan. Add the coriander, mint, spring onion and allspice, pour in 750 ml (26 fl oz/ 3 cups) water, and stir to combine.

Put the lid on and bring to the boil, then reduce the heat to low. Simmer for 10–12 minutes, or until the water has been absorbed and the rice is cooked.

Remove from the heat and allow to sit for 5–10 minutes.

Remove the lid and fluff up the rice with a fork. Add the butter and salt and continue to fluff the rice until the butter has been incorporated.

Put the lid back on and keep warm until ready to serve.

DIRTY RICE

ISLAND SLAW

CAULIFLOWER MAC'N'CHEESE

PREPARATION: 20 MINUTES // COOKING: 30 MINUTES // SERVES 8

There was an advertisement once, claiming that mushrooms are 'meat' for vegetarians. That's fair enough… but so is cauliflower! Because of its neutral flavour and meaty texture, you really could close your eyes and think you're eating chicken. Go on. CLOSE THEM.

1 litre (35 fl oz/4 cups) milk
1 brown onion, peeled
5 whole cloves
1 bay leaf
100 g (3½ oz) butter, diced
110 g (3¾ oz/¾ cup) plain
  (all-purpose) flour
125 g (4½ oz/1 cup) coarsely
  grated aged cheddar cheese
125 g (4½ oz/1 cup) coarsely
  grated smoked cheddar cheese
2 tablespoons dijon mustard
½ small cauliflower, cut into
  florets
500 g (1 lb 2 oz) macaroni

Pour the milk into a saucepan. Take the whole onion and stud it with the cloves, then add to the milk with the bay leaf. Warm the milk over medium–low heat until almost simmering. Remove from the heat, then discard the studded onion and bay leaf. Keep the milk warm.

In a heavy-based saucepan, melt the butter over medium heat. Once it starts to bubble, gradually add the flour, stirring vigorously to incorporate it into the butter. Continue cooking and stirring for about 4 minutes, until all the flour is incorporated and the mixture starts to become slightly coloured and smells biscuity.

Gradually whisk in the warm milk a little at a time, letting the mixture thicken slightly each time before adding more, until you have a thick white sauce bubbling away. Add the cheeses, reserving a small amount of each for the topping. Stir in the mustard and season to taste with sea salt and some freshly ground black pepper. Remove from the heat and keep warm.

Meanwhile, bring a large saucepan of water to a rolling boil, and preheat the grill (broiler) to medium.

Add the cauliflower to the pan of boiling water and cook for 2–3 minutes, or until tender. Remove with a slotted spoon, refresh under cold running water and set aside.

Now add the pasta to the pan of boiling water and cook according to the packet instructions until al dente — usually 8–10 minutes. Drain the pasta into a colander and return it to the pan, along with the cauliflower.

Pour in the white sauce and stir until everything is coated. Season to taste with salt and pepper, then spoon into a 2.5 litre (87 fl oz/10 cup) heatproof baking dish. Scatter the reserved grated cheese on top, then place the baking dish under the grill.

Cook for 6–8 minutes, or until the cheese on top of the pasta has started to become golden and bubbling. Remove from the oven and allow to cool slightly before serving.

BURNT-END BEANS

PREPARATION: 20 MINUTES // COOKING: 1¼ HOURS // SERVES 10

This dish is a staple of the Deep South of the US, and if you like baked beans, refried beans or any other kind of bean dish, this one is for you. Nothing goes better with juicy smoked meat than these beans and some fresh, tangy slaw.

Traditionally, in barbecue joints all across the South, the idea is that you throw your barbecued meat trimmings into the pot and keep cooking the beans away, so they take on all the rich, meaty goodness from the barbecue pit.

This is a great dish to make ahead; like a good curry, this bean dish actually benefits from sitting overnight. If you have any left over, you can use them in the Empanada rancheros on page 232.

Melt the butter in a large heavy-based saucepan over medium heat. Sauté the onion for 5 minutes, or until soft. Add the garlic and cook for a further 1 minute.

Pour in the tomato sauce, treacle, maple syrup and vinegar. Add the sugar, chilli, mustard and liquid smoke, if using. Stir until well combined.

Bring the mixture up to a boil and immediately reduce the heat to low. Add all the beans and leave to simmer gently in the sauce for 45 minutes to 1 hour, or until the sauce has thickened.

Season to taste with sea salt and freshly ground black pepper before serving.

50 g (1¾ oz) butter

3 large brown onions, finely diced

3 garlic cloves, finely chopped

750 ml (26 fl oz/3 cups) tomato sauce (ketchup)

115 g (4 oz/⅓ cup) treacle or molasses

80 ml (2½ fl oz/⅓ cup) maple syrup

125 ml (4 fl oz/½ cup) apple cider vinegar

165 g (5¾ oz/¾ cup, firmly packed) light brown sugar

1 whole dried ancho chilli (see glossary)

60 g (2¼ oz/¼ cup) American mustard

15 ml (½ fl oz) liquid smoke (see glossary); optional

2 x 400 g (14 oz) tins red kidney beans, drained and rinsed

2 x 400 g (14 oz) tins white beans, drained and rinsed

CAULIFLOWER MAC'N'CHEESE

BURNT-END BEANS

KALE and BROCCOLINI SALAD with GREEN GODDESS DRESSING

PREPARATION: 25 MINUTES // COOKING: 20 MINUTES // SERVES 6-8

To say the world has gone kale mad is an understatement. We have kale on almost all of our menus because it keeps the healthy homies happy, and that's not a bad thing. So if you're feeling like your chakras are out of alignment, assemble this green, green salad and get ready to *ommmm*.

You could also add some meat protein to it and transform it into a more substantial salad for lunches on the go.

table salt, for blanching
  the vegetables
5-6 cups of ice cubes (around
  3 ice cube trays)
3 bunches kale, each about 220 g
  (7¾ oz), stalks removed; you'll
  need about 450 g (1 lb) trimmed
  kale in total
100 g (3½ oz) sugar snap peas,
  trimmed
500 g (1 lb 2 oz) broccolini,
  cut into long florets
75 g (2½ oz/½ cup) sunflower seeds
pinch of chilli powder
pinch of sweet paprika
¼ teaspoon salt flakes

GREEN GODDESS DRESSING
250 g (9 oz/1 cup) whole-egg
  mayonnaise
250 g (9 oz/1 cup) sour cream
40 g (1½ oz/½ bunch) flat-leaf
  (Italian) parsley, leaves
  picked and finely chopped
2 tablespoons finely chopped dill
½ fresh jalapeño chilli, seeded
  and finely chopped
juice of 2 limes

Bring a large saucepan of water to the boil, adding about 2 tablespoons salt for every 1 litre (35 fl oz/4 cups) water.

Prepare an iced water bath by adding the ice cubes to a large bowl of cold water.

Blanch the kale in the boiling water for 2 minutes. Drain, then immediately refresh in the iced water bath until completely cold. Gently squeeze as much water as you can from the kale leaves and set aside.

Blanch, drain and refresh the sugar snap peas in the same way, then dry thoroughly and set aside. Repeat with the broccolini.

Set a dry frying pan over medium heat. Toast the sunflower seeds for 2–3 minutes, or until slightly coloured. Tip them into a small bowl and toss the chilli powder, paprika and salt through. Set aside.

Place all the green goddess dressing ingredients in a mixing bowl and mix together thoroughly.

TO SERVE
Make sure your blanched kale, sugar snap peas and broccolini are drained of as much water as possible and thoroughly dried, otherwise the dressing won't stick to them and you'll dilute your lovely dressing with excess water.

Place the vegies in a salad bowl. Add enough dressing to generously coat your salad. If you're a dressing fiend you can add a little more, or if you swing the other way you can add a little less; any left-over dressing can be sealed in a glass jar and will easily keep for a few days in the fridge.

Cover the salad and chill until required; it can be made several hours ahead. Top with the toasted sunflower seed mixture just before serving.

PINEAPPLE FRITTERS

PREPARATION: 10 MINUTES // COOKING: 20-25 MINUTES // SERVES 4

Almost every suburban Australian kid from the 1970s remembers buying
deep-fried potato scallops and pineapple rings from the corner takeaway shop.
This is a nod to nostalgia, using a secret ingredient: banana-flavoured
milk drink powder. It's a revelation, to be sure. Serve it up as a side
to a steak or a burger to make it tropical.

In a mixing bowl, combine the flour, milk drink powder, turmeric and coconut. Gradually pour in 750 ml (26 fl oz/ 3 cups) water, whisking until the mixture is the consistency of a thick, pancake-like batter.

Fill a deep-fryer or large heavy-based saucepan one-third full of vegetable oil. Heat over medium heat until it reaches 180°C (350°F) when tested with a cooking thermometer, or until a cube of bread dropped into the oil turns golden brown in 15 seconds.

Thoroughly dry the pineapple rings with paper towel. Coating and cooking them in batches, dip each pineapple ring in the batter and gently lower into the hot oil. Cook for 4–6 minutes, or until the batter is golden and crisp.

Remove from the oil using a slotted spoon and briefly drain on paper towel. Serve hot.

300 g (10½ oz/2 cups) plain (all-purpose) flour

50 g (1¾ oz/½ cup) banana-flavoured milk drink powder

2 teaspoons ground turmeric

30 g (1 oz/½ cup) shredded coconut

vegetable oil, for deep-frying

8 tinned pineapple rings, drained

YOU CAN WIN FRIENDS

WITH SALAD

'Salad' used to mean a leaf of iceberg lettuce, a few questionable Spanish olives, a cube of even more questionable feta cheese, and dressing that was French in name only. Thankfully the game has changed some!

We are personally fans of salads that think they're a meal. They have substance, texture, a touch of spice and sweetness, and a whole lotta body. It's time to get fresh…

SALMA HAYEK SALAD

PREPARATION: 20 MINUTES // COOKING: 15 MINUTES // SERVES 6-8

On some weekends, The Carrington morphs into a sultry den full of hot forty-something women in leather shorts out on the town, on a sexy party mission. We dedicate this salad to them.

Shaved fennel, candied walnuts, radish, goat's cheese... it's light, fresh and tasty, just as the ladies like it.

Preheat the oven to 220°C (425°F). Line a baking tray with baking paper.

To make the candied walnuts, place the sugar, maple syrup and a splash of water in a heavy-based saucepan over medium–high heat. Stir the sugar, then leave it until the liquid starts to bubble. After 1–2 minutes, add the walnuts and lemon zest.

Continue to stir for another 2 minutes, then carefully pour the walnuts onto the baking tray. Sprinkle with a pinch of salt flakes and bake for 7–8 minutes, or until the walnuts are golden and the mixture is bubbly.

Remove from the oven and set aside to cool. Once completely cool, break up any clusters and store in a dry, airtight container until needed. They'll be happy for a few days if kept in a cool pantry.

To make the dressing, whisk together the lemon juice and olive oil. Season to taste with salt and freshly ground black pepper and set aside.

Bring a small saucepan of lightly salted water to the boil. Add the frozen peas and blanch for 45 seconds. Drain and immediately refresh in very cold water to stop the cooking process and keep those babies bright green.

Using a mandoline or vegetable peeler, shave the zucchini lengthways into ribbons. Shave the fennel and radishes into super-thin slices. Place the shaved vegetables in a bowl. Roughly chop the mint leaves and add to the shaved vegetables, along with the blanched peas. Cover the bowl with a clean damp tea towel (dish towel) and refrigerate until just before serving.

Remove the vegetable mixture from the fridge about 5 minutes before serving. Whisk the salad dressing again, then dress the vegetables and transfer to a serving bowl.

Using your hands, crumble the cheese over the salad. Scatter the candied walnuts all over and finish with a good slug of olive oil.

CANDIED WALNUTS

115 g (4 oz/½ cup) caster (superfine) sugar

2 tablespoons maple syrup

230 g (8 oz/2 cups) walnuts

zest of 1 lemon

salt flakes, for seasoning

DRESSING

juice of 2 lemons

170 ml (5½ fl oz/⅔ cup) extra virgin olive oil

salt flakes, for seasoning

THE REST

100 g (3½ oz/¾ cup) frozen baby peas

4 zucchini (courgettes), ends trimmed

1 fennel bulb, halved and cored

4-6 radishes, trimmed

1 bunch (80 g/2¾ oz) mint, leaves picked, any larger ones torn

125 g (4½ oz) goat's cheese — or even better, goat's feta, if you can get it

extra virgin olive oil, for drizzling

ICEBERG WEDGE PARTY SALAD

PREPARATION: 30 MINUTES // COOKING: 25 MINUTES // SERVES 8

It was our life-long food dream to incorporate the word 'party' into the name of one of our dishes. I guess it just comes from our old lives as promoters and professional party tragics. We achieved that goal in this salad, and the name says it all: it's a goddamn party. On a plate. In a salad. For your face.

2 soft-poached free-range eggs (see page 224), refreshed in iced water

1 free-range egg

35 g (1¼ oz/¼ cup) plain (all-purpose) flour

30 g (1 oz/½ cup) panko (Japanese breadcrumbs; see glossary)

CREAMY MUSTARD DRESSING

85 g (3 oz/⅓ cup) sour cream

2 tablespoons whole-egg mayonnaise

2 teaspoons wholegrain mustard

2 teaspoons dijon mustard

THE REST

100 g (3½ oz) jamón serrano (or good pancetta or prosciutto), thinly sliced

vegetable oil, for pan-frying

½ bunch (40 g/1½ oz) flat-leaf (Italian) parsley, leaves picked

½ bunch (40 g/1½ oz) mint, leaves picked

8 radishes, trimmed, then thinly sliced using a mandoline

1 iceberg lettuce, cut in half down the middle, core removed

100 g (3½ oz) haloumi cheese, finely grated; parmesan also works well

salt flakes, for seasoning

2 tablespoons dukkah (see glossary)

There are plenty of how-tos on poaching the perfect soft egg. Look them up; it's a skill for life! Or see the Smoked paprika eggs benedict recipe on pages 223–224.

Lightly beat the other egg in a bowl. Put the flour and panko crumbs in separate bowls. Handling them gently, one at a time, dust your poached eggs with the flour, then dip into the beaten egg, then roll in the panko crumbs. Refrigerate until ready to serve; the eggs can be crumbed 6–12 hours ahead.

Combine the creamy mustard dressing ingredients in a bowl. Add 60 ml (2 fl oz/¼ cup) water and whisk to ensure everything is incorporated. Season to taste with sea salt and freshly ground black pepper and set aside.

Preheat the oven to 140°C (275°F). Line a baking tray with baking paper. Lay the ham slices on top and bake for 10–12 minutes, or until crisp. Remove from the oven.

Meanwhile, take your panko-crusted eggs out of the fridge and bring them to room temperature.

Fill a deep-fryer or large heavy-based saucepan one-third full of vegetable oil. Heat over medium–low heat until the temperature reaches 160°C (315°F) when tested with a cooking thermometer, or until a cube of bread dropped into the oil turns golden brown in 30–35 seconds. Gently lower in the panko-crusted eggs and fry for 2 minutes, or until golden. Remove from the oil and drain on paper towel.

In a mixing bowl, combine the parsley, mint and radish. Scatter most of the mixture over two serving plates. Add a lettuce half to each one. Using a spoon or a pastry brush, carefully separate each layer of lettuce leaves and spoon some of the dressing in between. Drizzle the remaining dressing around the platter.

Nestle a crumbed egg in the middle of each lettuce half. Break up the crisp ham slices and scatter over the top, along with the remaining herb mixture and the haloumi. Season with salt flakes and freshly ground black pepper and sprinkle the dukkah on top. Serve immediately, with steak knifes for slicing cleanly through the lettuce.

VAN KALEN SALAD

PREPARATION: 30 MINUTES // COOKING: 10 MINUTES // SERVES 4

Salmon, pomegranate, white beans, pumpkin seeds and kale.
Doesn't sound like a rock-star diet, does it? But when we first tested this dish,
we had 'Jump!' blasting from the stereo, so naming it after those 1980s
rock gods just seemed the right thing to do.

Heat a barbecue or chargrill pan to a medium–high heat.

Rub the salmon fillets with some salt flakes, freshly ground black pepper and olive oil. When your barbecue or pan is nice and hot, grill the salmon for 2–3 minutes on each side, keeping it pink in the centre. Remove from the heat and set aside to rest.

Meanwhile, start preparing the salad. Place the kale in a mixing bowl and sprinkle the lime juice over. Season with salt flakes and freshly ground black pepper and rub in thoroughly. Add all the cabbage, along with the fennel, radish, coriander and beans. In a separate bowl, mix together the dressing ingredients, then use it to dress the salad.

Returning to the fish, use a fork to gently break it up into large flakes.

Arrange the salad on a platter and top with the salmon chunks. Now hold one of the pomegranate halves, cut side down, over the salad. Whack the back of the pomegranate with a rolling pin and rain those little suckers over the salad. Give the other pomegranate half a good whacking too.

Garnish with the toasted pepitas and serve.

4 x 100 g (3½ oz) salmon fillets, pin-bones and skin removed
salt flakes, for seasoning
olive oil, for brushing

THE SALAD
16 large kale leaves, stalks removed, leaves finely shredded
juice of 1 lime
salt flakes, for seasoning
¼ red cabbage, finely shredded
¼ white cabbage, finely shredded
1 fennel, cored and finely shaved
4–6 radishes, trimmed and finely shaved
½ bunch (30 g/1 oz) coriander (cilantro), stems and leaves finely chopped
400 g (14 oz) tin cannellini beans, drained and rinsed
1 pomegranate, halved
3 tablespoons pepitas (pumpkin seeds), lightly toasted

DRESSING
2 chipotle chillies in adobo sauce (see glossary), finely chopped
160 g (5½ oz/⅔ cup) sour cream

MEX STREET SALAD

PREPARATION: 25 MINUTES // COOKING: 15 MINUTES
SERVES 4 AS A MAIN MEAL, OR 8 AS A SIDE

This, for us, is an old-school salad. It's messy, it's slaw-based, and replete with barbecued chicken... although left-over fried pork belly also makes a fantastic substitute. What's not to love?

500–600 g (1 lb 2 oz–1 lb 5 oz) boneless, skinless chicken thighs, marinated for 3 hours in our Achiote marinade (see the Barbecued chicken tacos recipe on page 59)

HONEY LIME DRESSING
125 ml (4 fl oz/½ cup) lime juice
125 ml (4 fl oz/½ cup) extra virgin olive oil
2 tablespoons runny honey
1 tablespoon American mustard
salt flakes, for seasoning

THE SALAD
½ red cabbage, finely shredded
½ white cabbage, finely shredded
120 g (4¼ oz/½ cup) pickled jalapeño chillies, drained and cut into thin rings
2 handfuls tortilla chips, crushed with your hands
1 green mango, flesh cut into matchsticks
1 bunch (60 g/2¼ oz) coriander (cilantro), stems and leaves roughly chopped
3–4 spring onions (scallions), including the green bits, thinly sliced
6–8 radishes, trimmed and finely shaved
60 g (2¼ oz) haloumi cheese

Heat a chargrill pan or barbecue to a medium–high heat. Once hot, grill the chicken for 4–5 minutes on each side, or until cooked through and slightly charred. Remove from the heat and set aside to rest for a few minutes, before chopping it into bite-sized pieces.

Meanwhile, make the honey lime dressing. In a small mixing bowl, whisk together the lime juice, olive oil, honey and mustard. Season to taste with salt flakes and freshly ground black pepper and set aside.

In a large mixing bowl, toss together all the salad ingredients, except the haloumi. Give the dressing another whisk and use it to dress the salad.

Add the chopped chicken to the salad and toss to combine. Season with to taste, then transfer the salad to individual serving plates, or a serving platter. Finely grate the haloumi over the top and serve.

GRILLED EGGPLANT SALAD
with LABNEH and HUMMUS

PREPARATION: 30 MINUTES + 24-48 HOURS FOR THE LABNEH
COOKING: 40 MINUTES // SERVES 4

Some people have pointed out that this is not really a salad. Maybe they're right. Maybe who cares? Regardless, this little wonder makes for an excellent solo dinner or a starter to share with your significant other/roommate/ future ex-husband. It's simple, tasty stuff.

Making your own labneh — a strained yoghurt cheese — is an excellent way to use up that tub of yoghurt in the back of your fridge that's about to turn… It's the easiest way to make cheese, and once you check it out, you'll never buy it again.

LABNEH

500 g (1 lb 2 oz/2 cups) Greek-style
   yoghurt
1 tablespoon salt flakes

Place a double layer of clean muslin (cheesecloth) over a colander or sieve.

Mix together the yoghurt and salt and pour the mixture into the cloth. Pick up the corners of the muslin and twist them, so you have a tight little pouch that will eventually squeeze most of the moisture out of the yoghurt. Secure with a knot or a rubber band.

Now you need to let the cheese drain for 24–48 hours… so, hang the cheese over a bowl to catch the whey and leave it in the fridge. You will see a fair amount of liquid gathering in the bowl, which is a good sign your labneh is happening!

Remove the labneh from the fridge and give it a final gentle squeeze to get rid of any more moisture. Take it out of the cloth and store it in the fridge, either in an airtight container, or rolled into small balls and stored in jars topped with olive oil. It will keep for a few days, depending on the original freshness of the yoghurt.

HUMMUS

2 x 400 g (14 oz) tins chickpeas,
   drained and rinsed
1 tablespoon tahini
juice of 3 lemons
3 garlic cloves, peeled
1 teaspoon ground cumin
½ teaspoon sweet paprika
salt flakes, for seasoning

Throw all the hummus ingedients into a blender and blitz until a smooth purée forms. If the mixture needs a little thinning out, add a splash of cold water — you are looking for a thick pouring consistency.

Season with freshly ground black pepper, decant into an airtight container and refrigerate until needed. It will keep for up to 3 days.

THE EGGPLANT

3 large eggplants (aubergines),
   cut into 3 cm (1¼ inch) cubes
185 ml (6 fl oz/¾ cup) olive oil
salt flakes, for seasoning
3 garlic cloves, thinly sliced
1 long red chilli, seeded and
   thinly sliced
1 long green chilli, seeded and
   thinly sliced
3 fresh bay leaves
10 thyme sprigs, leaves picked
juice of ½ lemon

Preheat the oven to 200°C (400°F). Line a baking tray with baking paper.

Meanwhile, heat a chargrill pan to a high heat. Working in batches, add the eggplant pieces to the pan and leave them alone for 1 minute, or until scored with char marks underneath. Turn them over and char them on the other side, then place in a mixing bowl.

When all the eggplant has been charred, drizzle with 60 ml (2 fl oz/¼ cup) of the olive oil. Season well with salt flakes and freshly ground black pepper and gently toss together to coat the eggplant pieces. Now spread them on the baking tray and bake for 15–20 minutes, or until soft and tender. Remove from the oven and set aside to cool.

Heat the remaining 125 ml (4 fl oz/½ cup) olive oil in a heavy-based frying pan over medium heat. Gently fry the garlic and chillies for 3–4 minutes, or until the garlic turns golden. Add the bay leaves and thyme, remove the pan from the heat and set aside to cool.

Put the cooled eggplant in a mixing bowl. Add the lemon juice and the garlic and chilli mixture and gently fold through. Season to taste with more salt and pepper as needed.

TO SERVE

salt flakes, for sprinkling
extra virgin olive oil, for drizzling
2 tablespoons coarsely chopped flat-leaf
   (Italian) parsley
a pinch of smoked or sweet paprika
toasted sourdough bread or warmed
   flatbread

Spoon the hummus onto a serving plate, spreading it out into a circular shape using the back of the spoon.

Scatter the eggplant pieces over the top, making sure there is some of the chilli and garlic in there too. Dollop the labneh evenly around the platter. Garnish with salt flakes, a good slug of olive oil and a scattering of parsley. Sprinkle a little paprika on each dollop of labneh.

Serve with warm bread on the side.

ROASTED CAULIFLOWER, ALMOND, GRAPE and DUKKAH SALAD

PREPARATION: 20 MINUTES // COOKING: 20 MINUTES // SERVES 6

This is a great winter salad that we serve when the cold rolls around each year.

Cauliflower is one of our ultimate favourite vegetables. It's substantial, meaty and takes on other flavours really well. Here, it provides a great background for the sweetness of grapes and the aromatic dukkah spices.

If you think salads are wimpy, you are a) in the wrong section of this book, or b) going to be converted by this salad.

Preheat the oven to 180°C (350°F). Line a baking tray with baking paper.

Lay the cauliflower florets out on the baking tray. Drizzle them with olive oil and sprinkle with a good pinch of salt. Transfer to the oven and roast for 15–20 minutes, or until golden.

Tip the cauliflower into a large heatproof bowl. Toss the spinach through, so that it wilts from the heat of the cauliflower.

Place the grapes on a flat plate and top it with another flat plate of the same size. Carefully slide a large, sharp knife between the plates and remove the top plate: voilá! You've just halved your grapes. (This nifty trick works a treat for cherry tomatoes too!) Add them to the roasted cauliflower mixture.

In a separate bowl, whisk together the sour cream, tahini and lemon juice to form a dressing. Season with salt and freshly ground black pepper to taste. Drizzle the dressing over the salad and toss to evenly coat all the ingredients.

Spoon the salad into a serving dish. Serve sprinkled with the dukkah and a good slug of olive oil.

2 cauliflowers, broken into florets
extra virgin olive oil, for drizzling
salt flakes, for seasoning
90 g (3¼ oz/2 cups) baby spinach leaves
100 g (3½ oz) red seedless grapes
2 tablespoons sour cream
1 tablespoon tahini
juice of 1 lemon
1 tablespoon dukkah (see glossary)

SMOKED OCTOPUS SALAD with FENNEL, ORANGE and CHILLI

PREPARATION: 40 MINUTES // COOKING: 20 MINUTES + 2½ HOURS FOR POACHING
THE OCTOPUS // SERVES 6–8

When a summer sojourn in the Mediterranean isn't possible, it's good to know there's *The Talented Mr Ripley* and recipes such as this. The combination of smoky charred octopus, aniseedy fennel and a citrus chilli kick is sure to fool anyone's tastebuds into thinking they're sitting in an old bistro on the Amalfi coast. Break out the Campari and soda and fire up the barbecue. Lunch is on its way…

1 kg (2 lb 4 oz) large octopus
  tentacles

olive oil, for drizzling

salt flakes, for seasoning

a handful of wood chips, suitable
  for smoking

THE SALAD

3 oranges

3 fennel bulbs, halved and cored

4–6 radishes, trimmed and finely
  shaved

½ bunch (40 g/1½ oz) flat-leaf
  (Italian) parsley, leaves
  picked

180 g (6 oz) rocket (arugula)

2 long red chillies, cut on the
  diagonal into thin rings

60 ml (2 fl oz/¼ cup) extra virgin
  olive oil

salt flakes, for seasoning

Follow the method for tenderising and poaching the octopus used in our Dragon dawgs recipe on page 102.

Meanwhile, light the coals in your barbecue and allow them to burn through until they start to ash; you want to cook the octopus at around 110°C (230°F). Soak the wood chips in water for at least 30 minutes.

Dress your poached octopus tentacles with olive oil and a pinch of salt. Scatter the soaked wood chips onto the coals. Place the tentacles on the barbecue and grill for 15–20 minutes, or until they're crisp and slightly blackened all over. Remove from the barbecue, season with an extra pinch of salt and set aside while preparing the salad.

Start by segmenting your oranges. Working with one orange at a time, cut off the top and bottom using a small sharp knife, so it will sit flat. Place the orange on a chopping board. Cutting from top to bottom, and working your way around the whole orange, cut away all the skin and bitter white pith, being careful not to cut into the flesh. Now, working over a mixing bowl to catch any juices that squirt out, carefully cut the oranges into segments. Do this by making a V-shaped cut along each side of an orange segment, between the white membranes, to release the lovely orange goodness within. Add the orange segments to the mixing bowl as you release each one.

Using a mandoline or vegetable peeler, finely shave the fennel bulbs lengthways, then shave the radishes into thin rounds. Add to the orange segments, along with the parsley, rocket and chilli. Drizzle the olive oil over the salad. Season to taste with salt flakes and freshly ground black pepper and toss to coat the salad.

Slice the octopus tentacles on the diagonal, into bite-sized pieces. Scatter them over the salad and serve.

* SWEET * THANGS

Okay. We're at the end of the meal now. The sweet end. Mains are finished. The coals on the barbecue have all but snuffed out. Snacks are in your stomach. Drinks have been drunk. You are pretty full, ready to recline and fall head first into your food coma.

But first, let's stuff in some sweets.

Pubs aren't really known for their desserts. People are far too busy drinking to bother, so we like to keep it fun. Nice and easy does it…

DEEP-FRIED ICE CREAMS

PREPARATION: 15 MINUTES // COOKING: 15 MINUTES // SERVES 6

We created this dessert to honour the great Scottish food tradition of deep-frying anything and everything. People's uniformly happy reactions are proof that sometimes the simple things in life are the best… deep-fried!

We use toffee and vanilla-flavoured ice creams that are coated in crushed honeycomb biscuits and sold impaled on a wooden popsicle-stick. If you can't find anything similar, ice-cream sandwich bars work well, as long as they are not choc-coated.

250 g (9 oz) packet of arrowroot milk biscuits (cookies)

4 eggs, beaten

2 tablespoons milk

110 g (3¾ oz/¾ cup) plain (all-purpose) flour, sifted

vegetable oil, for deep-frying

6 ice creams on wooden popsicle-sticks (or 6 ice-cream sandwich bars plus 6 wooden popsicle-sticks), frozen as long as possible in the coldest part of the freezer

hundreds and thousands, for sprinkling

CHOCOLATE SAUCE

125 ml (4 fl oz/½ cup) thin (pouring) cream

40 g (1½ oz) dark chocolate (70% cocoa), bashed into small pieces

Using a food processor, blitz the biscuits into fine crumbs. Tip them into a bowl and set aside.

In another bowl, lightly beat the eggs, then whisk in the milk. Put the flour in a third bowl. Set aside.

To make the chocolate sauce, pour the cream into a saucepan and gently bring up to the boil. Turn off the heat and whisk in the chocolate until smooth and silky. Set aside.

Fill a deep-fryer or large heavy-based saucepan one-third full of vegetable oil. Heat over medium heat until it reaches 180°C (350°F) when tested with a cooking thermometer, or until a cube of bread dropped into the oil turns golden brown in 15 seconds.

Once the oil has reached a constant temperature, remove the ice creams from the freezer. Working quickly, take off their wrappers. (If using ice cream bars, quickly impale each one on a wooden popsicle-stick, to make them easier to handle during coating and deep-frying.) Dust them in the flour, then the egg mixture, then into the crushed biscuits, ensuring the ice creams are evenly coated.

Carefully lower each ice cream into the deep-fryer and fry for 45 seconds to 1 minute, or until golden; you may need to cook them in two batches.

Remove directly to serving plates. Spoon on some chocolate sauce, sprinkle with hundreds and thousands and serve immediately.

SWEET CORN ICE CREAM
and CHICKEN CRISPS

PREPARATION: 30 MINUTES + 1 HOUR STEEPING + ICE CREAM CHURNING TIME
COOKING: 1¼ HOURS // SERVES 4–6

One of our favourite places to eat Indonesian is in a food court in Sydney's Chinatown called Eating World (because Eating Country isn't enough eating). They make an excellent dish called Baby Mummy Rice. It's essentially another way of saying 'chicken and egg' in the one dish. The name was so cute we decided to find a way to put it on one of our menus.

Originally, we wanted to do a Baby Mummy Burger — but somehow it turned into this dessert, which bears very little resemblance to the original idea… the 'chicken' element being the crisps, and the 'egg' being the yolks in the ice cream (because that's how we roll). Sometimes, though, a random segue into completely different territory can be a very good thing.

CORN ICE CREAM

3 corn cobs, husks and silks removed

500 ml (17 fl oz/2 cups) thin (pouring) cream

250 ml (9 fl oz/1 cup) milk

230 g (8 oz/1 cup) caster (superfine) sugar

6 free-range egg yolks

½ teaspoon salt flakes

1 teaspoon natural vanilla extract

Run the blade of a sharp knife down the corn cobs to slice off the kernels. Place the kernels in a heavy-based saucepan, along with the bare cobs, the cream, milk and half the sugar. Bring the mixture to a simmer over medium heat, then remove from the heat and allow the ingredients to steep for 1 hour.

Remove the bare cobs, then pour the rest of the mixture into a blender and blitz to a smooth purée. Pass the purée through a fine-mesh sieve to remove any small solids.

Pour the purée into a saucepan and bring to a simmer over medium–high heat.

Meanwhile, put the remaining sugar, egg yolks and salt in a mixing bowl. Using an electric mixer,

whisk together on medium speed for 2–3 minutes, or until light and airy.

When the corn purée has started to simmer, pour about 250 ml (9 fl oz/1 cup) of the purée into the yolk mixture, whisking continuously so the mixture doesn't scramble. Once combined, pour the entire contents of the mixing bowl into the simmering saucepan, whisking continuously. After 3–4 minutes, once the mixture is thick enough to coat the back of a spoon, remove the pan from the heat.

Strain the mixture through a sieve lined with muslin (cheesecloth), into a mixing bowl.

Place the mixing bowl in a sink full of iced water, whisk in the vanilla and leave to cool.

Once cool, churn that bad boy following your ice-cream maker's instructions. Freeze until ready to serve; the ice cream can be made up to 3 days ahead.

CHICKEN CRISPS

200 g (7 oz) chicken skin (ask your
    butcher for this)
1 tablespoon icing (confectioners') sugar

Preheat the oven to 180°C (350°F). Line a baking
tray with baking paper.

Pat the chicken skin dry with paper towel, then
lay it flat on the baking tray. Cover the chicken skin
with another layer of baking paper. On top, now
place a tray that fits inside the bottom baking tray
(you're trying to press the skin while roasting it).

Transfer the whole thing to the oven and roast
for 15 minutes. Rotate the trays to ensure even
cooking, then roast for a further 15 minutes.

Remove the trays from the oven. Remove the
top tray, then the top layer of baking paper, setting
these aside momentarily.

Dust the chicken skin with the icing sugar, then
place the baking paper and top tray back on top
of the skins. Return the trays to the oven and bake
for a final 15 minutes, or until the skins are golden
and crisp.

Remove the trays from the oven. Take off the
top tray and baking paper. Turn the chicken crisps
onto a wire rack to cool. Once cooled, they'll stay
crisp in an airtight container for up to 12 hours.

TO SERVE

60 ml (2 fl oz/¼ cup) maple syrup
4–6 ice-cream cones or cups

Brush the chicken skins with a little maple syrup.
Fill each ice-cream cone with a scoop of corn
ice cream, and stick a chicken skin wafer on top!

SWEET CORN ICE CREAM AND CHICKEN CRISPS

COLADA COOL DOWN

PREPARATION: 1 HOUR + CHURNING TIME + OVERNIGHT FREEZING
COOKING: 35 MINUTES // SERVES 6

As the name implies, this is a great dessert to chill things out a bit, clean off that palate and help everyone wind down some. Combining all the reasons we love a piña colada (rum, coconut, pineapple, cherry), into a super-refreshing ice/fruit/sorbet affair that is fantastic for late-summer get togethers. You'll need an ice cream maker for this one, so be good and hopefully Santa will bring you one next Christmas if you don't already have one.

SOUR CHERRY SORBET

115 g (4 oz/½ cup) caster (superfine) sugar
500 g (1 lb 2 oz) frozen sour cherries, thawed
1 free-range egg white
60 ml (2 fl oz/¼ cup) guava syrup
60 ml (2 fl oz/¼ cup) white rum

Put the sugar in a saucepan, pour in 125 ml (4 fl oz/½ cup) water and stir to dissolve the sugar. Bring to the boil over medium–high heat and cook for 5 minutes, or until a light syrup forms.

Add the cherries and stir continuously for 4 minutes. Remove from the heat and allow the mixture to cool completely.

Transfer the cherry mixture to a blender. Add the egg white, guava syrup and rum and blitz until smooth. Pour into an ice-cream maker and follow the manufacturer's instructions for making sorbet.

Freeze until ready to use; the sorbet will keep for up to 1 week.

COCONUT PUDDING

6 young green coconuts
200 ml (7 fl oz) coconut milk
230 g (8 oz/1 cup) caster (superfine) sugar
pinch of salt flakes
40 g (1½ oz/⅓ cup) cornflour (cornstarch)

First you want to get the coconut water out of the young coconuts. To do this, hold the coconuts over a tray to catch all the juices, and use a serrated knife to carefully slice off the top of each coconut, making sure you cut off enough to leave a hole big enough to fill the coconut shell up with the rest of your dessert goodies. Scoop out all the white flesh from inside the coconuts and reserve.

Pour 160 ml (5¼ fl oz) of your coconut water into a saucepan (reserve the rest for another use, such as rehydrating yourself after a big night on the cans). Add the coconut milk, sugar and salt. Bring to the boil over medium heat and cook for 6 minutes, or until the sugar has dissolved, stirring occasionally.

Pour the mixture into a food processor. Add all the reserved flesh from the scooped-out coconuts and blend until smooth. Return the mixture to the saucepan and bring to a simmer.

In a mixing bowl, whisk together the cornflour and a few tablespoons of water, to form a smooth slurry. Whisk the slurry a little at a time into the boiling coconut milk, until the mixture thickens.

Remove from the heat and strain the mixture through a fine-mesh sieve, into a container. Pour the mixture into your hollowed-out coconut shells and refrigerate for at least 3 hours, or until the mixture has set; overnight is best.

PINEAPPLE GRANITA

115 g (4 oz/½ cup) caster (superfine) sugar
500 ml (17 fl oz/2 cups) pineapple juice

In a small saucepan over medium–high heat, combine the sugar and 60 ml (2 fl oz/¼ cup) water. Bring the mixture to a simmer, stirring only once or twice. Once the sugar has dissolved, whisk in the pineapple juice.

Pour the mixture into a deep-sided metal baking tray, then carefully transfer to the freezer. Leave to freeze for 3 hours, or until ice begins to form around the edges.

Now rake a fork through the mixture every 30 minutes to break up the ice particles, then place back in the freezer, until the mixture has a granular consistency (AKA 'granita'). The more times you do this, the merrier; depending on the coldness of your freezer, you'll need to do this up to 8–10 times.

The granita can be made a day ahead.

CASSAVA CHIPS

1 cassava (see glossary)
vegetable oil, for deep-frying
salt flakes, for sprinkling

Peel the cassava, then use a vegetable peeler to shave the cassava lengthways, into ribbons.

Fill a deep-fryer or large heavy-based saucepan one-third full of vegetable oil. Heat over medium heat until it reaches 180°C (350°F) when tested with a cooking thermometer, or until a cube of bread dropped into the oil turns golden brown in 15 seconds.

Working in batches if necessary, cook the cassava ribbons for 2–3 minutes, or until golden and crisp. Drain on paper towel and sprinkle with salt flakes. Once cooled, the cassava chips will keep in an airtight container for 1 day.

TO SERVE

1 pomegranate, cut in half, seeds removed and reserved
2 passionfruit, cut in half, pulp removed and reserved
30 g (1 oz/¼ cup) icing (confectioners') sugar

In each hollowed-out coconut, on top of the coconut pudding, place a scoop of cherry sorbet and a few spoonfuls of pineapple granita.

Garnish with the pomegranate seeds, passionfruit pulp and cassava chips. Finish with a dusting of icing sugar.

JELLY WRESTLE

PREPARATION: 15 MINUTES + 3 HOURS SETTING TIME FOR THE JELLY
COOKING: 10 MINUTES // SERVES 6-10

Do you have two hands? Do you have three friends? Do you have
a competitive eating spirit? Yes? Then this is the dessert for you.

This dessert is dedicated to nostalgic childhood sweets, mashed into one dessert
of stoner proportions. It comes from our menu at The Oxford — in its former life,
the tavern was a working-man's bar where jelly-wrestling chicks were the highlight
of the week. This dessert pays homage to those heady days and is served with
no cutlery, just latex gloves. It's kind of like a gentrified food fight — just as much
fun to watch as it is to partake in.

This recipe is more of a raid down the cake aisle at your local supermarket
than a recipe, so anything goes.

Prepare the jelly according to the packet instructions and
allow to set. Once set, cut the jelly into cubes and set aside
until ready to serve.

In a huge trough of a serving platter, evenly distribute
the contents of your supermarket trolley as you see fit.

Hand everyone a pair of latex gloves and yell GO!

4 x 85 g (3 oz) packets of
your favourite jelly flavours

lots of thin waffles, cut into
triangles and toasted

300 g (10½ oz) can of whipped
cream, for spraying

220 g (7¾ oz) bottle of
Ice Magic (a chocolate syrup
that, when poured over ice
cream, hardens into a shell;
you'll find it or a similar
product in the supermarket
dessert aisle)

175 g (6 oz) bag of caramel
popcorn

280 g (10 oz/2 cups) salted
roasted peanuts, chopped

150 ml (5 fl oz) bottle of
raspberry sauce

2 litre (70 fl oz) tub of
vanilla-bean ice cream

250 g (9 oz) packet of
marshmallows

65 g (2½ oz) jar of hundreds
and thousands

maraschino cherries

GUAVA EMPANADAS

PREPARATION: 45 MINUTES + 1–2 HOURS COOLING FOR THE DULCE DE LECHE
+ 30 MINUTES CHILLING FOR THE EMPANADAS
COOKING: 1 HOUR + 4 HOURS FOR THE DULCE DE LECHE // MAKES 8 EMPANADAS

Did we come up with this dish 'cos the name rolls off your tongue so well? Yes.
Does that mean it isn't delicious? No.

Empanadas might sound like an odd choice for dessert, but they're really no
different from a sweet pastie or pie. We use guava purée for this version,
but you can use fresh guava… just watch out for the seeds.

DULCE DE LECHE

395 g (14 oz) tin condensed milk

Using a can opener, punch three small holes or slits in the top of the milk tin. Remove the paper label and place the naked tin in a small saucepan. Fill the saucepan with enough water to reach 2.5 cm (1 inch) below the top of the tin.

Bring the water to a boil, then immediately turn the heat down to a simmer. Leave to simmer for 4 hours, topping up the pan with more water as needed to maintain it at the same level.

After 4 hours, use a pair of tongs to remove the tin from the water. Set it aside to cool.

Remove the mixture from the tin; it will keep for up to 1 week in an airtight container in the fridge.

APPLE & GUAVA FILLING

2 ripe guavas, peeled and chopped
(use tinned ones if fresh ones
aren't available)
50 g (1¾ oz) butter
7 granny smith apples, peeled, cored
and cut into 1 cm (½ inch) cubes
170 g (6 oz/¾ cup) caster (superfine)
sugar
½ teaspoon freshly grated nutmeg
1 teaspoon ground cinnamon
1 teaspoon natural vanilla extract

Put the guava in a heavy-based saucepan with half the butter. Gently sauté over medium heat for 5–6 minutes, or until the guava is soft. Remove the guava from the pan and press through a sieve, into a bowl, to remove the seeds. Set aside.

In the same pan, sauté the apple with the remaining butter for 10 minutes, or until just softened. Add the sugar, spices and vanilla, along with the guava, and stir to combine.

Cook for a further 5 minutes, then set aside and leave to cool completely. The filling can be made a day ahead if needed; place it in an airtight container and keep it in the fridge.

THE EMPANADAS

8 sheets frozen puff pastry, thawed
2 free-range egg yolks, beaten

Line one large or two medium baking trays with baking paper. Cut each pastry sheet into a 15 cm (6 inch) round. Lay the pastry circles on a clean work surface and spoon a few tablespoons of the cold apple and guava filling onto one half of each disc. Fold the other half over the filling, then crimp the edges together with a fork to seal.

Lay the empanadas on the baking tray. Brush the tops with some of the beaten egg yolks, setting the remaining beaten egg yolks aside. Place the tray in the refrigerator for 30 minutes.

Meanwhile, preheat the oven to 220°C (425°F).

Remove the tray from the fridge and brush the empanadas again with the remaining beaten egg yolks. Transfer the tray to the oven and bake for 10 minutes.

Turn the oven temperature down to 180°C (350°F) and bake for a further 10–15 minutes, or until the empanadas are a deep golden colour.

Remove from the oven and let cool slightly.

TO SERVE

1 large plantain (see glossary),
    or 2 very unripe bananas
vegetable oil, for deep-frying
1 tablespoon icing (confectioners')
    sugar
8 scoops vanilla-bean ice cream

While the empanadas are in the oven, peel the plantain. Using a vegetable peeler or mandoline, thinly slice the plantain lengthways, into ribbons.

Fill a deep-fryer or large heavy-based saucepan one-third full of vegetable oil. Heat over medium heat until it reaches 180°C (350°F) when tested with a cooking thermometer, or until a cube of bread dropped into the oil turns golden brown in 15 seconds.

Add the plantain ribbons to the hot oil, in batches if necessary, and cook for 2–3 minutes, or until golden brown. Drain on paper towel and leave to cool, then dust with the icing sugar.

To serve, place one empanada on each serving plate. Top with a scoop of ice cream, then a dollop of the dulce de leche. Serve garnished with the fried plantain ribbons.

FRIED MILK BANANA SPLITS

PREPARATION: 30 MINUTES + 24 HOURS CHILLING // COOKING: 15 MINUTES
SERVES 6

In Spain and Central America, fried milk is a very common dessert or coffee companion. A bit like a set custard, it's basically thickened milk, coated in flour and fried. Here it stars in a kind of Latino ode to the banana split.

FRIED MILK

750 ml (26 fl oz/3 cups) milk
115 g (4 oz/½ cup) caster (superfine) sugar
60 g (2¼ oz/½ cup) cornflour (cornstarch)
¼ teaspoon freshly grated nutmeg
20 g (¾ oz) unsalted butter
zest of ½ lemon
30 g (1 oz/¼ cup) icing (confectioners')
  sugar
½ teaspoon ground cinnamon
2 free-range eggs
45 g (1½ oz/¾ cup) panko (see glossary)
250 ml (9 fl oz/1 cup) vegetable oil

Bring the milk to a simmer in a saucepan, over medium heat. In a bowl, whisk together the caster sugar, cornflour and nutmeg, then add the mixture to the simmering milk, stirring well. Bring the milk up to the boil for 1 minute, or until the mixture has thickened, then remove from the heat. Whisk in the butter and lemon zest until combined; set aside.

Line a 20 cm (8 inch) square cake tin with baking paper, allowing the sides to overhang by 5 cm (2 inches). Pour in the milk mixture, then refrigerate, uncovered, overnight.

The next day, sift the icing sugar and cinnamon onto a plate, reserving 1 tablespoon for the chocolate sauce. Lightly beat the eggs in a bowl, and place the panko crumbs in a separate bowl.

Remove the custardy milk mixture from the fridge and cut it into 5 cm (2 inch) squares. Dip them in the egg, then into the breadcrumbs.

In a heavy-based frying pan, heat the vegetable oil over medium–high heat. Fry the crumbed milk squares for about 2 minutes on each side, or until golden. Drain on paper towel, then dust with the cinnamon icing sugar mixture. Serve warm.

CHOCOLATE SAUCE

250 ml (9 fl oz/1 cup) thin (pouring) cream
50 g (1¾ oz) dark chocolate (70% cocoa),
  bashed into small pieces
25 g (1 oz) unsalted butter
1 tablespoon cinnamon icing sugar
  (reserved from the Fried milk)

Just before serving, heat the cream in a small pan until it starts to boil. Remove from the heat and whisk in the chocolate, butter and cinnamon icing sugar until glossy and incorporated. Keep warm.

TO SERVE

3 ripe bananas, peeled and cut into
  3–4 pieces each
55 g (2 oz/¼ cup) light brown sugar
6 large scoops of your favourite ice
  cream (chocolate, vanilla bean, salted
  caramel, banana or toffee work well!)
can of whipped cream, for squirting
70 g (2½ oz/½ cup) toasted salted
  peanuts, chopped
maraschino cherries, to garnish
icing (confectioners') sugar, for dusting

Just before serving, heat a non-stick frying pan over medium–high heat. Dip one end of each banana piece into the sugar. Add to the pan, sugared end down, and cook for 3–4 minutes, or until golden.

Divide the banana among serving plates. Add a big scoop of ice cream, and a few warm fried milk squares. Add a big drizzle of your warm chocolate sauce, and a few squirts of cream. Sprinkle with the peanuts, garnish with cherries, dust with icing sugar and serve.

✳ 3 PM BREAKFAST ✳

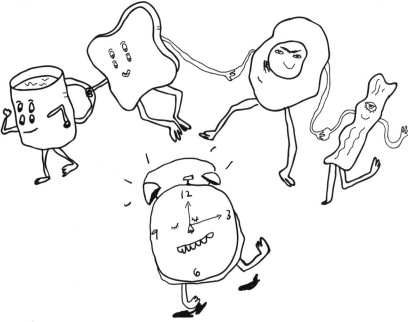

It all comes down to the business end of the book: breakfast. No, we're not jerking your chain. It's the most important meal of the day, and yet the one most often overlooked, which is a pity.

Rad things can happen at breakfast. And we're not talking about granola, muesli or fruit (zzzzzzzzz). If that's your jam, then you're not thumbing through the right book… after all, you didn't buy this book to learn to cut up fruit, did you?!

Instead, this chapter will inform you of the magical and ancient powers of sausages, fried chicken, bacon, waffles, bacon, coffee and also bacon. We tackle some stone-cold breakfast classics, but also offer you a few new contenders for the breakfast championship ring: from the United States to El Salvador, Mexico and Down Under, there's something in here for every kind of hangover you think you might have.

So good morning darlings, fire up the gas!

HANGTOWN FRY

PREPARATION: 20 MINUTES // COOKING: 25 MINUTES // SERVES 4

A breakfast dish not for the faint-hearted. It sorts the lads from the boys,
the girls from the ladies, and the forest from the trees.

There are lots of stories about where this dish originally came from. The first one
involves a gold prospector, who ordered it when he struck it rich. The second
involves a man on death row, who ordered it as his last ballin' meal before lights
out. We may never really know… but what we do know is that once you put all
the bits together, the results are rather magnificent.

8 bacon rashers, rind removed

12 free-range eggs

35 g (1¼ oz/¼ cup) plain
(all-purpose) flour

55 g (2 oz/½ cup) dry breadcrumbs

8 oysters, shucked

salt flakes, for seasoning

20 g (¾ oz) unsalted butter

4 spring onions (scallions),
thinly sliced

vegetable oil, for deep-frying

1 tablespoon sesame seeds,
toasted

sriracha hot chilli sauce
(see glossary), for drizzling

buttered bread or hot toast,
to serve

Preheat the grill (broiler) to medium–high. Place the bacon on a baking tray, then cook under the grill for 4–5 minutes, or until golden brown and crisp. Drain on paper towel, then break the bacon into small pieces and set aside.

Meanwhile, lightly beat one of the eggs in a bowl. Put the flour and breadcrumbs in separate bowls. Pat the oysters dry with paper towel and season with salt flakes and freshly ground black pepper. Dust each oyster in the flour, dip it in the egg, then into the breadcrumbs. Place the oysters on a floured plate until you're ready to fry them.

Whisk the remaining eggs in a bowl and season with salt and pepper. In a 25 cm (10 inch) non-stick frying pan (one with a lid), melt the butter over medium–high heat. Pour in the beaten eggs, then evenly scatter half the grilled bacon and half the spring onion over the top. After 3 minutes or so, when the eggs have just set, reduce the heat to low and put the lid on. Allow the omelette to cook for a further 5 minutes.

Meanwhile, fill a deep-fryer or heavy-based saucepan one-third full of vegetable oil. Heat over medium heat until it reaches 180°C (350°F) when tested with a cooking thermometer, or until a cube of bread dropped into the oil turns golden brown in 15 seconds.

Add the oysters to the hot oil and cook for 2 minutes, or until golden. Drain on paper towel.

Back to the eggs! Run a spatula all around the edge of the pan to loosen the omelette, then carefully turn it out onto a warmed serving plate. Top with the fried oysters, remaining bacon and spring onion. Sprinkle with the sesame seeds, finish with a good drizzle of sriracha and serve.

We eat ours between two slices of heavily buttered bread. Just because we can.

SMOKED PAPRIKA EGGS BENEDICT

PREPARATION: 50 MINUTES + 2 HOURS PROVING // COOKING: 50 MINUTES // SERVES 6

In the 1980s in Sydney, eggs benedict was the height of 'going out to breakfast' fashion. It's decadently rich, graced with a golden crown of cholesterol-inducing sauce. Giving it a bit of a 'Spanglish' twist, ham becomes jamón, and smoked paprika gives that pale English sauce a nice-looking tan, innit?

Shrug off that hangover and make your own English muffins too. Come on, you know you want to! But if it's all too much, you can always just buy them in, and then try making your own when you're feeling a little better...

ENGLISH MUFFINS

300 g (10½ oz/2 cups) strong flour (also called bread-making flour), plus extra for dusting
2 teaspoons dried yeast
1 teaspoon salt flakes
185 ml (6 fl oz/¾ cup) milk, at room temperature
2 teaspoons caster (superfine) sugar
15 g (½ oz) butter, at room temperature
1 free-range egg, lightly beaten
polenta, for dusting
20 g (¾ oz) lard

In a large mixing bowl, combine the flour, yeast, salt, milk, sugar, butter and egg. Mix together until a soft dough forms. If the dough feels a little dry, add a dash more milk to bring everything together. Turn the dough out onto a floured work surface and give it a good knead for 10 minutes, or until soft and stretchy.

Roll the dough into a large ball and place in a large oiled mixing bowl. Cover with damp paper towel and leave in a warm place for 1½ hours, or until the dough has doubled in size.

Turn the dough out onto a lighlty floured work surface dusted with a little polenta. Knead the dough, then roll it out to a 1.5 cm (⅝ inch) thickness. Cut out rounds of dough using a 9 cm (3½ inch) pastry cutter. Place on a lined baking tray, leaving a little breathing space between each one. Dust the tops with more polenta, cover with a tea towel (dish towel) and set aside to prove for a further 30 minutes.

Heat a heavy-based frying pan over medium–low heat. Add the lard. When it has melted, fry the muffins on one side for 5 minutes, or until golden underneath, then flip them over and cook the other side for 5 minutes, or until cooked through. Set aside to cool.

SMOKED PAPRIKA HOLLANDAISE

250 ml (9 fl oz/1 cup) white wine vinegar
2 tablespoons mixed whole peppercorns
1 tarragon sprig
3 large free-range egg yolks
185 g (6½ oz) butter, melted
1 tablespoon sweet paprika
juice of ¼ lemon
salt flakes, for seasoning

In a small heavy-based saucepan, combine the vinegar, peppercorns and tarragon. Boil over medium–high heat for 4–5 minutes, or until the mixture has reduced by half. Strain the liquid and store it in a glass jar until needed. You will only need a little of this vinegar reduction for the hollandaise, but the leftovers will easily keep in the fridge for a few weeks.

Bring a large saucepan of water to a simmer. Find a heatproof mixing bowl that fits snugly on top of the pan, so that the bottom of the bowl doesn't touch the simmering water. In the mixing bowl, whisk together the egg yolks and

CONTINUED OVER ➤

◀ **CONTINUED FROM PREVIOUS PAGE**

3 teaspoons of the vinegar reduction, beating vigorously until the mixture turns into a golden, airy foam.

In another bowl, whisk together the melted butter and sweet paprika until combined. A little at a time, gradually add the paprika butter to the egg yolk mixture, whisking vigorously each time until combined. Continue until all the butter is incorporated and the texture is similar to a thick mayonnaise.

Remove from the heat. Season to taste with the lemon juice, salt flakes and freshly ground black pepper. Set aside and keep warm.

SOFT-POACHED EGGS
1 tablespoon white vinegar
12 free-range eggs — the fresher
    the better

In a large wide saucepan, bring about 10 cm (4 inches) water to the boil. Add the vinegar and reduce the heat to a bare simmer.

Crack an egg into a cup or small bowl, then gently slide the egg into the barely simmering water. You can add a few more eggs; just make sure there's a good amount of space between them. Turn the heat off, pop the lid on and leave to gently poach for about 4 minutes, or until the whites have set, but the yolks are still soft.

Using a slotted spoon, gently scoop the eggs out, into a bowl of cold water to stop them cooking any further.

Poach the remaining eggs in the same way.

When you're done, you can reheat the eggs just before serving. To do this, bring a fresh saucepan of water to the boil, take it off the heat and add the eggs. Cover and stand for 1 minute. Remove using a slotted spoon and briefly drain on paper towel.

TO SERVE
200 g (7 oz) sobrasada (soft, cured
    spreadable spicy Spanish salami;
    see glossary) or nduja (the Italian
    version)
butter, for pan-frying
200 g (7 oz) baby spinach leaves
12 slices of jamón serrano or good
    prosciutto
salt flakes, for seasoning

Preheat the oven grill (broiler) to medium–high. Split your muffins in half, toast them, then spread them with the sobrasada. Place under the grill, sobrasada side up, for 3–4 minutes to warm through.

Meanwhile, melt some butter in a frying pan over medium heat. Add the spinach and cook for a minute or two, or until just wilted. Drain on paper towel.

Remove the muffins from the grill. Top each muffin half with a slice of jamón, a little pile of wilted spinach, a poached egg and a good spoonful of the hollandaise sauce. Sprinkle with salt flakes and some freshly ground black pepper and serve at once.

BLFT

PREPARATION: 25 MINUTES // COOKING: 15 MINUTES // SERVES 4

BLTs tick all the boxes — if those boxes involve bacon, bacon, some other stuff and bread. There are some breakfasts that are best enjoyed in the sun, at a table, with all the trimmings laid out in front of you. This is not one of them.

All it needs is the BLT (we jammed some fried green tomatoes in ours, so you do the deduction), your hands, and most importantly, your face.

Preheat the grill (broiler) to medium–high. Place the bacon on a baking tray, then cook under the grill for 4–5 minutes, or until golden brown and crisp.

Meanwhile, get cracking on your fried green tomatoes. In a small bowl, lightly beat the egg. Place the flour and breadcrumbs in two separate small bowls. Season the tomato slices with salt flakes and freshly ground black pepper, then dust them in the flour, dip them in the egg, then the breadcrumbs.

Pour enough vegetable oil into a heavy-based frying pan to reach a depth of 1 cm (½ inch). Place the pan over medium–high heat. When the oil is hot, pan-fry the tomatoes for 2–3 minutes on each side, or until golden. Drain on paper towel and set aside.

Meanwhile, split the rolls in half and toast them.

Spread the mayo over the bottom half of each roll. Add a leaf or two of lettuce, then layer the grilled bacon and roast pork on top. Add two fried green tomato slices to each roll. Drizzle with sriracha sauce, pop the lids on, and into those hungry mouths they go.

8 bacon rashers, rind removed

4 soft bread rolls

85 g (3 oz/⅓ cup) whole-egg mayonnaise

¼ iceberg lettuce, cored, leaves separated

8 slices roast pork (from your local delicatessen)

sriracha hot chilli sauce (see glossary), for drizzling

FRIED GREEN TOMATOES

2 green tomatoes, cored, then cut into 4 slices each; you'll need 8 tomato slices all up

1 free-range egg

35 g (1¼ oz/¼ cup) plain (all-purpose) flour

30 g (1 oz/¼ cup) dry breadcrumbs

salt flakes, for seasoning

vegetable oil, for pan-frying

FRIED CHICKEN with WAFFLES and MAPLE HOT SAUCE

PREPARATION: 30 MINUTES + 24 HOURS TO SOAK THE CHICKEN
COOKING: ABOUT 30 MINUTES // SERVES 6

On paper, fried chicken and waffles together on one plate seems ludicrous. Anywhere outside the United States, people think this combination is insanity… especially for breakfast. Those people have clearly never eaten fried chicken and waffles at the same meal. This is a brunch-time superstar, no doubt about it, hangover or not — but you'll need to plan ahead, as the chicken needs to soak in buttermilk for 24 hours, to make it super juicy.

6 large boneless, skinless chicken thighs

250 ml (9 fl oz/1 cup) buttermilk (see glossary)

vegetable oil, for deep-frying

½ quantity Herb and chilli flour (from the Fried chicken burgers recipe on page 88)

salt flakes, for seasoning

3 limes, halved

MAPLE HOT SAUCE

250 ml (9 fl oz/1 cup) maple syrup

60 ml (2 fl oz/¼ cup) of your favourite hot sauce (sriracha or Tabasco sauce work well)

WAFFLES

300 g (10½ oz/2 cups) plain (all-purpose) flour, sifted

2 teaspoons baking powder

2 tablespoons caster (superfine) sugar

1 tablespoon olive oil

3 free-range eggs, separated

500 ml (17 fl oz/2 cups) milk

pinch of salt flakes

Place the chicken in a large plastic container. Pour the buttermilk over and mix to combine. Put the lid on and leave to soak in the refrigerator for 24 hours.

On the day of cooking, remove the chicken from the fridge and leave at room temperature for 20 minutes.

Fill a deep-fryer or large heavy-based saucepan one-third full of vegetable oil. Heat over medium–low heat until it reaches 160°C (315°F) when tested with a cooking thermometer, or until a cube of bread dropped into the oil turns golden brown in 30 seconds.

Working in batches, remove each chicken thigh from the buttermilk and dredge it through the herb and chilli flour. Fry each batch for 10–12 minutes, or until golden and cooked through. Remove and drain on paper towel, then immediately season with salt flakes.

Meanwhile, heat a waffle iron according to the manufacturer's instructions. Whisk the maple hot sauce ingredients together in a small jug and set aside.

To make the waffles, whisk together the flour, baking powder, sugar, olive oil, egg yolks and milk in a mixing bowl until thoroughly combined.

In a separate bowl, whisk the egg whites and salt flakes using an electric mixer until soft peaks form.

Gently fold the egg whites into the flour mixture, to make a smooth batter. Spoon into a hot waffle iron and cook according to the manufacturer's instructions. Keep warm while cooking the remaining waffles; you will need 12 waffles all up.

Place two warm waffles on each serving plate and top with the fried chicken. Liberally douse the chicken and waffles with the maple hot sauce. Serve with the lime halves for squeezing over.

'SHROOMS, GOAT'S CHEESE and AREPAS

PREPARATION: 20 MINUTES // COOKING: 15 MINUTES // SERVES 6

Sourdough bread seems to be a fixture on every cafe breakfast plate these days. It's okay, but there are other carbs that can do the job in style.

We take our arepas from the Talking Taco chapter and jam them full of mushrooms and tangy goat's cheese, creating a textural flavour sensation to delight vegetarians and omnivores alike.

You can bulk these up by topping the mushrooms with a poached egg. For a vegie version, simply hold off on the sobrasada.

In a large heavy-based frying pan, heat a splash of the olive oil over high heat. Fry the button mushrooms for 10 minutes, or until golden brown and softened. Add the oyster mushrooms, chilli and garlic and cook for a further 1–2 minutes, or until the oyster mushrooms have taken on some colour.

Add the butter and kale. Turn the heat down slightly and sauté for 2 minutes, then stir in the lemon zest and juice. Season to taste with salt flakes and some freshly ground black pepper.

Spread a little sobrasada on each arepa. Crumble the cheese over the mushroom mixture, in large chunks. Mix briefly, then sandwich between the arepas and serve.

60 ml (2 fl oz/¼ cup) olive oil

500 g (1 lb 2 oz) small button mushrooms, cleaned

300 g (10½ oz) oyster mushrooms, sliced

1 fresh jalapeño chilli, seeded and finely chopped

2 garlic cloves, crushed

50 g (1¾ oz) butter

4 kale leaves (about 200 g/7 oz), white central stalks removed, leaves finely chopped

zest and juice of 1 lemon

salt flakes, for seasoning

THE REST

200 g (7 oz) sobrasada (soft, cured, spreadable spicy Spanish salami; see glossary)

6 Arepas (see page 58), warmed and split in half

180 g (6 oz) soft goat's cheese

KINGFISH PASTRAMI BAGEL

PREPARATION: 10 MINUTES // SERVES 6

If tuna is the chicken of the sea, kingfish is surely the duck. It's our pick of all the fin-fishes around for sure, thanks to its sturdy, meaty nature and the fact that it doesn't wimp out in the presence of strong flavours.

A great bagel is the foil for this dish, so choose the best one you can find, or get YouTubing and learn how to make a legit, New York–style bagel. Another skill for life.

We serve these bagels with some salted potato crisps on the side.

6 best-quality bagels

250 g (9 oz) spreadable cream cheese

300 g (10½ oz) Kingfish pastrami (see page 43)

560 g (1 lb 4 oz) jar of crinkle-cut bread and butter pickles

extra virgin olive oil, for drizzling

salt flakes, for seasoning

a few dill sprigs, torn up

Split the bagels in half and toast them. Smear all the cut sides with the cream cheese, then layer the kingfish slices on the bottom halves.

Top with the pickles. Add a drizzle of olive oil, then a sprinkling of salt flakes and freshly ground black pepper. Top with the dill, pop the lids on and get noshing.

EMPANADA RANCHEROS

PREPARATION: 30 MINUTES // COOKING: 1¼ HOURS // SERVES 6

In our version of huevos rancheros, or 'rancher's eggs', we put a spicy bean mix inside an empanada, on a pool of creamed corn, and crown it with a fried egg. It's deconstructed reconstructed Latin logic, so just go with it. Any left-over Burnt-end beans (see page 179) would also be brilliant in these empanadas.

SPICY BEANS

1 tablespoon olive oil

150 g (5½ oz) smoked pancetta, diced

2 brown onions, diced

2 garlic cloves, crushed

1 tablespoon English mustard

½ teaspoon smoked paprika

4 chipotle chillies in adobo sauce (see glossary), drained, then coarsely chopped

1 teaspoon treacle

400 g (14 oz) tin chopped tomatoes

1 teaspoon light brown sugar

1 teaspoon tomato paste (concentrated purée)

400 g (14 oz) tin white beans or butterbeans, drained and rinsed

worcestershire sauce, for seasoning

salt flakes, for seasoning

THE REST

6 sheets frozen puff pastry, thawed

2 free-range egg yolks, beaten

olive oil, for pan-frying

6 free-range eggs

400 g (14 oz) tin creamed corn

1 pickled jalapeño chilli, finely chopped

coriander (cilantro) leaves, to garnish

Start by making the spicy beans. Heat the olive oil in a heavy-based saucepan over medium heat. Add the pancetta and cook for 3–4 minutes, or until nicely browned and a little crisp. Remove and drain on paper towel.

Sauté the onion in the same pan for 2 minutes, or until it softens. Add the garlic, mustard and paprika and sauté for a minute or so, until fragrant. Stir in the chilli, treacle, tomatoes, sugar and tomato paste, then bring to a simmer and cook for 10 minutes, stirring regularly.

Stir in the beans and pancetta, mixing well. Simmer for 30 minutes, or until the mixture has thickened. Add a few good shakes of worcestershire sauce, and salt flakes and freshly ground black pepper to taste. Set aside to cool completely. You could easily prepare the beans a few days ahead and stash them in the fridge until required.

When you're ready to roll, preheat the oven to 200°C (400°F). Line a baking tray with baking paper.

Using a 15 cm (6 inch) cutter or a small plate as a guide, cut out six rounds from the pastry. Evenly spoon the bean mixture onto one half of each round. Dampen the edges with a little water, then fold the other pastry half over, to make a half-moon. Gently crimp the sealed edges using a fork, then use a pastry brush to glaze the empanadas with the egg yolk. Place on the baking tray and bake for 10 minutes, or until lightly golden. Turn the oven down to 180°C (350°F) and bake for a further 10 minutes, or until golden brown and puffed.

About 10 minutes before the empanadas are done, heat some olive oil in a large heavy-based frying pan over medium heat. Fry the eggs for about 2 minutes, without turning them over; you want them sunny side up, so the centre of the yolk is still a little runny.

Meanwhile, gently warm the creamed corn in a small saucepan over medium–low heat, stirring occasionally.

Spoon some creamed corn in the middle of each plate. Place an empanada on the creamed corn, and top with a fried egg. Garnish with the chilli and coriander and serve.

AZTEC BREAKFAST

PREPARATION: 30 MINUTES // COOKING: 55 MINUTES // SERVES 6

Here's a breakfast dish for those times when a fry-up isn't quite justified, but a fruit salad isn't going to scratch that itch: introducing The Breakfast Salad.

Give yourself a head start by cooking the barley and quinoa the night before.

In a saucepan, bring 1 litre (35 fl oz/4 cups) water to the boil. Add a good pinch of salt flakes, stir in the barley and reduce the heat to low. Simmer for 40 minutes, or until tender, then set aside to cool.

Meanwhile, in a separate saucepan, bring 250 ml (9 fl oz/1 cup) water to the boil. Add a good pinch of salt flakes and add the thoroughly rinsed quinoa. Reduce the heat and simmer for 10–12 minutes, or until the quinoa is tender and the liquid has been absorbed. Set aside to cool.

Place the grains in a mixing bowl. Add the lime juice and olive oil and mix until thoroughly combined. Now add the herbs, kale and chilli and toss to combine. Season to taste with salt flakes and freshly ground black pepper; the salad should be on the slightly acidic side, to balance out the richness of the poached eggs, so add a little extra lime juice if needed.

Divide the salad among six serving bowls, then top each one with a poached egg. Garnish with a dollop of tomatillo salsa and serve a rolled-up tortilla on the side.

salt flakes, for seasoning

200 g (7 oz/1 cup) pearl barley, rinsed

200 g (7 oz/1 cup) quinoa, thoroughly rinsed

juice of 2 limes

60 ml (2 fl oz/¼ cup) extra virgin olive oil

1 bunch (80 g/2¾ oz) mint, leaves picked and finely chopped

1 bunch (80 g/2¾ oz) flat-leaf (Italian) parsley, leaves picked and finely chopped

1 bunch (60 g/2¼ oz) coriander (cilantro), stems and leaves finely chopped

4 kale leaves (about 200 g/7 oz), white central stalks removed, leaves very finely chopped

1 fresh jalapeño chilli, finely chopped

6 free-range eggs, poached (see the Smoked paprika eggs benedict recipe on pages 223–224)

250 g (9 oz/1 cup) Tomatillo salsa verde (see page 277)

6 flour tortillas, about 25 cm (10 inches) in size, warmed

DRINK ALL

THE DRINKS

Do you know what is way more important than food? Drinks. That's right. You've spent the last 200 pages warming up for this section. So now that you're limber, let's get rolling.

Like our food, our drinks are free of fanciness and hi-tech wizardry. There is no nitrogen gas, triple-frozen ice balls or rare tea infusions. We leave that to the experts. We like our drinks heavy on the booze, big on the juice, hectic on the garnish, ridiculous with the names and high on life.

These are drinks for an instant good time, easily produced with minimal set-up or fuss. They should get you moving and laughing quicker than it takes to shoot a shooter. All of them are plucked straight off our menus. They are our all-time favourites — a lot of them house specials — that best sum up our drinking spirit.

These are drinks to be drunk, not looked at. Drinks should be drinkable, right? Right. Cheers.

AROUND THE WORLD
WITH MARY

Almost the whole 3pm Breakfast chapter was created within reach of booze. So it made sense to follow up those dishes with the things we like to drink them with.

Throughout our venues, we've collected nearly 30 different bloody Mary variations. On the next few pages you'll find the ones we love best. Using the basic 'Mary mix' on the opposite page, you can travel 'around the world' with Mary by incorporating the flavours and liquors of different countries.

And remember: a bloody Mary should never be shaken. Repeat after us: 'Roll and stir. Roll and stir.' Serve it in a tall glass with an insane garnish and you'll get top marks, for sure.

MARY MIX

PREPARATION: 5 MINUTES // MAKES ENOUGH TO SEASON MANY, MANY BLOODY MARYS

Bloody Marys are a big deal to us. A bloody Mary with a late breakfast or brunch is an institution that should be honoured by anyone who works hard for the money. And everyone else. The bloody Mary seems to be the one cocktail that is permissible at any given time of the day, no matter where you are. In our view, there is no drink better suited to a hungover Sunday afternoon or a serious breakfast session with mates than a bloody Mary of one kind or another.

A basic Mary seasoning mix should contain worcestershire sauce and horseradish paste. Apart from that you can kind of go crazy. Additions can include pickled onions, olive brine, dry vermouth, brown sugar, sweet paprika, or anything else that tickles your fancy. Here's our basic recipe to get the ball rolling.

Mix everything thoroughly and store in a large squeeze bottle until needed. Your Mary seasoning mix will keep in the fridge for up to 2 weeks.

1 litre (35 fl oz/4 cups) worcestershire sauce

1 tablespoon horseradish paste

1 teaspoon cayenne pepper

2 teaspoons smoked paprika

60 ml (2 fl oz/¼ cup) pickled onion juice (from a jar of pickled onions)

BLOODY BANGKOK

PREPARATION: 5 MINUTES

ESSENCE OF TOM YUM
3 tablespoons tom yum paste
375 ml (13 fl oz/1½ cups) freshly
   boiled hot water

PER SERVE
ice cubes
45 ml (1 fl ½ oz) whisky
30 ml (1 fl oz) Essence of tom yum
15 ml (½ fl oz) lime juice
90 ml (3 fl oz) tomato juice
   (or enough to fill the glass)
15 ml (½ fl oz) Mary mix (page 237)
a dash of soy sauce
a dash of Tabasco sauce

GARNISH
Thai basil sprig
olive on a toothpick

In a small bowl, whisk the tom yum essence ingredients together and set aside. You can store the mixture in an airtight container in the fridge for a few days, but be sure to give it a good whisk or stir before using, as it can separate a bit. Makes enough essence for 12 drinks.

To serve, fill a tall glass with a handful of ice cubes. Pour in the whisky, tom yum essence, lime juice, tomato juice and enough Mary mix to suit your taste. Season with a dash of soy and Tabasco sauce.

Top with the garnish and #suckitdown.

BLOODY MEXICAN

PREPARATION: 5 MINUTES // MAKES 1

ice cubes
45 ml (1½ fl oz) tequila
15 ml (½ fl oz) lime juice
90 ml (3 fl oz) tomato juice
   (or enough to fill the glass)
20 ml (½ fl oz) Mary mix (page 237)
a dash of Tabasco sauce
a dash of Mexican-style hot
   chilli sauce, such as Tapatío

GARNISH
cherry tomato and pickled
   jalapeño rings on a toothpick
lemon or lime wedge

Fill a tall glass with a handful of ice cubes. Pour in the tequila, lime juice, tomato juice and enough Mary mix to suit your taste. Season with a dash each of Tabasco and Tapatío sauce.

Top with the garnish and #suckitdown.

BLOODY INDIAN

PREPARATION: 5 MINUTES // MAKES 1

Fill a tall glass with a handful of ice cubes. Add the curry powder and cumin. Pour in the gin, lemon juice, tomato juice and enough Mary mix to suit your taste.

Top with the garnish and #suckitdown.

ice cubes
1 teaspoon curry powder
pinch of ground cumin
45 ml (1½ fl oz) gin
15 ml (½ fl oz) lemon juice
90 ml (3 fl oz) tomato juice
   (or enough to fill the glass)
20 ml (½ fl oz) Mary mix
   (page 237)

GARNISH
olive, cherry tomato and bird's
   eye chilli on a toothpick

BLOODY ITALIAN

PREPARATION: 5 MINUTES + 4 DAYS INFUSING

Combine the Italian vodka ingredients in a clean plastic container with a lid. Seal and refrigerate for 4 days.

Strain out the solids, pour the vodka back into the bottle and you're ready to go. Makes enough for 16 drinks.

To serve, fill a tall glass with a handful of ice cubes. Pour in the Italian vodka, lemon juice, tomato juice and enough Mary mix to suit your taste.

Top with the garnish and #suckitdown.

ITALIAN VODKA
750 ml (26 fl oz) bottle of vodka
2 rosemary sprigs
60 ml (2 fl oz/¼ cup) balsamic
   vinegar
2 garlic cloves, crushed

PER SERVE
ice cubes
45 ml (1½ fl oz) Italian vodka
15 ml (½ fl oz) lemon juice
90 ml (3 fl oz) tomato juice
   (or enough to fill the glass)
20 ml (½ fl oz) Mary mix (page 237)

GARNISH
rosemary sprig
cherry tomato, olive and cocktail
   onion on a toothpick

BLOODY BANGKOK

BLOODY MEXICAN

BLOODY INDIAN

BLOODY ITALIAN

FILTHY HORCHATA

PREPARATION: 10 MINUTES // MAKES 1

While at Guisados taco house (a magical place) in Los Angeles on an eating vacation, we experienced a dirty horchata for the first time.

A horchata is a Latino spiced-milk drink. A dirty horchata is one of those, with a shot of coffee in it. A revelation!

We added rum to the revelation and the Filthy horchata was born. The misconception with horchata is that it's a heavy, creamy drink, but when you load this baby up with a stack of ice, what you actually have is a light, refreshing drink you won't want to miss.

ice cubes

15 ml (½ fl oz) Sugar syrup (see page 276)

30 ml (1 fl oz) shot of cold espresso coffee

30 ml (1 fl oz) dark rum

185 ml (6 fl oz/¾ cup) rice milk, approximately

60 ml (2 fl oz/¼ cup) milk

½ teaspoon ground cinnamon

Load a tall glass up with ice to chill the glass. Pour in the sugar syrup, coffee and rum. Fill the glass three-quarters full with the rice milk and top up with regular milk.

Dust some cinnamon over the top.

BIG B COLADA

PREPARATION: 5 MINUTES // MAKES 1

This is a dedicated multi-tasker of a drink. The rum gets you moving along, while the vitamin B tackles last night's hangover that is still lingering in the background. It might sound like a goofy drink, but the result is delicious and (dare we say it) nutritious. As well as clearing your head, it gets your heart pumping like only a hit of vitamin B can. That's a win, win, win situation.

Muddle the vitamin B tablet in a cocktail shaker. Add the rum, lime juice, sugar syrup and some ice cubes. Shake until the tablet is fully dissolved.

Strain into a big glass filled with ice cubes, then top up with the Irn-Bru. Garnish with the maraschino cherries.

1 soluble vitamin B tablet, such as Berocca

45 ml (1½ fl oz) white rum

15 ml (½ fl oz) lime juice

10 ml (⅓ fl oz) Sugar syrup (see page 276)

ice cubes

120 ml (4 fl oz) Irn-Bru (see glossary), or enough to fill the glass

2 maraschino cherries

ROBERT MITCHUM

PREPARATION: 5 MINUTES // MAKES 1

Robert Mitchum was a legend. An American actor, author, composer and singer, he was once voted the 23rd greatest screen legend of all time.

He was also fond of a drink or three — so much so that we named this breakfast tipple after him. We like imagining he lived on a diet consisting only of these, but he probably didn't, because he lived until he was nearly 80.

This cocktail tastes a lot like a banana milkshake for adults.

Add the whisky, orange juice, egg and maple syrup to a cocktail shaker. Pop in an ice cube, close the lid and shake vigorously for at least 30 seconds.

Add a handful of ice cubes and shake again. Strain into a rocks glass. Using a microplane, grate some nutmeg over the top.

45 ml (1½ fl oz) bourbon whisky

20 ml (½ fl oz) orange juice

1 free-range egg

20 ml (½ fl oz) maple syrup

ice cubes

fresh whole nutmeg

FILTHY HORCHATA

BIG B COLADA

ROBERT MITCHUM

LAGERITA

PREPARATION: 5 MINUTES // MAKES 1

It's hot. You're sweating. You need a beer. But a beer just won't do. Sounds like you need a LAGERITA, mate. What's better than beer? The answer is TURBO BEER!

ice cubes
20 ml (½ fl oz) agave syrup
  (see glossary)
30 ml (1 fl oz) tequila
juice of ½ lime (save the
  squeezed-out shell for
  garnishing)
about half a 350 ml (12 fl oz)
  bottle of a pale Mexican-style
  lager, such as Corona

GARNISH
reserved squeezed-out lime half,
  pushed halfway inside out to
  create a lime wheel

Fill a pint glass three-quarters of the way with ice cubes. Add the agave syrup, tequila and lime juice.

Stir with a long spoon and pour in enough beer to fill the glass.

Garnish with the lime wheel.

$10 ROOT

PREPARATION: 10 MINUTES // MAKES 1

We ran this drink as a house special, but we aren't entirely sure if we've ever actually sold any. Beetroot as a drink, as it turns out, is not everyone's thing.

Having said that, it's worth taking some time to try this guy. It's a great drink for winter, for saunas, for hot springs, or a date with a Polish gentleman.

ice cubes
45 ml (1½ fl oz) vodka
10 ml (⅓ fl oz) grape liqueur,
  such as Pavan (see glossary)
20 ml (½ fl oz) lemon juice
10 ml (⅓ fl oz) Sugar syrup
  (see page 276)
30 ml (1 fl oz) beetroot (beet)
  juice

Fill a martini glass or champagne coupe with ice cubes and leave to chill for at least a minute.

To a cocktail shaker, add the remaining ingredients and another handful of ice. Shake vigorously for 30 seconds.

Tip out the ice cubes from the martini glass and strain the cocktail into the martini glass.

TENGO HUEVA

PREPARATION: 5 MINUTES // MAKES 1

Pisco is a really hectic, unpalatable booze, even in cocktails, as you have to try your best to hide its petrol-like taste. This drink, however, pulls it off — and that's with two types of pisco. If miracles are real, then this is surely one of them.

Add the piscos, bitters, lime juice, sugar syrup and a handful of ice cubes to a cocktail shaker. Shake vigorously and strain into a tall glass over ice.

Garnish with a lime peel ribbon.

30 ml (1 fl oz) pisco
 (see glossary)
30 ml (1 fl oz) plum pisco
2 dashes of plum bitters
20 ml (½ fl oz) lime juice
15 ml (½ fl oz) Sugar syrup
 (see page 276)
ice cubes

GARNISH
lime peel ribbon, peeled using
 a vegetable peeler

GOLDEN STATE MARTINI

PREPARATION: 5 MINUTES // MAKES 1

This was a drink at our short-lived Santa Barbara, which had a restaurant devoted to Californian-style cuisine called The Californian (no points for originality). It's what you'd drink by the pool after a nose job, all goofed up on Quaaludes. The orange curaçao is a nod to the Golden State… and nothing says 'I'm rich, bitch!' quite like gold leaf. One for the showpeeps and Hollywood types.

Place a handful of ice cubes into a martini glass to chill it. Once chilled, dump the ice and turn the glass upside down onto the sheet of gold leaf to give the glass a golden rim.

Pour the curaçao into the glass. Rinse the glass with the liqueur by slowly rotating the liquid around the inside of the glass, to coat it, then tip the liqueur out.

Fill a cocktail shaker full of ice. Add the vodka and vermouth and stir with a bar spoon for 1 minute. Double-strain the cocktail into the glass, then set an orange twist alight over the glass. Additional gold leaf coating optional.

ice cubes
gold leaf sheet
1 teaspoon orange curaçao
60 ml (2 fl oz/¼ cup) top-shelf
 vodka
1 teaspoon dry vermouth

GARNISH
orange twist, wound with gold
 leaf

TENGO HUEVA

LAGERITA

$10 ROOT

GOLDEN STATE MARTINI

RAVE JUICE

PREPARATION: 5 MINUTES // MAKES 1

Our designer Michael Delany invented this drink. Back in the day he owned a nightclub called Third Class. In the late '90s and early '00s, Melbourne was famous for a dance move called the 'Melbourne Shuffle'. This is a drink dedicated to those shufflers. It's the ultimate drink to help you power through an all-nighter, but be warned — more than two isn't the best idea you'll ever have.

ice cubes

45 ml (1½ fl oz) Agwa liqueur
   (see glossary)

250 ml (9 fl oz) can of high-energy
   drink, such as Red Bull

1 glow stick

1 rubber band

Fill a large zip-lock bag with a cup of ice cubes. Pour in the liqueur and energy drink. Activate the glow stick to light it up, then place it in the bag, ensuring it cannot possibly leak.

Put a straw in one corner and tie the top of the bag with a rubber band. Drink out of the straw — not the glow stick!

COCONUT DAIQUIRI

PREPARATION: 10 MINUTES // MAKES 1

The same principles that make salted caramel great are at work here. Simply, salt has the magical ability to enhance, but also balance out sweetness. Which is the case in point when it comes to the coconut purée and salt-rim combo in this cocktail.

30 ml (1 fl oz) coconut purée,
   such as Monin Coconut Fruit
   Purée; don't use coconut cream
   as it will separate

30 ml (1 fl oz) white Cuban rum

30 ml (1 fl oz) lime juice

ice cubes

CHILLI SALT RIM

80 g (2¾ oz/¼ cup) rock salt,
   pulverised

1 long mild red chilli, seeded
   and finely diced

1 lime wedge

Start by rimming a martini glass or champagne coupe glass with chilli salt. To do this, thoroughly combine the salt and chilli in a small bowl, then evenly spread the chilli salt out on a small plate. Rim the glass with the lime wedge, then place the glass, upside down, onto the plate of chilli salt to coat the rim.

Pour the coconut purée, rum and lime juice into a cocktail shaker. Add a handful of ice cubes, pop the top on and shake for your life.

Strain into the rimmed glass.

PORTO COLADA

PREPARATION: 5 MINUTES // MAKES 1

The Oxford Tavern is in a Sydney suburb called Petersham, known for its amazing Portuguese chicken shops. We pay tribute to these chicken establishments with this drink — a Portuguese-ish take on a piña colada.

Pour the cherry juice into a tall glass, then top with a handful of ice cubes. Tilt the glass on an angle and carefully pour in the soda, to create a layer.

Into a cocktail shaker, pour the rum, lime juice and cachaça. Add another handful of ice, pop the lid on and shake. Very carefully strain the booze on top of the soda layer.

Garnish with a maraschino cherry.

15 ml (½ fl oz) cherry juice
ice cubes
pineapple-flavoured soda, for topping up the glass
15 ml (½ fl oz) coconut-flavoured rum, such as Malibu Rum
20 ml (½ fl oz) lime juice
30 ml (1 fl oz) cachaça (see glossary)

GARNISH
maraschino cherry

BLACK NAGA

PREPARATION: 5 MINUTES // MAKES 1

Our version of an Old Fashioned involves a decent-quality tequila and chocolate bitters. It's the kind of stiff drink that puts hairs on your chest and galvanises our staff when work is done and it's time to play. The cucumber garnish is no garnish. It's vital. So don't go skipping it, okay?

It's named after our favourite Pachanga Boys song of the same name. Look it up while you mix up one of these… it's a hectic combo.

Put the sugar and bitters in a rocks glass. Using a muddling stick, grind the ingredients into a paste.

Add 6–8 ice cubes and pour in half the tequila. Stir for 2 minutes. Now add another 6–8 ice cubes, then the rest of the shot of tequila. Stir for a further 2 minutes, or until the sugar has dissolved.

Serve with a cucumber wedge jammed into the glass.

1½ teaspoons dark brown sugar
4 dashes of chocolate bitters
ice cubes
60 ml (2 fl oz/¼ cup) aged ('añejo') tequila

GARNISH
1 large cucumber wedge

RAVE JUICE

COCONUT DAIQUIRI

BLACK NAGA

PORTO COLADA

PANAMARGARITA

PREPARATION: 5 MINUTES + 5–7 DAYS INFUSING

Possibly the best drink in this book. Margaritas should only be played with under exceptional circumstances… and this is one of them. Aloe vera–flavoured juice lends a grape bubblegum taste, which does something alchemic when mixed with jalapeño-infused tequila. The trick is to use aloe juice that doesn't contain the pulp. The juice is for flavour here, not texture.

JALAPEÑO-INFUSED TEQUILA

6 fresh jalapeño chillies,
    roughly chopped

750 ml (26 fl oz) bottle of
    tequila

PER SERVE

50 ml (1¾ fl oz) Jalapeño-infused
    tequila (see above)

45 ml (1½ fl oz) aloe vera juice
    (a pulp-free variety)

40 ml (1¼ fl oz) lime juice

20 ml (½ fl oz) agave syrup
    (see glossary)

ice cubes

GARNISH

lime wedge

salt flakes, to rim the glass

whole long green chilli

To infuse the tequila, add the jalapeño chillies to the bottle of tequila and allow to infuse at room temperature for 5–7 days. During this time, turn the bottle upside down daily and taste it to ensure that the heat from the chillies is adequately developing, adding a little more chopped jalapeño if you think it needs more kick. If you like it really spicy, feel free to keep the chilli in a few days longer; the infusion is all about trial and error.

Note that the jalapeño-infused tequila makes enough for 15 margaritas.

To serve, add the infused tequila, aloe vera juice, lime juice and agave syrup to a cocktail shaker with a handful of ice cubes. Shake it like a mad dog.

Rim half the lip of a tumbler with the lime wedge, then dip it into a plate of salt flakes to coat.

Strain the margarita into the glass and pop the green chilli in as a garnish.

SINGAPORE SLANG

PREPARATION: 5 MINUTES // MAKES 1

As soon as you put a drink in a hurricane glass, it stops being an okay drink and becomes a GREAT drink. This is such a drink. We take a Singapore Sling and bastardise it with maraschino liqueur and almond syrup. A riff on the Raffles classic.

Into a cocktail shaker, pour the gin, lemon juice, orgeat syrup, pineapple juice and grenadine. Add a handful of ice cubes, pop the lid on and give it a shake.

Strain into a hurricane glass or other tall glass and add a few drops of bitters on top.

Garnish with the maraschino cherries, and pineapple leaves if you have some handy.

45 ml (1½ fl oz) gin
15 ml (½ fl oz) lemon juice
15 ml (½ fl oz) orgeat syrup
  (see glossary)
40 ml (1¼ fl oz) pineapple juice
10 ml (⅓ fl oz) grenadine
  (see glossary)
ice cubes
a dash of bitters

GARNISH
3 maraschino cherries
pineapple leaves (optional)

MANTINNY

PREPARATION: 5 MINUTES // MAKES 1

For our money, we offer this up as the best name we've ever come up with for a drink. This is simply beer, gin, vermouth and a few olives served to you in the can from whence it was born. This is booze for the discerning yobbo, who appreciates the okay things in life.

Open the can of beer and drink about 80 ml (2½ fl oz/⅓ cup) of it.

Pour the gin, lime juice, vermouth and sugar syrup into the can.

Garnish with the toothpick of olives.

375 ml (13 fl oz) can of cold
  pale lager
30 ml (1 fl oz) gin
15 ml (½ fl oz) lime juice
10 ml (⅓ fl oz) dry vermouth
15 ml (½ fl oz) Sugar syrup
  (see page 276)

GARNISH
3 stuffed olives on a toothpick

PANAMARGARITA

SINGAPORE SLANG

MANTINNY

SATAN'S BREAKFAST

SATAN'S BREAKFAST

PREPARATION: 5 MINUTES // MAKES 1

Our bar manager extraordinaire at The Norfolk, Zana, is responsible for the majority of the cocktails on the lists at our venues. His take on cocktails is a bit loose and spicy for some; suffice to say he's come up with some of the crazier concoctions on the menu.

He has also developed a philosophy called 'The Squint Method'. He claims that the harder you squint at a customer while suggesting drinks, the more the customer is convinced that the cocktail must be delicious and therefore the higher the success rate at suggestion-to-purchase conversion. Apparently it works. Next time you're at the bar, see if it works on you.

Satan's Breakfast requires the deepest of squints to sell. Black cherry bourbon tends to freak people out, but once tried, people are converted. It is here that we see The Squint Method benefit the people.

45 ml (1½ fl oz) Jim Beam Black Cherry, or other cherry-flavoured bourbon

15 ml (½ fl oz) coffee liqueur, such as Kahlúa

30 ml (1 fl oz) shot of cold espresso coffee

10 ml (⅓ fl oz) Sugar syrup (see page 276)

ice cubes

a pinch of salt flakes

GARNISH
maraschino cherry

Pour the booze, coffee and sugar syrup into a cocktail shaker full of ice cubes. Add the salt flakes, pop the lid on and shake vigorously.

Strain into a tumbler full of ice and garnish with a maraschino cherry.

SUGAR MAMA

PREPARATION: 5 MINUTES // MAKES 1

This drink is summer in a glass. A cross between a caipirinha and a Dark & Stormy, it's zesty, rum-soaked and sweet, just like the partner of your dreams.

Sugarcane juice can be found at Vietnamese or South-East Asian fruit and vegetable grocers, and is the key ingredient in making this cocktail a success. If you can't find it, we're fresh out of ideas.

Into a tall glass, add a small scoop of ice cubes and the rum. Pour the sugarcane juice and lime juice over the top, then charge the glass with ginger ale.
    Garnish with a lime wheel.

ice cubes
30 ml (1 fl oz) spiced rum
30 ml (1 fl oz) sugarcane juice
15 ml (½ fl oz) lime juice
150 ml (5 fl oz) dry ginger ale

GARNISH
1 lime wheel

SINGLE MOTHER

PREPARATION: 5 MINUTES // MAKES 1

Our house drink at one of our venues is this baby, the Single Mother. It's a red wine mixed drink akin to sangria. Red wine is really an underrated mixer for cocktails, and while the Spanish have long known this, now you all do.

We thought the name would offend everyone, but it actually took about two years for us to receive our first complaint. That's a record for us. How hard is it to offend people these days? Sheesh.

Add all the liquids to a tall glass. Grate some nutmeg over the top, then garnish with an orange wheel.

30 ml (1 fl oz) Southern Comfort, or other spicy peach liqueur
60 ml (2 fl oz/¼ cup) chilled red wine
a dash of orange juice
a dash of ginger beer

GARNISH
fresh whole nutmeg
orange wheel

YARDBIRD

PREPARATION: 10 MINUTES

Chicken salt — that most dubious of salty, yellow-hued seasonings — takes a shot of tequila to surprising places. Chased down with a pineappley sangrita, it'll make you want to ruffle your feathers and fly the coop.

SANGRITA

1 bunch (60 g/2½ oz) coriander
  (cilantro), roots trimmed

1.5 litres (52 fl oz/6 cups)
  pineapple juice

1 fresh jalapeño chilli

1 teaspoon hot green chilli
  sauce, such as green Tapatío
  or Tabasco

PER SHOT

1 lime wedge

chicken salt, to rim the glass

30 ml (1 fl oz) tequila

30 ml (1 fl oz) Sangrita (see
  above)

Add all the sangrita ingredients to a blender and blitz until completely combined.

Strain through a fine-mesh sieve, then bottle the mixture. The sangrita will keep in the fridge for up to 1 week; make sure you shake the bottle vigorously before each use, as the ingredients will separate.

To serve, rim a shot glass with the lime wedge, then coat it with chicken salt. Fill the glass with the tequila.

Fill a second shot glass with sangrita (that's your chase). You can chase each shot with as little or as much sangrita as you wish; it is also delicious as a refreshing juice, if you like coriander and a bit of spice.

Shoot the tequila, then the sangrita.

BARFLY

PREPARATION: 5 MINUTES // MAKES 1

Everything is cuter in miniature. This is a mini Manhattan, for those who fancy themselves a bit more serious than others.

15 ml (½ fl oz) rye whisky

10 ml (⅓ fl oz) red vermouth

1 teaspoon cherry-flavoured syrup

1 teaspoon lemon juice

ice cubes

PRETZEL RIM

a handful of pretzels, crushed

1 lime wedge

To make the pretzel rim, place the crushed pretzels on a plate. Rim a shot glass with the lime wedge, then up-end it onto the crushed pretzels to coat.

Add the whisky, vermouth, cherry syrup and lemon juice to a cocktail shaker, along with a handful of ice cubes. Pop the lid on, shake, then strain into the pretzel-rimmed shot glass. Et voilà!

WATERMELON MAN

PREPARATION: 5 MINUTES // MAKES 1

The only flavour better than watermelon is synthetic watermelon.
And it doesn't get any more fake-tasting than this one. This is a layered shot,
so take your time to get it right.

Pour the watermelon syrup into a shot glass. Carefully pour the lime juice over the back of a teaspoon into the glass, then do the same with the tequila.

Top off the glass with one small drop of green food colouring and stir very gently to retain the layered effect.

Garnish with a watermelon wedge sprinkled with the salt flakes.

1 teaspoon watermelon-flavoured syrup
1 teaspoon lime juice
20 ml (½ fl oz) tequila
1 drop of green food colouring
1 small watermelon wedge
a pinch of salt flakes

BURNIN' PASSION

PREPARATION: 5 MINUTES // MAKES 1

A shot on fire, inside a passionfruit shell! Great for the next time you want to
listen to Sunn O))) while watching an eclipse, then eat a whole pineapple with
the skin on before sacrificing a virgin goat.

Add the vodka, liqueur and passionfruit pulp to a cocktail shaker. Pop the lid on and shake, then double-strain into the passionfruit shell.

Place on a shot glass, then pour in the rum and light it on fire!

15 ml (½ fl oz) vodka
15 ml (½ fl oz) Licor 43 (see glossary)
10 ml (⅓ fl oz) passionfruit pulp
½ passionfruit shell, hollowed out
½ teaspoon Bacardi 151, or other 75.5% alcohol rum

YARDBIRD

BURNIN' PASSION

WATERMELON MAN

BARFLY

LADY HAIR

SWINGING TIT

FIRE DOWN BELOW

LADY HAIR

PREPARATION: 5 MINUTES // MAKES 1

Garnishing anything with floss is pretty wanky. We don't usually do it, but this one makes people so confused when they are served it for the first time that it's worth including just for the reaction alone.

15 ml (½ fl oz) aged golden
    Cuban rum
15 ml (½ fl oz) grape liqueur,
    such as Pavan (see glossary)
10 ml (⅓ fl oz) grape juice
ice cubes

GARNISH
fairy floss

Pour the rum, liqueur and grape juice into a cocktail shaker and add a handful of ice cubes.

Pop the lid on and shake well, then strain into a shot glass. Garnish with a pile of fairy floss.

SWINGING TIT

PREPARATION: 5 MINUTES + SEVERAL HOURS TO SET THE JELLY // MAKES 1 SHOT + 1 CHASER

Before we took over the Oxford Tavern, it was a working-man's bar with strip shows and jelly wrestling. The locals nicknamed it the Swinging Tit. How could we not name a drink after such a salubrious history?

PER SHOT
1 x 85 g (3 oz) packet of jelly
    crystals
30 ml (1 fl oz) rye whisky

Prepare the jelly as instructed on the packet.

Once the jelly has set, empty the jelly into a soda siphon and charge the siphon with two bulbs, shaking vigorously after each charge.

Pour the rye into a shot glass. Squirt the jelly foam into another shot glass (or over your other hand).

Shoot the rye and swallow the jelly chase.

FIRE DOWN BELOW

PREPARATION: 10 MINUTES + UP TO 24 HOURS INFUSING

This one comes packed with not-to-be-messed-with fire. Make sure you strain the habanero chillies from the tequila and don't let the strained tequila sit for days on end, or the tequila will just keep getting hotter and hotter until it'll blow your head off! Okay, so it won't actually blow your head off, but you might need a new mouth.

To infuse the tequila, pour the entire bottle of tequila into a blender. Throw in the chilli and blitz until combined. Strain right away, or pour it all back into the bottle and let it settle for 24 hours maximum, depending on your tolerance for heat. The infusion is all about trial and error, but this chilli one being particularly hot, infusing it for any longer than 24 hours is going to result in extreme heat!

Strain the tequila through a fine-mesh sieve, then pour the tequila back into the bottle and seal it up. Even though the chilli has been strained out, the longer the tequila rests, the hotter it will become. You have been warned. Again.

Makes enough for 30 shots.

To serve, pour some salt flakes onto a clean plate. Rim a shot glass with the lime wedge, then up-end it onto the salt. Dust the orange wheel with the cinnamon. Pour the tequila into the salt-rimmed shot glass and garnish with the orange wheel.

HABANERO-INFUSED TEQUILA
750 ml (26 fl oz) bottle of
    tequila
1 fresh habanero chilli
    (see glossary)

PER SHOT
30 ml (1 fl oz) Habanero-infused
    tequila (see above)

GARNISH
salt flakes, to rim the glass
lime wedge
orange wheel
pinch of ground cinnamon

GARNISH CORNER

Drinks can never really have too many garnishes. Subtlety is the enemy of awesomeness. Less isn't more. More is more! Garnish like no one is watching.

BANANA DOLPHIN

Using a sharp knife, cut the banana in half across the middle, on a slight diagonal.

Trim off the stalky end of the banana to neaten it.

Now make a 5 cm (2 inch) incision into the neck of the banana, cutting all the way through, to make a mouth.

Use a grape to wedge the mouth of your dolphin open.

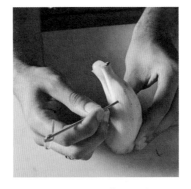

Poke a cocktail stick or other sharp implement into the banana, to make an eye on each side of the head.

Voilà, your banana dolphin is now complete!

VIKING SHIP

Cut an orange in half, from top to bottom, using a sharp knife.

Cut each half in half. Discard one of the orange quarters.

On two quarters, cut away the rind, including the white pith.

Trim your two pieces of orange peel into rectangles, keeping them as large as you can.

You'll now have one full orange quarter, and two rectangular orange peel strips.

Fold each orange peel strip in half, with the rind inside, then skewer them on a cocktail stick.

Use your full orange quarter as the base of your viking ship, then attach your toothpick 'mast and sails' in the middle.

Push a toothpick into each side of your viking ship, to create a set of oars.

LIME ORB

Take a lime, place it on its side, then use a sharp knife to trim off the round end.

Cut off one thick, round disc and set it aside.

Cut off another disc, the same thickness as the last. Discard the stumpy ends.

Lay the two lime discs flat on your chopping board.

Cut a small wedge out of each lime disc.

Here's a closer view of what your discs should look like.

Now simply slot the discs into each other, wedge to wedge.

Your lime orb masterpiece is now finished.

ESSENTIALS

AJI & PINEAPPLE SALSA

PREPARATION: 15 MINUTES
MAKES ABOUT 500 G (1 LB 2 OZ/2 CUPS)

1 pineapple
2 bottled aji chillies in vinegar,
   or 2 pickled jalapeño chillies
   (see glossary), finely chopped
juice of 2 limes
100 ml (3½ fl oz) extra virgin olive oil
1 bunch (60 g/2¼ oz) coriander
   (cilantro), finely chopped (including
   the roots and stems)
1 red capsicum (pepper), seeded and
   finely diced
salt flakes, for seasoning

Cut away the skin and inner core of the pineapple.
Finely dice the flesh and place in a mixing bowl.

Add the remaining ingredients and mix well.
Cover and refrigerate until needed; this salsa is
best eaten the same day.

BARBECUE SAUCE

PREPARATION: 15 MINUTES
COOKING: 1¼ HOURS
MAKES 1.5 LITRES (52 FL OZ/6 CUPS)

40 g (1½ oz) butter
1 white onion, finely diced
2 garlic cloves, finely chopped
1 teaspoon cayenne pepper
125 g (4½ oz/½ cup) American mustard
350 g (12 oz/1 cup) black treacle or
   molasses
220 g (7¾ oz/1 cup, firmly packed)
   brown sugar
125 ml (4 fl oz/½ cup) tomato sauce
   (ketchup)
250 ml (9 fl oz/1 cup) apple cider
   vinegar
250 ml (9 fl oz/1 cup) orange juice
125 ml (4 fl oz/½ cup) worcestershire
   sauce

Melt the butter in a heavy-based saucepan over
medium–low heat. Add the onion and garlic and
cook for 5–6 minutes, or until the onion is soft.

Stir in the cayenne pepper and mustard and
continue to cook for 3–4 minutes.

Add the remaining ingredients, stirring them
in well. Turn the heat up and bring the sauce to a
gentle boil, then immediately turn the heat down
as low as it will go. Cook for a further 1 hour, or
until the sauce has thickened, stirring occasionally.

Set aside to cool, then pour into clean jars or
squeeze bottles and refrigerate until needed. The
sauce will keep in the fridge for up to 2 weeks.

CHILLI MINCE

PREPARATION: 20 MINUTES
COOKING: 1 HOUR
MAKES ABOUT 1.25 KG (2 LB 12 OZ)

2 tablespoons olive oil
1 brown onion, finely chopped
750 g (1 lb 10 oz) minced (ground) beef
½ large red capsicum (pepper), diced
½ large green capsicum (pepper), diced
1¼ teaspoons chilli powder
1 teaspoon ground cumin
1 teaspoon ground coriander
½ teaspoon ground cinnamon
1 teaspoon smoked paprika
2 x 400 g (14 oz) tins chopped tomatoes
300 g (10½ oz) tin red kidney beans,
  drained and rinsed
salt flakes, for seasoning
½ bunch (30 g/1 oz) coriander
  (cilantro), stems and leaves chopped

Heat the olive oil in a large heavy-based saucepan over medium heat. Cook off the onion for about 5 minutes, until soft and translucent.

Add the beef and turn the heat up to high. Brown off the beef for 5–6 minutes, making sure to break it all up nicely, then add the capsicums and sauté together for 2 minutes.

Stir in the spices, turning the heat down to medium again so they don't burn. Cook out the spices for 2–3 minutes, then add the tomatoes and reduce the heat to a gentle simmer. Leave to bubble away for 20 minutes.

Stir in the beans, then cook for a further 20 minutes, or until the sauce is rich and slightly thickened. Season with salt flakes and freshly ground black pepper.

Just before serving, add the fresh coriander.

Your chilli mince will keep in an airtight container in the fridge for several days.

CHIPOTLE MAYO

PREPARATION: 5 MINUTES
MAKES 500 G (1 LB 2 OZ/2 CUPS)

4 chipotle chillies in adobo sauce
  (see glossary)
400 g (14 oz/1⅔ cups) whole-egg
  mayonnaise
juice of 2 limes
½ teaspoon dried oregano
salt flakes, for seasoning

Place the chillies, mayonnaise, lime juice and oregano in a blender. Blitz to a smooth paste, then season to taste with salt flakes and freshly ground black pepper.

Spoon into a clean jar or squeeze bottle and refrigerate until needed. The mayo will keep in the fridge for up to 2 weeks.

CORN SALSA

PREPARATION: 15 MINUTES
COOKING: 20 MINUTES
MAKES 400 G (14 OZ/2 CUPS)

5 corn cobs, husks and silks removed
1 red onion, finely diced
2 long red chillies, seeded and finely
   chopped
½ bunch (30 g/1 oz) coriander
   (cilantro), finely chopped
125 ml (4 fl oz/½ cup) extra virgin
   olive oil
juice of 1 lime
salt flakes, for seasoning

Heat a chargrill pan or barbecue to medium.
Add the corn cobs and cook, turning now and
then, for 10–15 minutes, or until they develop a
few char marks. Remove from the heat and leave
until cool enough to handle, then use a sharp knife
to cut the kernels off the cob, breaking them up
into individual kernels.

Place the corn kernels in a mixing bowl with the
onion, chilli and coriander. Drizzle with the olive oil
and lime juice and toss together. Season to taste
with salt flakes. Cover and refrigerate until needed;
the salsa will keep in the fridge for up to 2 days.

HONEY & CHIPOTLE GLAZE

PREPARATION: 10 MINUTES
MAKES 1 LITRE (35 FL OZ/4 CUPS)

350 g (12 oz/1 cup) honey
250 g (9 oz) chipotle chillies
   in adobo sauce (see glossary),
   roughly chopped
500 ml (17 fl oz/2 cups) of your
   favourite barbecue sauce
½ teaspoon ground cumin
½ teaspoon smoked paprika
2 tablespoons liquid smoke
   (see glossary)

Place all the ingredients in a blender and blitz
until smooth.

Pour into clean jars or squeeze bottles and
refrigerate until needed. The glaze will keep in
the fridge for up to 1 month.

This recipe can also be halved if you think
you won't need all the glaze.

JERK MAYO

PREPARATION: 5 MINUTES
MAKES 500 G (1 LB 2 OZ/2 CUPS)

1 tablespoon Jerk paste (see page 273)
500 g (1 lb 2 oz/2 cups) whole-egg
   mayonnaise

Mix the jerk paste through the mayonnaise until
thoroughly combined.

Pour into a clean jar or squeeze bottle and
refrigerate until needed. The mayo will keep in
the fridge for up to 2 weeks.

JERK PASTE

PREPARATION: 15 MINUTES

MAKES ABOUT 250 G (9 OZ/1 CUP)

6–10 fresh habanero or scotch bonnet
  chillies (see glossary), finely chopped
2 brown onions, finely chopped
3–4 spring onions (scallions), finely
  chopped
1 garlic clove, roughly chopped
1 tablespoon fresh thyme leaves
2 teaspoons sea salt
1 teaspoon freshly ground black pepper
1 teaspoon sugar
1 teaspoon ground allspice
½ teaspoon ground cinnamon
¼ teaspoon freshly grated nutmeg

Place all the ingredients in a blender. Add a splash of water and blitz to a smooth paste.

Scrape the paste into a clean jar and refrigerate until needed. The paste will keep in the fridge for about 2 weeks.

KOREAN RED PEPPER DRESSING

PREPARATION: 10 MINUTES

COOKING: 5 MINUTES

MAKES ABOUT 375 ML (13 FL OZ/1½ CUPS)

2 teaspoons black sesame seeds
2 teaspoons white sesame seeds
250 g (9 oz/1 cup) gochujang (Korean
  hot red pepper paste; see glossary)
1½ tablespoons caster (superfine) sugar
1½ tablespoons sesame oil

Add the sesame seeds to a small dry frying pan. Toast them over medium heat for about 3 minutes, or until they darken and become fragrant, shaking the pan frequently and keeping an eye on them so they don't burn. Tip them into a mixing bowl.

Add the remaining ingredients. Pour in 170 ml (5½ fl oz/⅔ cup) water and whisk to combine.

Pour into a clean jar or squeeze bottle and refrigerate until needed. The dressing will keep in the fridge for up to 2 weeks.

MANGO SALSA

PREPARATION: 10 MINUTES

MAKES 500 G (1 LB 2 OZ/2 CUPS)

2 firm but ripe mangoes, flesh cut into
  1 cm (½ inch) dice
1 red onion, cut into 1 cm (½ inch) dice
1 long red chilli, seeded and finely diced
½ bunch (30 g/1 oz) coriander
  (cilantro), finely chopped
zest and juice of 1 lime
60 ml (2 fl oz/¼ cup) extra virgin
  olive oil

Place all the ingredients in a mixing bowl and gently mix together. Season to taste with sea salt. This salsa is best served straightaway.

MEXICAN CREMA

PREPARATION: 5–10 MINUTES

MAKES ABOUT 500 G (1 LB 2 OZ/2 CUPS)

375 g (13 oz/1½ cups) sour cream
60 ml (2 fl oz/¼ cup) buttermilk
  (see glossary)
2 chipotle chillies in adobo sauce
  (see glossary), finely chopped
zest of 1 lime
1 teaspoon sea salt

Whisk all the ingredients together in a mixing bowl. Pour into a clean jar or squeeze bottle and refrigerate until needed. It will keep in the fridge for up to 3 days.

PICO DE GALLO

PREPARATION: 15 MINUTES

MAKES ABOUT 1 KG (2 LB 4 OZ/4 CUPS)

8 ripe red tomatoes (about 1 kg/2 lb
   4 oz), halved, cored and finely diced
1 small red onion, finely diced
3 tablespoons finely chopped coriander
   (cilantro)
1 long green chilli, finely diced
1 teaspoon sea salt
1 teaspoon caster (superfine) sugar
juice of 1 lime
2½ teaspoons extra virgin olive oil

Place all the ingredients in a mixing bowl and mix thoroughly to combine.

Transfer to a clean airtight container and refrigerate until needed. The salsa will keep in the fridge for up to 3 days.

QUICK RANCH DRESSING

PREPARATION: 5 MINUTES

MAKES 500 ML (17 FL OZ/2 CUPS)

125 ml (4 fl oz/½ cup) buttermilk
   (see glossary)
375 g (13 oz/1½ cups) whole-egg
   mayonnaise
1 teaspoon garlic powder
3 teaspoons finely chopped chives, mint
   and/or flat-leaf (Italian) parsley

Put all the ingredients in a large clean jar. Pop the lid on and shake well. Season with sea salt and freshly ground black pepper to taste.

Store in the refrigerator until needed; the dressing will keep in the fridge for up to 1 week.

QUICK SLAW

PREPARATION: 15 MINUTES

SERVES 6

¼ red cabbage
¼ white cabbage
juice of ½ lemon
60 g (2¼ oz/¼ cup) whole-egg mayonnaise
4 spring onions (scallions), finely
   chopped
3-4 tablespoons chopped flat-leaf
   (Italian) parsley
sea salt flakes, for seasoning

Using a mandoline or a food processor, slice the cabbages as thinly as possible.

In a large mixing bowl, thoroughly combine the lemon juice and mayonnaise. Add the cabbage, spring onion and parsley and toss until well combined. Season to taste with salt flakes and freshly ground black pepper and serve.

SALSA ROJA

PREPARATION: 20 MINUTES

COOKING: 5 MINUTES

MAKES ABOUT 1 KG (2 LB 4 OZ/4 CUPS)

1-2 tablespoons vegetable oil
3 red onions, finely diced
5 garlic cloves, finely diced
zest of 1 lemon
1 cm (½ inch) knob of fresh ginger,
   peeled and grated
½ teaspoon dried oregano
30 g (1 oz/¼ cup) peri peri herb
   seasoning (available from spice stores
   and gourmet grocers)
185 g (6½ oz/¾ cup) tomato paste
   (concentrated purée)
2 tinned chipotle chillies
   (see glossary), finely diced
250 ml (9 fl oz/1 cup) red wine vinegar

1½ tablespoons caster (superfine) sugar
½ bunch (30 g/1 oz) coriander
  (cilantro), roughly chopped
185 ml (6 fl oz/¾ cup) extra virgin
  olive oil
juice of 2 limes

Heat a frying pan over medium–low heat. Add the vegetable oil and gently sauté the onion, garlic, lemon zest, ginger and dried herbs for 2–3 minutes, or until the herbs have become aromatic and the garlic has softened.

Add the tomato paste and chilli and stir for about 1 minute. Deglaze the pan with the vinegar, stirring to dislodge any stuck-on bits, then add the sugar and stir until the sugar has dissolved.

Remove from the heat and leave to cool slightly, then decant the mixture into a blender.

Add the coriander, then turn the blender on, adding the olive oil in a steady stream until the mixture emulsifies into a paste.

Add the lime juice and blitz again to combine. Season to taste with sea salt and freshly ground black pepper. Transfer to a clean airtight container and refrigerate until needed. The salsa will keep in the fridge for up to 1 month.

SALT & PEPPER MIX

PREPARATION: 10 MINUTES
MAKES ABOUT 3 TABLESPOONS

2 teaspoons sichuan peppercorns
2 teaspoons ground white pepper
2 teaspoons chilli powder
1½ tablespoons sea salt

Using a mortar and pestle, grind the sichuan peppercorns. Tip into a mixing bowl, add the remaining ingredients and mix until well combined.

This spice mix works well as a seasoning on everything from fried fish to grilled chicken. It will keep indefinitely in an airtight container in the pantry.

SCOTCH BONNET SAUCE

PREPARATION: 15 MINUTES +
10 MINUTES SOAKING
COOKING: 10 MINUTES
MAKES 500 ML (17 FL OZ/2 CUPS)

20 dried scotch bonnet chillies
  (see glossary)
1–2 tablespoons vegetable oil,
  for pan-frying
5 fresh jalapeño chillies, seeded
  and chopped
4 garlic cloves, finely chopped
1 white onion, finely chopped
2 tablespoons sugar
125 ml (4 fl oz/½ cup) apple cider
  vinegar
salt flakes, for seasoning

Soak the dried chillies in a bowl of hot water for 10 minutes. Drain the chillies and chop them up a bit.

Heat a frying pan over low heat. Add the vegetable oil and sauté the rehydrated chillies, jalapeño chillies, garlic and onion for 3–5 minutes, or until everything has softened, but hasn't coloured. Add the sugar and vinegar and stir until the sugar has dissolved.

Remove from the heat and leave to cool slightly, then decant the mixture into a blender. Add a splash of water and a good pinch of salt flakes. Blitz until a smooth paste forms.

Pour the sauce into a clean jar or squeeze bottle and refrigerate until needed. It will keep in the fridge for about 1 week.

SESAME & GARLIC MAYO

PREPARATION: 5 MINUTES
MAKES ABOUT 500 G (1 LB 2 OZ/2 CUPS)

250 g (9 oz/1 cup) whole-egg mayonnaise
3 garlic cloves, peeled and smashed
juice of ½ lime
170 ml (5½ fl oz/⅔ cup) sesame oil
salt flakes, for seasoning

Spoon one-third of the mayonnaise into a blender. Add the garlic and blitz together. Add the lime juice and blitz again.

Add the sesame oil, blending to form a smooth paste. Season to taste with salt flakes.

Pour into a clean jar or squeeze bottle and refrigerate until needed. The mayo will keep in the fridge for up to 2 weeks.

SPECIAL SAUCE

PREPARATION: 5 MINUTES
MAKES ABOUT 500 G (1 LB 2 OZ/2 CUPS)

250 g (9 oz/1 cup) whole-egg mayonnaise
3 tablespoons American mustard
60 ml (2 fl oz/¼ cup) tomato sauce
  (ketchup)
3 tablespoons grated dill pickles,
  squeezed of excess juice
¼ white onion, finely diced

In a small bowl, whisk together all the ingredients until well combined.

Pour into a clean jar or squeeze bottle and refrigerate until needed. The mayo will keep in the fridge for up to 1 week.

SUGAR SYRUP

PREPARATION: 5 MINUTES
COOKING: 5 MINUTES
MAKES ABOUT 500 ML (17 FL OZ/2 CUPS)

460 g (1 lb/2 cups) caster (superfine)
  sugar

Sugar syrup is basically equal parts water and caster sugar. Mix it up in batches to suit the quantity of cocktails you are making.

Place the sugar in a saucepan and pour in 500 ml (17 fl oz/2 cups) water. Stir over low heat until all the sugar has dissolved.

Set aside to cool, then pour into a clean squeeze bottle. The sugar syrup will keep for up to 1 month in the fridge.

TAMARILLO SALSA

PREPARATION: 15 MINUTES
COOKING: 5 MINUTES
MAKES 500 G (1 LB 2 OZ/2 CUPS)

10 tamarillos
5 pickled aji chillies or jalapeño
  chillies (see glossary)
1 bunch (60 g/2¼ oz) coriander
  (cilantro), stems and leaves chopped
100 g (3½ oz/⅔ cup) very finely diced
  brown onion
juice of 3 limes
salt flakes, for seasoning

Bring a saucepan of water to the boil. Blanch the tamarillos in the boiling water for 20–30 seconds. Remove with a slotted spoon and leave until cool enough to handle.

Peel off and discard all the skin from the tamarillos. Place the flesh in a food processor with the chillies. Blend until smooth, adding about 125 ml (4 fl oz/½ cup) water to help things along.

Tip the mixture into a saucepan and heat to a gentle simmer, then tip into a large non-metallic bowl and leave to cool.

Stir in the coriander, onion and lime juice to taste. Season with salt flakes and freshly ground black pepper.

Cover and refrigerate until required; the salsa will keep for up to 2 weeks in the fridge.

TOMATILLO SALSA VERDE

PREPARATION: 15 MINUTES
MAKES ABOUT 500 ML (17 FL OZ/2 CUPS)

800 g (1 lb 12 oz) tin tomatillos
  (see glossary), drained
1 fresh jalapeño chilli (see glossary),
  roughly chopped
1 bunch (60 g/2¼ oz) coriander
  (cilantro), roughly chopped
½ bunch (40 g/1½ oz) mint, leaves
  picked
2 garlic cloves, roughly chopped
juice of 1 lime
60 ml (2 fl oz/¼ cup) extra virgin
  olive oil
1 teaspoon sea salt
½ brown onion, finely diced

Place all the ingredients, except the onion, in a blender. Blitz to a smooth purée.

Pour the purée into a mixing bowl and stir the onion through. Season to taste with some freshly ground black pepper.

Store in an airtight container in the refrigerator until needed. The salsa verde will keep in the fridge for up to 1 week, and is at its best around day two or three.

TEMPURA BATTER

PREPARATION: 10 MINUTES
MAKES 500 ML (17 FL OZ/2 CUPS)

125 g (4½ oz/1 cup) tempura flour
  (see glossary)
30 g (1 oz/½ cup) shredded coconut
150 ml (5 fl oz) chilled soda water
juice of 1 lime
1 egg
4-5 ice cubes

Sift the flour into a mixing bowl, then stir in the coconut. Gently whisk in the soda water and lime juice, breaking up any lumps with your fingers if necessary.

Whisk in the egg; the mixture should be the consistency of pancake batter.

Add the ice cubes and use the batter before they melt; the ice cubes make the batter colder, which gives a lighter, sharper batter when it hits the hot oil.

A GUIDE TO DEEP-FRYING YOUR DREAMS

A good portion of this recipe book involves deep-frying. Why? Because we're a pub group. Have you seen punters in pubs? They're there for booze, friends and fried food.

If you are going to deep-fry at home, though, there are a few pointers worth noting so that you nail it. When done the right way, deep-frying isn't actually as unhealthy as you'd think. A good batter cooked at the right temperature will basically steam whatever's inside the batter.

Greasy fried food happens when the oil isn't the right temperature, the right kind or handled in the right way.

Here's a hit list of tips to get you on track.

SAFETY FIRST

At the end of the day, it goes without saying that if you're dealing with boiling oil, be careful. Using the correct implements to do the job will save your skin. Good-quality, long-handled stainless steel tongs are the go.

OIL AND WATER

… DON'T MIX!
Never put anything wet (other than batter) into hot oil — it will spit. And you'll end up with nasty third-degree burns.

THE OIL

The kind of oil you fry your food in does matter. It must have a high smoking point, which means the oil can be heated to a high temperature without starting to smoke or even burn. Good frying oil should also have a neutral flavour, so it doesn't add a taste to your food that you don't want.

Great oils to use for deep-frying that tick both these boxes are peanut, rice bran and canola oil.

THE TEMPERATURE

A rookie error in deep-frying is believing that the oil must be at its absolute hottest. This is a sure-fire way to burn the bejesus out of something. The truth is, the correct temperature of the oil really depends on what you're deep-frying.

For example, hand-cut potatoes for fries should be cooked at 150°C (300°F) for 5 minutes, before turning up the temperature to 185°C (365°F) to crisp and colour the fries.

Fried chicken should be kept at the lower end of the spectrum — around 150°C (300°F) — to give the meat a chance to cook without burning the coveted crunchy coating on the outside.

A wetter batter, like a tempura, should be cooked at a higher temperature —180°C (350°F) — so the oil doesn't seep into the batter during the cooking process.

HOW HOT?

A cooking thermometer that can handle high heat is a must. Clip it to the side of your heavy-based saucepan or deep-fryer to keep an eye on the temperature.

LOAD BEARING

Never overcrowd your pan or deep-fryer. This will drop the temperature of the oil faster than you can yell, 'WHY AREN'T YOU CRISPY, DAMMIT?!' Frying food in smaller batches will help ensure you keep an optimum frying oil temperature, giving you a better end result.

DISPLACEMENT

When filling a heavy-based saucepan or deep-fryer, think about how much oil will be displaced by what you're frying. It might sound obvious, but don't overfill your pan or fryer with oil… otherwise, when you go to fry, you're going to end up with a boiling oil spill! Not smart, or safe.

AFTERCARE

Paper towel is a deep-fryer's best mate. Always rest whatever you've just fried on some crumpled-up paper towel to absorb any excess oil.

'TIS THE REASON FOR THE SEASON

Season food *after* you fry, and not before. Salt draws moisture from food, but it also lowers the temperature of the oil.

Always season immediately after removing food from the fryer, when the salt has the best opportunity to stick to the food.

KEEP IT CLEAN

Know what that stale smell is when you walk into a dodgy fish and chip shop? It's stale oil.

Oil can be reused a few times before being responsibly disposed of; simply wait until it has cooled, pour the oil through a sieve to filter out any bits of batter or food, then store it in a bottle in a cool, dry place.

When the oil starts to get a little dark, it's time to vote it off the island. The best way to dispose of it is to recycle it. Scout around and you may come across a local dude in your neighbourhood who is turning it into biofuel; they may even pick it up and pay you for it!

GLOSSARY

ACHIOTE PASTE a spice blend used in Mexican cooking. It takes its vibrant red colour from achiote seeds (also called annatto seeds) that are native to the tropical Americas, and usually also contains garlic, black pepper, cinnamon, cloves, allspice, oregano and salt. It is available from Latin specialist spice stores and providores.

AGAVE SYRUP sweeter than sugar or honey, this syrup is made from the sap of the agave plant, which is native to the Mexico region, and is the same plant from which tequila is derived. It isn't as thick as honey, has a milder flavour and dissolves quickly in cold drinks. Look for it in health food stores.

AGWA LIQUEUR a bright green herbal elixir featuring Bolivian-grown coca leaves and dozens of botanical extracts, including guarana, ginseng and green tea.

AJI CHILLIES are also known as amarillo chillies. They're bright orange, slightly sweet and a little hot. They are usually sold in brine and are available from most South American specialty food stores, and can also be ordered online.

ANCHO CHILLI the dried form of the Mexican poblano chilli pepper. Ancho chillies are large, dark, heart-shaped and wrinkly, with a smoky, sweet flavour and a generally mild heat level.

BLUE CORN TORTILLAS are made from blue corn, which has long been a staple grown by the Hopi people in the south-western regions of the United States. And yes, the tortillas really are blue!

BUTTERMILK a dairy product that has been inoculated with harmless bacteria. It is much thicker than regular milk and has a tangy flavour, and is great in baking and pancakes as it acts as a leavening agent. You'll find it in the dairy aisle of larger supermarkets.

CACHAÇA the national drink of Brazil, cachaça is an almost rum-like spirit distilled from sugarcane, and a key ingredient in Brazil's most widely enjoyed cocktail, the caipirinha.

CASSAVA a tuberous, yam-like tropical root, also known as manioc or tapioca. You can buy fresh cassava from most Fijian and Indian markets; it is also available frozen.

CASSAVA CRACKERS are made from cassava (see above). They are sold in packets, ready to be deep-fried.

CHILLI PEPPER EXTRACT these extracts come in various heat intensities, measured in Scoville units. The higher the score, the more incendiary the heat! Pepper extracts can be found online, in barbecue stores or at specialty grocers; try stores that specialise in Mexican produce for the best chance of success.

CHINESE PANCAKES you can buy these ready-made, from Asian grocers and some good supermarkets. They are sold in packets, usually frozen. Also known as 'bing' or Peking/Beijing pancakes, they are used in dishes such as Peking duck pancakes.

CHINESE RED PORK SEASONING traditionally used for seasoning and colouring roast pork, and also called char siu, this powdered spice mix is available from Asian grocers, and not to be confused with achiote/annatto. It is actually made in Thailand, rather than China, and is often called 'khao moo daeng'.

CHIPOTLE CHILLIES IN ADOBO SAUCE you'll find tins of these in Latin grocers and spice stores. Chipotles are dried, ripe, smoked jalapeño chillies with a rich, deep, smoky flavour, marinated in a piquant red adobo sauce.

CLAMATO JUICE   a clam-flavoured tomato juice, used in bloody Caesars — a variation on a bloody Mary. You'll find it in good delicatessens and food halls.

CORN MEAL   a roughly textured, gritty 'flour', ground from dried corn. Not to be confused with cornflour (cornstarch), it is available in various grades of coarseness and is used to make cornbread and spoonbread.

DUKKAH   a toasted nut, seed and spice mix, often used for dunking bread in after first dunking it in olive oil. The exact ingredients vary, but dukkah is easy to find in just about any decent food store. Recipes are also available online.

FURIKAKE   a Japanese seasoning mix, traditionally sprinkled on rice, and usually containing sesame seeds, seaweed, sugar, dried fish flakes and salt. You'll find it in stores stocking Japanese ingredients.

GOCHUGARU (Korean red chilli flakes)   hot, sweet and slightly smoky, gochugaru is made from red chillies that have been dried (traditionally sun-dried), then ground into fine bright red flakes or a powder. Korean stores stock it.

GOCHUJANG (Korean hot red pepper paste)   described as a 'spicy miso', this thick, pungent condiment is made from red chillies, glutinous rice flour, fermented soy beans and other seasonings, and is used widely in Korean cooking. Look for it in South-East Asian food stores.

GRENADINE   traditionally made from pomegranate, this sweetly tart, pinkish-red bar syrup adds a lurid blush to cocktails and other drinks. Large supermarkets and liquor stores stock it.

HABANERO CHILLI   quite small and wide shouldered, these chillies are stupidly, intensely hot. They begin life green and turn yellow, orange and then red as they ripen. Approach with caution and wear gloves when chopping these fiery devils as they will burn.

IRN-BRU   Scotland's favourite soft drink, Irn-Bru has a mild orange sports drink flavour. Appealing, right?! It should be pretty easy to find in most cities.

JALAPEÑO CHILLI   moderately hot, this popular thick-fleshed Mexican variety is usually picked green, but is red when fully ripe. Fresh green ones are ideal for stuffing as little bite-sized snacks. Green ones are often sold pickled in brine.

JICAMA   also called a Mexican yam, this turnip-shaped tuber has a slightly sweet, nutty, juicy interior and a crisp crunchy texture. Once peeled, it can be eaten raw and used in salads. You'll find it in Asian and Latin greengrocers.

KIMCHI   a spicy, sour Korean fermented vegetable pickle that is usually cabbage-based. Traditionally it is fermented for months in underground jars. You'll find bottles of it in Asian food stores.

KOREAN RED CHILLI FLAKES   see gochugaru

LICOR 43   a golden Spanish liqueur containing 43 fruits, herbs and spices. It has a sweet, citrusy vanilla flavour.

LIQUID SMOKE   this liquid flavouring adds a smoky flavour to foods and should be used very sparingly, by the drop. It is available from barbecue stores, good supermarkets, and can be ordered online.

MANCHEGO CHEESE a firm, pale Spanish cheese made from Manchego sheep that graze across the plains of La Mancha. Salty and slightly nutty, it develops a peppery bite as it ages, and a crumblier texture. Any good cheese market will have it.

MASA HARINA also called harina de maíz, this specially treated corn-based flour is used for making tortillas, tamales and other Mexican doughs. You'll find it in stores specialising in Mexican and Spanish ingredients, as well as some health food stores. Masa harina is gluten free.

MORCILLA a Spanish sausage stuffed with pig's blood, onion, rice and spices. Look for it in providores and Spanish specialty stores.

OLD BAY SEASONING an American blend of 18 herbs and spices, including celery seeds, mustard, salt, paprika, bay leaf, ginger, allspice and red and black pepper. It is widely used in Southern US cuisine and is available from American specialist stores and online.

ORGEAT SYRUP a cocktail syrup made from almonds and flavoured with orange flower water or rose water. A prime ingredient in the classic mai tai. Some specialty stores stock it, or you can track it down online.

PANKO (JAPANESE BREADCRUMBS) made from crustless bread, panko crumbs are larger, lighter and flakier than regular breadcrumbs, giving a crisper, crunchier crust to traditional Japanese fried dishes such as tonkatsu. You'll find panko in most supermarkets these days.

PAVAN a fortified liqueur made from small Muscat grapes grown in the south of France, aged in old oak casks and infused with orange blossom.

PEDRO XIMÉNEZ also known by the initials PX, this dark, rich, sweet Spanish dessert sherry is made from grapes of the same name, which are partially dried on the vine to concentrate their sweetness.

PISCO an essential component of pisco sours, this clear to amber-coloured brandy is distilled from Muscat grapes. Both Peru and Chile claim pisco as their own, with Peru celebrating a national Pisco Sour Day on the first Saturday of each February.

PLANTAIN also called a 'cooking banana', or a 'potato of the air', a plantain looks like a green banana, but has a thicker skin, and must be cooked before being eaten as it is starchy rather than sweet. Unlike bananas, plantains keep their shape when cooked. They are a staple food throughout the Caribbean, Western Africa, Latin America and Asia.

SAMBAL OELEK a thin, red, sharp-tasting South-East Asian chilli paste, made with pounded chillies, salt and vinegar, used as a cooking sauce rather than a table condiment. You'll find it in the Asian section of larger supermarkets.

SAZÒN SEASONING a Caribbean spice mix used to flavour all manner of meats, rice and bean dishes and stews. It generally contains achiote (also called annatto), coriander (cilantro), garlic and salt. You'll find it in Latino grocers and online.

SCOTCH BONNET CHILLI an infernally hot Caribbean chilli, so named because someone thought it resembled a Scottish tam o'shanter, and also known as a Bahama Mama. It's similar in heat to a habanero, but is slightly sweeter, and is the signature chilli used in Jamaican jerk dishes.

SHICHIMI TOGAGRASHI ('seven flavour chilli pepper') a Japanese spice mix, usually containing chilli, dried orange peel, sesame seeds, seaweed and sichuan peppercorns. It is widely available from Asian supermarkets and spice stores.

SMOKED SALT salt that has been wood smoked, intensifying its flavour and adding a subtle smoky character, depending on the wood chips used (such as hickory, apple, alder or oak). You'll find smoked salt in spice shops and fine food markets.

SOBRASADA a soft, cured, spreadable Spanish salami, made from ground pork and spiced with paprika, sold in Spanish delicatessens and fine food and charcuterie stores.

SQUID INK a liquid extracted from the ink sac of squid. It has a rich, intriguing flavour and adds an attractive deep, dark, glossy sheen to dishes. It is sold in sachets or bottles and is available from fancier fishmongers and gourmet food retailers.

SRIRACHA HOT CHILLI SAUCE a spicy sauce made with chilli and garlic, named after Si Racha, a coastal city in eastern Thailand. It is widely served with Thai and Vietnamese food.

TACO FLOUR see masa harina

TEMPURA FLOUR a very fine, light flour used in Japanese tempura dishes. It is available from the Asian section of good supermarkets. To make your own, simply mix 1 tablespoon cornflour (cornstarch) with every 150 g (5½ oz/1 cup) plain (all-purpose) flour.

TOMATILLO widely used in Mexican cuisine, especially in green sauces and salsas, the unripe tomatillo looks like a green tomato once its inedible outer papery husk is removed, and has a tangy flavour. Tomatillos are more closely related to cape gooseberries than tomatoes. Ripe fruits range in colour from yellow to purple, depending on the variety. You can buy tinned tomatillos from Latino grocery stores.

OUR RESTAURANTS

THE NORFOLK

Our first child and a massive learning process. We honestly had no idea what we were doing when we took this project on. The head chef walked out on his first shift, the menu changed nearly every day and we were WAY busier than we thought we would be. Whoops. There were grease traps overflowing, roofs leaking, late-night parties in our offices and we only just managed to navigate our way through it.

The Norfolk was a serious junk pile before we renovated it. Only half of the pub was used; the front was boarded up and in it lived an old dude/handyman who sometimes ran the kitchen. The idea for The Norfolk was to combine the charms of a classic Aussie pub with Mexican street food. Tacos sat next to schnitzels, quesadillas beside pies.

Some 500,000 tacos later, The Norfolk is still kicking (at the time of writing, at least). This combination of relaxed Australianism and exotic cultural references has become the cornerstone of Drink'n'Dine's operation.

THE CARRINGTON

Just as The Norfolk was getting on its feet, things were turned back on their head when we decided to take on The Carrington. This time, we had slightly more of an idea of what to expect, and what to do. Through it, we met our executive chef Jamie Thomas. To our surprise, the relaunch went off with a huge bang.

Before we took on The Carrington, it was known only as the crappy place across the road from a (then) successful Italian restaurant. People would wait at The Carrington for a table to come up at the restaurant across the road, and for a time, The Carrington survived by turning part of itself into a bottle shop to cater for the restaurant-across-the-road's BYO wine policy. Aside from then, you could only describe it as an old man's drinking den, but what many people don't know is that in a former life it was a transvestite day club.

Our approach here was to combine a classic English pub menu with Spanish pintxos. Jamie's experience at St John and The Anglesea Arms came into play, and bangers and mash sat on the menu alongside empanadas and nose-to-tail pies. As usual, it was weird, but it worked.

THE ABERCROMBIE

A week after opening The Carrington, we opened The Abercrombie. We didn't say we were smart operators. Two pubs in two weeks? You bet we did. The Abercrombie already had a reputation for being pretty ghetto, so we took that ball and ran with it. A short-term lease meant we did everything on the cheap: no locks on toilet doors, dodgy air conditioning, half-finished paint work… but the charm oozed from every dank corner.

The food was a rough mix of Scottish deep-fried favourites, American diner classics and Mexican hits. The 24-hour licence meant that the clientele were mainly students who wanted to party, eat badly and cheaply, and have a lot of fun. Hot dogs for lunch, techno for dinner. We were sad to close the doors just two years later when the lease expired.

THE FORRESTERS

This pub came with a reputation in Sydney. Home of the famous $5 steak, it had formerly been owned by a bunch of NRL football players, and was a rowdy mix of sports, steak, and secretaries on the prowl. The three-storey monster was a huge thing to bite off and chew, and if you thought we'd learnt our lesson by then, you would be wrong. We went with an American–Italian vibe, serving pizzas with sloppy American toppings, made in an electric oven by a Brazilian chef. So authentic!

QUEENIES

Six months into The Forresters, we decided that there was enough real estate within the building to do something else. Three weeks later, Queenies was born. Our own little slice of the Caribbean came to life. Think part jungle pick-up joint, part Jamaican booty bar, and you're halfway there. Reggae and jerk chicken with a side of fried plantains is the order of the day, washed down with coconut daiquiris.

SANTA BARBARA/ THE CALIFORNIAN

Kings Cross's iconic Coca-Cola sign was our home for a brief minute. This bar and club had a vaguely LA Korean street food meets Mexican vibe, and The Californian was the restaurant we decided to open within it. It was, for many reasons, a disaster. We closed a year later and have kept with pubs ever since. Now let's not speak of it anymore.

HOUSE OF CRABS

Three years after opening The Norfolk, we started to get restless (as you do). We wanted to do something new with the venue and had a function space and some offices in the same building that we thought we could turn into a restaurant. One day, our designer Mike Delany shouted across the office, 'CRAB SHACK!' And with those words, House of Crabs was born.

It's a bibs-on, eat-with-your-hands affair. Order some boil, eat it straight out of the bag and throw the scraps on the table. ZZ Top, Sheryl Crow and Nelly play loud and proud while a few cruise-ships worth of nautical gear swing above your head. It's the messiest and possibly funniest meal you will ever eat.

THE OXFORD

Infamous for midday strip shows, jelly wrestling, early opening hours and a 'colourful' clientele, The Oxford Tavern was the kind of pub everyone knew for all the wrong reasons. Situated in the suburb of Petersham, it was our first foray into Sydney's Inner (Wild) West. We retained a strong presence of the past — the strip stage became the back bar, the neon lights were modified to read 'Hot Live BBQ', and the gambling room was hacked up to become booth seating. The Oxford is a real locals' boozer with a seriously Aussie vibe that you need to experience to understand.

Much like The Abercrombie, our menu is real mix of pub classics, Mexican street food and American diner eats. We also run Black Betty's BBQ on the weekends in the beer garden. Black Betty is our barbecue smoker and she churns out huge slabs of low- and slow-smoked meats, while you neck a can of beer under the stars.

CHICA LINDA

After three years, The Carrington needed a refresh. Chica Linda is our version of a Central American eating house. The menu is your ticket to a bus trip around El Salvador, Nicaragua, Honduras and then deep (deep) into the Amazon. Latino rock'n'roll is your soundtrack to pork arepas, smoked chickens, banana coladas and guava empanadas. The phoenix to the ashes of The Carrington.

INDEX

ACKNOWLEDGMENTS

Woah! What a long, long ride, and lots of people to thank who helped so much along our journey.

Big thanks to Jamie Thomas, who wrote, rewrote, rewrote again, added, changed, tested and plated *every* dish. THANK YOU. Danny for his huge help through the testing and photo stages. To Mike Delany for helping with the design and VIBEZ, Jacqui for fine-tuning all the drinks and making them look mega pretty, Matty for his drink testing, Joel for helping to write the first draft and supplying the funnies, Mel Leong for coming aboard and saving us with her expert writing skills and pro-tips. Thanks to Benito for his photo excellence, Lynsey for the styling and Sherbs for his all-filler-all-killer shots. Thanks to all the Murdoch party people (not even that many fights in the end!) — Hugh for the design/photos/email sparring, Katri for her editing and patience, Sue, Barbara, Diana, Matt and everyone else at Murdoch for putting up with us and putting this project together. Also original thanks to Jill and Terry, for thinking we had a book within us in the first place. Also thanks to my babe, Aimee, because without her the sun would never shine.

And of course thanks to all our staff, chef superstars and customers, without whom we would be nowhere. THANKS LEGENDS.

Published in 2015 by Murdoch Books, an imprint of Allen & Unwin

Murdoch Books Australia
83 Alexander Street
Crows Nest NSW 2065
Phone: +61 (0) 2 8425 0100
Fax: +61 (0) 2 9906 2218
murdochbooks.com.au
info@murdochbooks.com.au

Murdoch Books UK
Erico House, 6th Floor
93–99 Upper Richmond Road
Putney, London SW15 2TG
Phone: +44 (0) 20 8785 5995
murdochbooks.co.uk
info@murdochbooks.co.uk

For Corporate Orders & Custom Publishing contact
Noel Hammond, National Business Development Manager,
Murdoch Books Australia

Publisher: Diana Hill
Designer: Hugh Ford
Editorial Manager: Barbara McClenahan
Project Editor: Katri Hilden
Food photographer: Benito Martin
Stylist: Lynsey Fryers
Illustrations: Carla Uriarte
Food Editor: Wendy Quisumbing
Production Manager: Mary Bjelobrk

Text © James Wirth 2015
The moral rights of the author have been asserted.
Design © Murdoch Books 2015
Food photography © Benito Martin 2015
Additional photography © Drink'n'Dine 2015

A cataloguing-in-publication entry is available from the
catalogue of the National Library of Australia at nla.gov.au.

ISBN 978 1 74336 405 5 Australia
ISBN 978 1 74336 426 0 UK

A catalogue record for this book is available
from the British Library.

Colour reproduction by Splitting Image Colour Studio
Pty Ltd, Clayton, Victoria

Printed by C & C Offset Printing Co. Ltd., China

IMPORTANT: Those who might be at risk
from the effects of salmonella poisoning
(the elderly, pregnant women, young
children and those suffering from immune
deficiency diseases) should consult their
doctor with any concerns about eating
raw eggs.

OVEN GUIDE: You may find cooking times
vary depending on the oven you are using.
For fan-forced ovens, as a general rule, set
the oven temperature to 20°C (35°F) lower
than indicated in the recipe.

MEASURES GUIDE: We have used 20 ml
(4 teaspoon) tablespoon measures. If you
are using a 15 ml (3 teaspoon) tablespoon
add an extra teaspoon of the ingredient
for each tablespoon specified.